Good HAIR Days

Good HAIR Days

A Personal Journey with the American Tribal Love-Rock Musical *HAIR*

By Jonathon Johnson

iUniverse, Inc.

New York Lincoln Shanghai

Good HAIR Days
A Personal Journey with the American Tribal Love-Rock Musical *HAIR*

iUniverse books may be ordered through booksellers or by contacting:

iUniverse
2021 Pine Lake Road, Suite 100
Lincoln, NE 68512
www.iuniverse.com
1-800-Authors (1-800-288-4677)

Cover Graphics by Kevin Mason, www.alkiave.com

ISBN: 0-595-31297-7

Printed in the United States of America

Contents

Prayer For A Peaceful World

May all the races in every country on this little blue planet, be led to the truth that all men and women, regardless of spiritual paths, are one. We are the children of one God; none more favored or loved than the other, equal in the eyes of our Divine Creator. We were born into this imperfect world as mortals, potential immortals, to strive for perfection, to be as perfect as the First Source and Center of all things.

On this journey, let us not be divided by our physical boundaries, our color, our class, a political party, ideals, or any number of meaningless and hurtful prejudices. Help us not to show malice and hate for our brothers and sisters, for when we do so we harm the very source of all creation, the eternal gift of all the ages, the divine spark of the creator that resides within us all.

Guide us to the understanding that although we are each unique individuals, we are also one in spirit. As children of God we honor our brotherhood by learning to love and by mastering tolerance for one another. As we seek to love let us also learn to accept, understand and celebrate our differences. Through this we will grow in spirit and find peace. Peace is born of love and love is infectious. So let us gather together in spirit and offer a prayer for a peaceful world.

Jonathon Johnson   © 2004

Introduction

Destined For Greatness or Madness

Life is but a journey each one of us takes individually. I believe our destiny is indeed mapped out in advance, but because of free will there are many paths we can choose to reach it. Each one of these paths can provide an adventure in itself and in many ways a destiny of its own.

I also know there are many others who have a destiny similar to mine but they will choose different paths than I have chosen. There is a quote that comes to mind that sums up my feelings on this subject. It goes something like this—"There are as many paths to God as there are people to walk them." It's a simple truth that could resolve so many differences if only more people in the world could recognize it.

This is a story of only one of the paths I chose to follow. Primarily it's a story about my journey through the sixties and eventually into the seventies with the Broadway Musical "Hair." Although there were around 2,000 young people, in approximately 35 casts of "Hair" worldwide between the years of 1967 through 1975, only one other person I know of has ever written their story to date.

In my case, my personal experience with "Hair" was so life altering that I felt a calling to finally write it down. There are undoubtedly many other stories of similar journeys from those who were in "Hair" just waiting to be told and most likely more compelling than mine. Maybe this body of work will inspire them to do so.

Because of the times I am writing about there will be many issues and personal revelations that I myself will have to come to grips with. A lot has changed in my life during the past 30 years, most definitely my own lifestyle. The most difficulty I can foresee having will be discussing the drugs and free sex of the times. Although this writing is not intended to be a "tell all" story, I do after all have children who will most likely read this journal and wonder if I have succumbed to the proverbial double standard. Regardless, believing that honesty is always the best policy, I will attempt to portray things as they were rather than as I would have wished them to be now.

As I begin this belated journal I have set some personal guidelines for myself that I hope to be able to abide by. While sharing the story of my journey, if at all possible I will try and keep it all on a positive note. What I mean by that is I do not want to say anything bad about any of the participants who shared in my journey. There are also many great people and stories that touched my life throughout this period that I will not talk about. Their omissions may be necessary for me to stay on track with the story itself or simply as an oversight on my part.

Like most other people, there have also been some not so great people and events that occurred along the way. Therefore in order to adhere to my objective, I will simply avoid elaborating about them and in some cases, not talk about them at all. Not that all you read here will be bright and cheerful, that is not the way in life. I have personally come to understand and appreciate the positive learning experiences that oftentimes are the outcome of a dark event.

For the most part this journal covers a short and intense period of my life. As you peruse its pages, think of it as a personal recollection of the past by just another human being on the planet. Nobody famous, nothing fancy, just a diary, a scrapbook of sorts filled with events, thoughts, and musings about a very special time in someone's life. Perhaps it will even help you to recollect some of the good things that went on in the 60's and 70's.

Although there have been many great and successful musicals throughout history none have been as markedly influential in changing the thoughts and feelings of audiences worldwide as the musical "Hair" has. Conceptualizing the major events of the sixties, the authors of "Hair" lovingly created a palatable mix of music, dance and a message of love and peace that still moves audiences to this day. "Hair" provided a unifying voice of reason to millions of people around the globe, many of whom may not have been reached through any other medium. To really understand the importance of "Hair," you must first understand the sixties.

During the turbulent sixties there was an incredible amount of unrest in America. So much so, that there are many who still feel we were very close to having another civil war. In the comfort of our homes we watched on television the "supposed" typical American family on "Father Knows Best," but few families resembled the Anderson's. The reality of the Vietnam War hit us hard with daily news coverage of body bags and body counts. There were also vivid pictures of race riots in our streets and the suspicious activities of the Soviet Union. Imagine this, in our schools we were taught to "duck and roll" to protect ourselves from nuclear annihilation (should the dirty commies decide to nuke us) and we were introduced to the dangers of drugs through the often shown movie, "Reefer Madness."

We were inadvertently taught to hate, fear and distrust anyone or anything different and expected to blindly trust all that we were taught. Racism, bigotry and homophobia ran rampant in society as a whole and those who were against these values were considered "Un-American." Even though they were not old enough to vote, at the age of eighteen young boys were expected to go off to a foreign country, kill (and quite possibly die), for reasons no one could properly explain. Failure to do so, or to disagree, or even to ask why, was oftentimes considered cowardice and an act of treason. This was after all, "America, love it or leave it."

In stark contrast to these ideals implanted by the generations before us, the youth of America began to question everything and on every level—we felt disenfranchised. Here we were being asked to sacrifice our lives and yet we were not given a voice. There were few political or religious figures who were willing to speak for us, and those few who offered us hope were assassinated. We rejected the notion that liberty is for some but not for all. We felt a unity with those groups who had long experienced social isolation and persecution. We wanted a voice and needed to be heard, but no one listened, so we rebelled.

At first they simply called it a "generation gap." The older generation was not quite able to understand the younger generation and the youth was too immature to understand their elders. In reality, people as a whole were increasingly becoming aware of the paradoxicalness of our society in general. But it wasn't just the youth who were rebelling, as there were waves of new ideas and thoughts that were converging from many directions. We were openly seeking spiritual enlightenment and were awakening to new ideas, almost as if we had been in a deep sleep. We were becoming aware of our relation to God, to the planet and to each other. At the same time we were rejecting bigotry, racism, pollution, sexism and homophobia. Above all we were rejecting the concepts of hate and war—and we were embracing peace and love. We were on the brink of a paradigm change, a new age. This was "The Dawning of the Age of Aquarius."

In creating "Hair," Rado, Ragni and MacDermot were able to encapsulate all these elements of the sixties into a form that is easily communicated and warmly accepted. The music, the lyrics, and its messages of love, peace and understanding far transcend that of the typical musical play. "Hair" was and is anything but typical. Some call "Hair" a time-piece because of its direct relation to the sixties, but in my opinion "Hair" is timeless. It is timeless because its messages are timeless. Until we eliminate war, racism and hatred—until we achieve world peace, "Hair" will remain timeless.

Although "Hair's" effects on the peace movement in the sixties cannot be quantified, its influence certainly shouldn't be underestimated. "Hair" was able to reach those people who were not able to comprehend what was really going on from any other source. It allowed parents who were not able to communicate with their children, to get a glimpse into what their children were thinking. It allowed audiences to see that people of all colors and of all sexual preferences, could live peacefully together. If this could happen on a stage it could certainly happen in real life. From an insider's perspective, I personally heard many stories of changed lives directly from audience members. Other former tribe members have also expressed this phenomenon.

I believe "Hair" also contributed greatly to unifying the anti-war movement. As the Vietnam War was the first televised war, America had become numbed to the loss of humanity. We saw so much death and destruction on the nightly news, that unless you had personally lost someone dear, the facts became surreal. With "Hair," people were able to connect for two and a half hours with this loving group of young people and then dramatically experience the senseless loss of one of its leading characters to the war in Vietnam. By the time "Hair" closed on Broadway in 1972, America had finally pulled out of the Vietnam War.

The fact is, millions of people came to see "Hair" to be entertained, but many of these same people walked away with something much more. "Hair" was speaking out for those without a voice, and became their voice of reason and their hope for love and peace.

Today there is still a need for "Hair" and its antiwar message of love and peace. Even though the Vietnam War has long since ended, there are currently many serious conflicts around the globe. Many of these new conflicts are much more alarming and dangerous than Vietnam ever was. At the time of this writing, America has already felt a great loss in the tragedy of the events known as 9/11, which led to the worldwide "War on Terror." This war is already becoming a world war of sorts. It has spread to Afghanistan, Iraq,

Indonesia, and is threatening to break wide open in both Iran and on the Korean Peninsula.

In the efforts to fight this new kind of war (the war on terror) our current political leaders have once again begun the process of unilaterally disenfranchising and silencing those who disagree with the direction America is heading. Once again we hear the sounds of "America, love it or leave it." If you don't agree with the direction and policies of the current political administration, you must either be silent or face accusations of treason. The time is again ripe for "Hair" and all it stands for.

Besides its political and sociological importance, "Hair" became a phenomenal business success, reaching over 30 million people worldwide over its first 4 years alone, preaching its message of peace, love and understanding. By the year 1969 "Hair" was grossing over $350,000 a week, over $18 million a year, all on an initial investment of $250,000. "Hair" returned 40 times to its original investors. An April 1970 article stated that—"More than 600 recordings have been made from the score and half the songs its cast sings have become recorded hits. There are now 20 road companies of "Hair" playing the show in different cities of the world and more than 3,400,000 people have bought tickets to see it." By 1972, unlike any other show in history, "Hair" had 35 companies of the show running worldwide. In a 2001 article about "Hair" Michael Butler said, "The show grossed $80 million ($800 million in today's dollars) globally before the last love bead was put away."

I consider myself blessed in that I was one of around two thousand young people who were lucky enough to be cast into several of the original productions of "Hair." When I joined my first tribe I thought I was just going to be in another show. It did not take me long to realize that I was a part of something much greater. Besides being welcomed into this worldwide family, in many ways the entire "Hair" experience has assisted me in my spiritual journey.

One might ask, "How could anything having to do with "Hair" have a bearing on ones spiritual journey?" Wasn't "Hair" a hippie rock musical that promoted sex, drugs and rock and roll? Yes it was all that and more, but the underlying theme was one of love. Love for your brothers and sisters, love for the family, love for the planet, love for freedom of expression, love for life, peace, and love for God. Although it may not seem plausible, "Hair" was in many ways a spiritual experience to those who were involved with the show and to many of the millions of people who saw the show.

Some say if you can remember the sixties then you did not participate. There must be some truth to that because as each year goes by I find my recollections of those days becoming increasingly difficult to recall. When I first met Gerry Ragni in 1970, he advised I should always keep a journal to write down my thoughts, events of the day, poems, songs or whatever. He felt strongly enough about this concept that he even bought me my first journal. Unfortunately I only used the journal for writing down the lyrics to a few of my songs, some poems and nothing more. Now as I begin this tome I highly regret not taking his advice. Due to my memory handicaps, my recollection of events, places and times, might be a little off.

In this book you will find the history of "Hair" from an insider's point of view, plus original cast lists, first-hand stories, Playbill bio's, and quotes from articles that start from "Hair's" beginnings on up to the release of the movie. This book does not contain all that's available, there's simply too much out there for one book. What I've gathered here is more like volume one of a historical scrapbook.

Before I go any further, I have many people to thank. First I would like to thank the authors of "Hair," Gerome Ragni, James Rado and Galt MacDermot. Had it not been for their extremely unique, visionary approach to the theatre, the theatre as we know it today may not have evolved at all. "Hair" was after all, the very first Rock Musical.

Jim, besides co-writing one of the greatest shows of all time, I want to especially thank you for bringing Claude to life and for your friendship.

Galt, to this very day the fantastic music you wrote still makes the hair on the back of my neck stand on end. It's outstanding, it's beautiful and will surely transcend all time.

And Gerry, although you are no longer here to share this with, I want to thank you for co-writing this masterpiece, for sharing your incredible free spirit, for being Berger, for helping me discover my child inside and most of all, for your friendship.

Next, I want to thank Michael Butler for taking the show under his wing and sharing it with the world. Michael took a giant step and an even larger gamble by investing his time, love and monetary resources in "Hair." I'm sure there were many in his circle of friends and peers who thought he had lost all sense of reason. Michael, you were always more than just a boss and will always remain a great friend. I am indebted to your assistance with this project, your advice and tremendous stories. Your insight, perspective, thoughts and feelings are core to the essence of "Hair." You are indeed, "Hair's" Silver Indian.

A very, very special thanks goes out to the many former tribe members who took the time to contribute their thoughts in this book as well. Some of their stories are scattered about this volume, and you'll find even more in a special chapter called "Voices of the Tribe" towards the back of the book.

I would also like to thank the worldwide "tribe" of "Hair," which includes not only the casts, musicians, producers, directors, and other crew members of the shows I was privileged to work with, but it also includes "all" the above, in "all" productions of this marvelous show. Because "Hair" grows, there is not sufficient room in any book to contain all of the members of the tribe. However, in the back of this volume I have made an attempt at documenting those who were involved between the years of 1967 and 1975. My sincere apologies to those folks I have inadvertently omitted.

I am indebted to my family and friends who long ago thought it wise to keep copies of articles, programs, souvenir books, pictures and miscellaneous mementos. They have turned out to be very helpful to me while piecing this project together. I personally kept very little to remember those times by, which has ended up costing me much time, not to mention money, trying to find and buy them 30 plus years after the fact.

This all brings to mind that I also appreciate my family's patience in my spending so many hours each day on the computer. You'll have my undivided attention once this project is completed, at least until the next one comes along.

Lastly and most importantly, I would like to thank God for giving me the opportunity to have been a part of "Hair." I will forever treasure my association with the show and the extended family it brought into my life.

These things having been said, let the sunshine in.

1

What do you want to do with your life?
What do you want to be?

Having been born on June 25, 1951 at 8:36 am, my astrological sign is Cancer. My given name was Glen Arthur Johnson, which for some reason I always hated with a passion. I was named after my father's uncle who was a very special person to my father. For me though, I had met the man only once or twice when I was very young and was left with no impression of him at all.

My mom and dad divorced when I was very young and I would visit with my father only a couple of times each year. He had remarried, started a new family and moved north of Seattle.

Television was always a great focus of my attention. Although I would be content to watch almost anything on TV, I mostly loved the movies and would fantasize for hours on end that I was an actor. Much to my parent's chagrin, whenever I was asked what I wanted to be when I grew up, I wouldn't hesitate to answer with resolve, "An actor in the movies." This of course was always followed up with a resounding lecture from my parents, trying to convince me what I really wanted to be was a doctor, a lawyer, or anything other than an actor.

Another great love of mine was music. Music spoke to my soul and the love of it was something I shared with my sister. I especially loved the R&B and rock music of the fifties. Although my sister was older than me, I would sit and listen with her and her friends as they played and shared their 45's with one another.

When I was three or four I discovered an old guitar up in a closet in our attic. It was an old Harmony arch top with one or two strings missing. I would strum on it for hours when left idle. It was my mom's guitar, was used, and was given to her by her father on her 18th birthday. It was forbidden for any of us to even open the case let alone play with mom's guitar. My sisters knew of my passion for this instrument and blackmailed me for years to keep my mom from finding out. Many years later my mother let me play it and sometime in my twenties she relented and gave it to me.

Eventually my mom remarried and we moved to a new house in Renton. It was a welcomed move as the house was much larger and it was new.

One of the first friends I made after moving in our house was Brenda. She was very pretty, petite and had long dark straight hair. We got along extremely well and although we both had strong feelings for each other, we were also too painfully shy to act upon them. Inevitably our friendship grew and we remained friends over many years. The two of us would spend countless hours in my basement talking, listening to records and experimenting with recording sound and music. Brenda was truly one of my best friends.

Over the next couple of years most of my friends started playing some sort of musical instrument in hopes of starting a band. My parents however, were not receptive to buying or renting an instrument for me let alone pay for lessons. This of course depressed me to no end. Although I did have some harmonicas, bongos, and a tape recorder, I really wanted an electric guitar and amp. To make things even tougher, my oldest sister was asked to be a lead singer with a local group of guys who were all my friends. They called themselves The Acoustics.

Meanwhile, I pulled that old Harmony guitar of my mom's out of the closet and began to teach myself how to play it. I was on a mission. I would literally play it until my fingers would bleed, eventually wearing off much of the fingerboard. It took me about 6 months to learn the basics of guitar. Soon after learning how to play I started jamming periodically with some of the members of The Acoustics, hoping to join up.

Folk music was my all time favorite music until the Beatles came along. The Beatles were very influential to me at this time along with Dylan, The Rolling Stones, The Byrds and Barry McGuire. I insert Barry into this mix because of his hit rendition of PF Sloan's "Eve of Destruction." That song cut right to the chase for me. It was that song that helped me to see the potential of music. It really gave me the desire to write my own music, which I started to do right away. I also mention his influence because later on Barry and I would cross paths twice, through "Hair" and "The New Christy Minstrels." Barry and I were members of both, but at different times. Amazingly though, we never personally met.

I had a friend named David whose mom was a music promoter and owned a popular coffee shop in Seattle called "The Door." The Door was the quintessential bohemian hangout of its time in Seattle. There was lots of music there, folk, rock, poetry readings and beatniks. Yes, that's what they called the earlier version of hippies and they all seemed pretty cool to me.

Many great acts came to play at The Door. Because there was no alcohol served, only coffee and hot cider, anyone of any age could enter the premises. My friend often invited me to stay when he visited his mother and we would of course always hang out at The Door.

One of the great local bands that played there was "The Daily Flash." When they did the Beatles, it was as if you were listening to a Beatles record. I loved their sound, they were hot and they were always willing to show us younger guys a few of their tricks.

The Daily Flash had a strong following and they played in many of the major clubs up and down the west coast. They eventually got a contract, released a couple of singles, and got a spot on the show, "The Girl from U.N.C.L.E." They eventually broke up spawning two other successful west coast bands, "Bodine" and "Rhinoceros."

It was during this period that I also decided to grow my hair long. I was only one of a handful of boys in town who had long hair. It was definitely an issue at the time, especially with the school authorities. I would often have to conceal it from them by putting water on it, pushing it behind my ears and down my collar.

This year I also had my first psychic reading. I was out and about with a friend one evening and we were invited by some girls to stop by their house. One of the girls was in her twenties, claimed to be psychic and wanted to know if we wanted a reading. That sounded fun so we said yes. During my reading she predicted that I would fall in love with a girl but we would be separated by some sort of tragedy. This freaked me out because over the years I had already experienced a reoccurring dream with similar content. In the dream there was a girl, I knew we were in love, and in the dream we were being pulled apart from one another. Anyway, she also said I would be rich and famous which is what I really wanted to hear and believe at the time. It was all in fun and soon forgotten.

This same year I was asked to join The Acoustics to play rhythm guitar and share with vocals. Soon after I joined the group my sister decided to leave it. When she left she gave me her PA system and I took over the spot of lead vocals. The band became my central focus and we played anywhere and everywhere we could.

On one summer night there was a free outdoor concert by a rival group at a local shopping center parking lot. I wanted to hear this group and hitch hiked with a friend to see them play. Two girls stopped and gave us a lift. We didn't know them, but they were pretty cute so what more could you ask for. It turns out they were sisters. I sat in the front with the older sister Billie and my friend sat in the back with Robin. We hadn't met before because Billie was a senior in High School, while Robin was a grade behind us and attended a Junior High School.

Billie was older and very cute, but there was something very special about Robin. I can still remember peeking at her in the back seat through the rear view mirror. I was wishing I had picked the back seat to sit in. By the twinkle in Robin's eye and the smile on her face, I believed she was wishing the same.

Besides being cute, one of the things about Robin that impressed me was her voice. She had a unique, high-pitched and sort of cartoonish, raspy sounding voice. It was very endearing and sexy to say the least. Thinking we might get lucky, we asked them both to come to the concert with us. Unfortunately they had someplace else to go so they just dropped us off.

Later that year we were having a band rehearsal during the day on a weekend. Our bass player Dan drove up and brought his new girlfriend. She was a cutie, about my height, with shoulder length brown hair and sparkling brown eyes. She was wearing one of those red and white striped surfer tee shirts and faded blue jeans. As they came closer, Dan introduced her to all of us. Her name was Robin Ball and I was green with envy. She was the same Robin who picked me up hitchhiking. Lucky Dan.

Dan soon left the band to join another group that was more show oriented. So when he left we were in desperate need of a bass player. Our drummer asked his parents (who were very supportive of us) to buy him a bass guitar and amp which I used. From this point on I handled lead vocals and on occasion, bass as well.

Just as summer was to begin (the Summer of Love in 1967) The Acoustics entered a battle of the bands at the Seattle Center. We went over real well and although we didn't win an official prize, we did get an offer to go on tour. There was this eighty something year old man, Mr. C. L. Cooper, who ran a traveling fair. He wanted a band to play as an added attraction to attract the teen crowd. We were on!

This was a first for a band from Renton. Just before we left on tour The Beatles released Sgt. Pepper. We immediately used some of the songs from the album in our set, along with "My Back Pages," a Dylan song the Byrds had performed. This was very cool because where we were going the folks didn't hear much of any new music, so often they thought our covers were originals.

Our first stop on the tour was Great Falls Montana. Mr. Cooper had refurbished an old fun house building for us with a stage and bandstand. The lighting wasn't the best but we made do. Because of the popularity of British bands, Mr. Cooper also had an idea it would be good publicity if one or all of us could pretend to be from England. I was volunteered because I could fake an English accent a little better than the others. When developing my fake identity I decided to say I was from Manchester, England if asked. I chose Manchester completely out of the air; having no idea one day I would play a similar role in "Hair."

"Manchester England, England, across the Atlantic sea. And I'm a genius, genius, I believe in God, and I believe that God, believes in Claude, that's me."

We played for 20 minutes with 20 minutes of break time following each set, from around noon until around 9:00 P.M. everyday. It was a grueling schedule, but we were making $150 each per week cash with free rooms, which was good pay for a bunch of 16 year olds.

After the first few days we met a guy who had just returned from San Francisco. He had worked the light shows at the Avalon Ballroom and the Fillmore Auditorium in San Francisco. He liked our music and with Mr. Cooper's approval, we asked him to join up with the show. The addition of a professional San Francisco type light show really spiced up the act. The folks in the towns we were visiting had only heard of such things. He was also the first person we knew who smoked pot. He offered it to us, but none of us were willing to try it at the time.

Some time later the tour moved on up into Canada. After a week or so in Lethbridge, Alberta, the toll of being the only singer and playing so much finally got to me. I developed both bronchitis and laryngitis. This was really bad because the group was not an instrumental band. I stayed back at the hotel for a couple of days, being nursed by a few young girls and sweating my butt off while the guys tried to improvise the show. Apparently they didn't do too well because Mr. Cooper gave us our walking papers and replaced The Acoustics with an R&B show band called Pit and the Pendulums. The tour was over and we had to go back home.

When we returned to Renton I was still ill and nursing myself at home. One of the guys in the band was sent over to my house to inform me that The Acoustics were replacing me with another singer. I guess they wanted someone who was a bit healthier and although I was a little hurt, I also viewed it as an opportunity. I really desired to join a band that wanted to work more on original material. The Acoustics was just another High School band that was playing for fun and extra money. Not one of them was in the business for the long run. They all had different plans for life which was great for them, but not for me.

Having no band to belong to left me with a great deal of time on my hands in both the evenings and on weekends. I had been having an overwhelming desire to develop spiritually and used much of this spare time to search through the plethora of religions and cults that were in abundance. Although more of my friends were experimenting with drugs, I was still apprehensive about using drugs and steered away from them completely.

I started visiting my grandmother in Seattle more often throughout this year. She lived on the west side of Queen Anne Hill in the same house where my dad was raised. Even though my hair was getting longer and my clothes a bit weirder, I could tell my grandmother was enjoying our visits just as much if not more than me. We got along really well in spite of the fact she was both a racist and a republican. Not that those two necessarily went hand in hand. But from my point of view, both those ideologies were seriously flawed belief systems that I would constantly debate with her.

Over the years I think I chipped away at her beliefs enough to sway her to a more liberal philosophy. She had a picture of Nixon and a picture of Jesus on a wall in her entryway side by side. That really bothered me and although it took a long while, she finally consented to moving them apart from one another. It was a minor victory for me.

I usually got to my grandmother's by a combination of hitchhiking and buses when my thumb wasn't successful. On a few occasions however, I actually walked the entire 20 something miles from my mother's home in Renton all the way to my grandmother's house on Queen Anne Hill. On these visits I would usually take a detour to Pike Place Market and the Seattle Center, where a lot of the hip things were happening at the time. Pike Place Market had some great antique and resale shops while the Seattle Center offered a laid back festival type atmosphere. This is where the hippies were usually gathering.

Up the street from my grandmother was an old house that was being used as a crash pad. She would always point out to me that the house was filled with hippies and it would be a good idea for me to stay clear. To me her gentle warnings just fueled my curiosity. One sunny day several people were out in the front yard and the front door was wide open. As I was passing on my way to visit my grandmother I heard some people chanting. One of the folks outside invited me to come in and to learn about Buddhism. I wholeheartedly accepted their invite and from that point on I visited with them quite often. Although I was never convinced Buddhism was for me, I appreciated their friendship and enjoyed hanging out with them. My grandmother never knew of these visits to the notorious "house of hippies."

During this time I also encountered my first experience with channeling. Although it was not called channeling at the time, that is what it was. I went with a girlfriend and her family to attend a Rosicrucian's meeting in Olympia Washington. At the meeting there was a man who appeared to be in his early fifties, dressed in business attire, lying on his back on a cot. People were gathered around him and were asking questions as he lay in a trance. He would answer the questions in a strange voice. It was all very weird and I didn't glean any spiritual significance from the experience.

So my search for my spiritual identity continued. Although I had a firm belief in both God and Jesus I had a tremendous feeling I was missing something. There had to be more, some deeper explanations to life. I was convinced there was something or someone on the planet somewhere who had the answers to all my innermost questions. So from this time forward I spent a great deal of my time soul searching and checking out different spiritual groups. Somehow I had the notion the answers to the spiritual questions I had might be found in the form of a book. So I also spent a lot of time browsing the metaphysical, religious and occult sections in bookstores and libraries.

A couple of my friends were determined to experiment with pot. I still wasn't ready myself but I was curious enough to go along for the ride. On this one night, my friends had purchased a lid of pot and wanted to drive to someplace secluded to smoke it. So the three of us drove out to a dirt road behind our subdivision where the two of them proceeded to smoke the entire bag! Lucky for them this was just cheap, run of the mill Mexican pot. The two of them were laughing hysterically and uncontrollably. I remember one of the guys kept saying he felt as though he was butter in a frying pan and some other nonsense. The air was so thick inside the car I'm sure I got a slight contact high just from breathing. Anyway, we drove around town the rest of the evening with the windows rolled down to air out the car. The three of us kept the events of this evening a secret from our other friends for quite sometime.

During another one of our evening adventures, we all decided to drive to Seattle and stop by my grandmother's for a visit. It was all very innocent and my grandmother was pleased to meet my friends. After meeting them, she retired upstairs while we all watched TV and visited downstairs. A few of us were smokers (me included at the time) and we had a few cigarettes. About a half hour after my grandmother had left she returned, sliding open the door that separated the living room from the stairwell. As she slid the door open, she gasped for air and exclaimed,

"POT!! POT!! I SMELL POT!! Are you boys smoking pot?"

All was silent except for a few murmurs of a chuckle or two. Other than that one night out with my friends, none of us had ever had any pot. I gave my grandmother a big hug, assured her there was no pot in the house, and walked her back up the stairs to her room. When I came back down I asked everyone to put out their cigarettes and we left shortly thereafter. I hope she didn't hear the roar of laughter once we reached the car!

A few months later my sister and her husband had visited my grandmother. My grandmother proceeded to show them a few cigarette butts she had kept from our visit. She asked them if it was pot and they assured her it was not. They even went so far as to point out the filters to her. After all, joints were not mass-produced with filters. I don't think she was ever convinced though.

This story reminds me of another pot story that happened a year or so later. I had been visiting my mom in Renton and was on my way back to my grandma's house in Seattle. I was supposed to be taking the bus but got tired of waiting in the cold rain for it to arrive. So somewhere down in the Rainier Beach area I decided to hitchhike instead. The first ride I got was from a cute girl with a deep sexy voice. Her name was Janis Gotti and the ride with her was quite fun.

Soon after saying hello, she took a joint out of her purse and lit it up. We proceeded to smoke the whole thing together, all the while talking and sharing a few laughs. I distinctly remember her telling me I looked like a fox. She wasn't saying I looked "foxy," but that I really reminded her of a fox or maybe a wolf somehow. We were both laughing about it and I remember her saying that "Fox" should be my nickname.

I'm still not sure where this was all coming from. Perhaps it was a premonition on her part. Only a couple of years later, Janis would play the role of Sheila in the Seattle cast of "Hair," while I was to play the role of "Woof." When we had this chance meeting, neither of us had any idea we were both budding entertainers, or that our paths would cross again in the near future. I simply thanked her for the ride and off she drove.

2

The Dawning

Sometime around 1964 in New York, two young actors met and became friends while performing in an off-Broadway production called, "Hang Down Your Head and Die." Both Gerome Ragni and James Rado had Shakespearean training and they were also very interested in improvisational theatre. Although the two actors were very well respected within New York Theatre circles, they were little known to the general public.

Gerry was one of the founders of the Open Theatre, a winner of a Barter Theatre award for acting, and had appeared on Broadway in "Hamlet" with Richard Burton and John Gielgud. He also acted in the off-Broadway production of "The Knack."

Jim had worked on Broadway in "Lion in Winter," with Robert Preston and Christopher Walken, and in "Luther," with Albert Finney. Not long after they met, they decided to collaborate as authors.

JAMES RADO, Richard—The past two seasons have been demanding ones for James Rado who has been with six productions during this short period. Most recently, he was an understudy in the current hit *Generation* which he left to play Richard. Last season, Mr. Rado was featured in *Quality Street* at the Bucks County Playhouse, played Tolen in the New York and Chicago companies of *The Knack* and rounded out his 1965 schedule at Boston's Charles Playhouse as George Nowack in *She Loves Me*. In 1964, he was the ringmaster in Roger L. Stevens' off-Broadway production *Hang Down*

Your Head and Die, and understudied the title role in *Luther* both on Broadway and on tour. Previously, Mr. Rado played a variety of roles in stock and worked as a nightclub vocalist. ~ *From the LION IN WINTER Playbill on Broadway, May 1966.*

GEROME RAGNI (Tom) is no stranger to *The Knack*, having played his current role in the Chicago company last winter. Born in Pittsburgh, he attended two schools in Washington, D.C., Georgetown University and the Mildred Greet Dramatic Academy. A call to join the armed forces interrupted his university studies. After his discharge, interested in the theatre, he came to New York, and studied with Philip Burton and Nola Chilton. Mr. Ragni made his New York debut off-Broadway as Mathias in *Legend of Lovers*. His Off and On Broadway credits since include Bernardo in Richard Burton's *Hamlet*, the lead in *Hang Down Your Head and Die*, Angel in *Dead End*, Dunois in *St. Joan*, and Treploff in *The Seagull*, the N.Y. Shakespeare Festival's *Julius Caesar* and last season's experimental plays, *Theatre 1964*. He also acted at Washington's Arena Stage. Abe Burrows chose Mr. Ragni for the Barter Theatre award in 1962, and at that playhouse he performed Gaston in *Waltz of the Toreadors*, Gradeau in *No Exit*, El Gallo in *The Fantasticks*, and Jack Chesney in *Where's Charlie?* He has appeared on a number of leading television drama programs, including *Naked City*. ~ *From THE KNACK Showcard, The New Theatre, off-Broadway, August 1965.*

Jim and Gerry had a great deal of experience in the off-off-Broadway experimental theatre projects that were going on in New York at the time. They had done quite a bit of work with Ellen Stewart at the La Mama Experimental Theatre Club and others. They were both bored with theatre as it was happening on Broadway at the time as were many of its critics and patrons.

The idea of "Hair" came to them when the realization that what was happening on the streets in Greenwich Village and around the world, was far more exciting and meaningful than what was currently on the stage. They very cleverly took the real bits and pieces of events that were impinging on their lives and with the help of Galt MacDermot, put it all together into a story, song and dance. For this incredible stroke of genius I will personally, forever be grateful to these three men.

Galt MacDermot was born in Montreal and educated at Capetown (South Africa) University, as his father was a Canadian diplomat. Galt had been a church organist, dance band musician, jazz musician, rock musician and composer of "African Waltz"—a smash hit in London and winner of a Grammy Award in the USA. "Hair" was Galt's first theatrical musical adventure as well.

Galt didn't approach "Hair" with any idea of writing it for Broadway. He hadn't seen that many shows, but of those he had, his opinion was they often seemed formalized and pointless. When Galt met Gerry and Jim, Joe Papp was already interested in producing "Hair" only they hadn't any music for it as yet. After reading the script, Galt liked it enough to join the project. Within a very short period of time the music for "Hair" was completed.

The first venue for "Hair" was a limited run at the Public Theatre in New York. It was the first production of any show to open at the new Florence Sutro Anspacher Theatre. The show was directed by Gerald Freedman and produced by Joseph Papp. Opening night for previews was on October 17, 1967 while the official Opening night was on October 29, 1967.

THE ORIGINAL SHAKESPEARE FESTIVAL COMPANY,
Opening Night October 29, 1967 at The Public Theatre

Jonelle Allen	William Herter
Susan Batson	Paul Jabara
Warren Burton	Bob Johnson
Thommie Bush	Jane Levin
Linda Compton	Marijane Maricle
Ed Crowley	Edward Murphy Jr
Walker Daniels	Jill O'Hara
Steve Dean	Shelley Plimpton
Sally Eaton	Gerome Ragni
Suzannah Evans	Alma Robinson
Lynda Gudde	Arnold Wilkerson

Although there were several reviews of "Hair" during its run at the Public Theatre, I will only include excerpts from a few.

In October of 1967, Clive Barnes of the New York Times wrote his first review of "Hair" as it was performed at the Public Theatre in New York. "Hair" was the first presentation at the newly remodeled Florence Sutro Anspacher Theatre and Joseph Papp produced it.

Clive wrote, "If it had a story—which to be honest it hasn't—that story would be about the young disenchanted, turned on by pot, switched off by the draft, living and loving, the new products of affluence, the dispossessed dropouts. That, if it had a story, would be what "Hair" is about."

He went on to say that "it is a mood picture of a generation—a generation dominated by drugs, sex and the two wars, the one about color and the one about Vietnam. Not that these two are made so separate. As someone says: "The draft is white people sending black people to fight yellow people to protect the country they stole from the red people."

He described the music by Mr. MacDermot as "rock and swingy, and while not especially original in itself, at least it does not sound like a deliberate pastiche of Rogers and Hammerstein." He also wrote "the other quality is simply the likeability and honesty of its cast."

One of the most intriguing comments I found in his review was the following. "Protesting, laughing, fighting, loving, rebel-without-a-causing, these young people spill across the stage with a sprawling, grinning arrogance. They seem to believe totally in what they are doing, which is always wonderful to see in the theatre, and their rather uncivil disobedience is made sharp and to the point." With that statement I believe that Clive got the essence of what "Hair" was all about.

Howard Taubman, another writer for the New York Times also reviewed "Hair" as presented at the New York Public Theatre in November 1967. Howard wrote, "The story line of "Hair" is so attenuated that it would be merciful to label the piece a revue. Examined under this rubric, it can be appreciated for what it essentially is—a wild, indiscriminate explosion of exuberant, impertinent youthful talents. What if coherence is lacking, discipline meager and taste often deplorable? The youngsters—authors and performers—have the kind of vitality that sends the memories of an older theatregoer wandering back to the twenties—to the bright impudence of "The Grand Street Follies" and "The Garrick Gaieties."

He also said "Hair" is much more concerned with the larger issues than its predecessors of the twenties. Although it devotes a good deal of its time to the tribal rites of the hippies, it lashed out at public figures. Its comment on the war in Vietnam is biting, and its contempt for contemporary institutions is unmistakable."

Howard summed up his review with, "The fundamental viewpoint and freshness of "Hair" make their mark not through the diffuse targetry of the lines but through the liveliness of the young people who sing, dance and shuffle in the open playing space of the delightful Florence Sutro Anspacher Theatre, and particularly through the score."

In November 1967, an article in Newsweek magazine said, "Hair" is many different things, but most important, it is alive and a sign of life. The whole idea of Joseph Papp's new Public Theatre is wonderful and the first of his working arenas immediately becomes the most delightful show-space in New York, jumping into life with a young company positively pop-eyed with conviction and energy."

"Square and hip will argue endlessly over whether "Hair" is the first real hippie show or a crass betrayal of the hippie ethos. But what it quite properly tries to do is present the hippie phenomenon as the mixed-up but inescapably alive eruption of energy that it is." "Watching one of its people is like watching one peppy proton in an atomic reaction—speaking lines, breaking into song, pivoting into dance, shooting into the audience to become a flash point in a constant crackle of music and movement."

Yes, a new era in the theatre had been born at the Public Theatre in 1967. Gerry, Jim and Galt had created a piece of history that would soon develop a life of its own. It was indeed the dawning of a new age.

HAIR Moves Uptown

Michael Butler was the young scion of the Butler family of Chicago, which held vast industrial and financial interests throughout the world. Michael, who had attended exclusive private schools, was a world traveler on his own yacht with John F. Kennedy (who was then a congressman from Massachusetts), a tycoon of the Butler Overseas Corp., organizer of new industries in India, the Middle East and Africa (and writing secret reports on international trade for his sailing companion, who had meanwhile been elected Senator), dealing personally with Arab and Persian kings, directing a South American publishing firm, a resort construction company in the Caribbean and on Fire Island, a sports preserve in Oak Brook, where he was Captain of the polo team, founding a fashionable ski resort, and running for State Senator on the Democratic ticket in Illinois' Du Page County, a Republican bastion for the previous hundred years. Although he eventually lost the election, Michael's real destiny and place in time was with "Hair," which he was soon to find out.

In the fall of 1967 Michael was in New York on a political business trip. While sitting in the Racquet and Tennis Club on Park Avenue, he idly picked up the New York Times. In the theatre section there was an ad for a show he'd never heard of, "Hair." In the ad was a picture of several Indians. In actuality, it was the same picture that was eventually used for the first "Hair" LP from the Public Theatre performance. It was titled, "Hair, An American Tribal Love-Rock Musical." This was before the first preview of "Hair" at the Public Theatre.

Michael had developed a passion for the American Indians, which was passed on from his grandfather, who had learned to appreciate the Indian way of life first hand. The family had owned vast acreage in the Black Hills and the Big-horn area of Montana, at a time when "shooting Indians was almost considered a sport." The treatment of the American Indians appalled the elder Butler, and he passed along those feelings to a young, impressionable, Michael Butler. Besides Michael's strong feelings about the American Indians, he was also very passionate about our countries involvement in the war in Vietnam. He was very much against it and even saw the division in our country as the catalyst for a possible civil war. He held great concerns over the many divisions in our country.

Excited about seeing a show with American Indians, he bought tickets to the first preview. Along with his good friends, Nancy Friday and Olivier Coquelin, he went to see the play. Mr. Coquelin, who was a business partner of Michael's, had interests in several discotheques which included the Cheetah in uptown Manhattan.

What Michael saw truly surprised him. In his opinion, "Hair" was the strongest anti-war statement ever written. No, this was not a show about the American Indians; it was about young men and women, the war, peace and love. In Michael Butler's own words, "It blew my mind." The same truth and honesty that attracted the authors and the young cast members of the show also drew in Michael Butler, whose very life was in direct contrast to much of the play itself.

Michael saw much potential in "Hair" as it was presented at the Public Theatre. But at this time the script had Claude going off to war and dying and that was that. There was no happy ending, no apparent hope, and no "Let the Sunshine In." Although the plot was a bit of a "bummer," to Michael it also appeared to be a great forum to express the anti-war sentiment in a positive, peaceful manner. After all, Michael was at this time more a politician than a producer. He was incredibly impressed with "Hair."

Michael went back home to Chicago with deep thoughts about "Hair." He made the decision he would like to bring the show to his own constituents in his hometown of Chicago. With that thought in mind he contacted Joseph Papp who was running the non-profit New York Public Theatre. When he told Joseph Papp of his desires to bring the show to Chicago, Joe Papp disappointed him by saying, "No." Papp then said something to the effect of, "We do shows like this all the time. We present them for a few weeks; close them and then go on to another."

Disappointed nearly to the point of giving up, Michael went about his business and daily affairs. Within a few weeks however, while doing business in Florida, Michael received a call from Joseph Papp. "Hair's" short run at the Public Theatre was coming to an end and Mr. Papp asked Michael if he would be interested in producing a joint venture of "Hair" at a different venue in New York. Without hesitation Michael agreed to the arrangement and he immediately started searching for a new location. First in mind was of course his friend, Olivier Coquelin. They quickly made arrangements to take "Hair" on to the Cheetah discotheque on the upper east side of New York.

I can't be certain, but logic leaves me to believe, had it not been for Michael Butler seeing that Indian picture on the poster and subsequently getting involved with 'Hair" when he did, the world would not have benefited from this great piece of work. The foundation of talent was there from the artistic side but what was really needed was the infusion of Michael's worldly business, political prowess, financial expertise and capital. With his "eyes wide open," Michael assembled the additional talents necessary to blow the minds of the world sky high. The stage was set and ready for "Hair" to truly "fly in the breeze and get caught in the trees."

In December 1967, not long after "Hair's" limited and successful run at the Public Theatre came to an end, Michael Butler and Joseph Papp joined forces to co-produce a new production of "Hair" uptown. They chose the Cheetah, which was still a working discotheque. In an unusual move the show opened with no advanced ticket sales. Unfortunately ticket sales were weak and for many various reasons, the Cheetah did not turn out to be a good venue for the show.

The lineup at the Cheetah was as follows:

THE CHEETAH COMPANY,
Opened December, 1967 at The Cheetah Theatre

Joseph Papp, Producer
Michael Butler, Executive Producer
Bernard Gersten, Associate Producer
Gerald Freedman, Director
Julie Arenal, Dance Director
Theoni V. Aldredge, Costumes
Ming Cho Lee, Scenery
Lawrence Metzler, Lighting
John Morris, Musical Director

The Cast

Jonelle Allen
Susan Batson
Steve Curry
Thommie Bush
Linda Compton
Ed Crowley
Walker Daniels
Steven Dean
Sally Eaton
Suzannah Norstrand
William Herter

Paul Jabara
Jane Levin
Marijane Maricle
Edward Murphy Jr
Jill O'Hara
Gale Dixon
B. J. Johnson
Alma Robinson
Arnold Wilkerson
Warren Burton

Musicians

Greg Ferrara   Steve Gillette   Jimmy Lewis

Galt MacDermot   Leonard Seed

Even though the box office said differently, Michael was still convinced in the potential of the show. He expressed his concerns to his father and his father's advice was, "If you really believe in this show and love it so much, go for the rights and give it your best shot."

Could Broadway be ready for "Hair?" Michael Butler believed the time was ripe. After further discussions with Joseph Papp, it became apparent to Michael that neither Joseph Papp, nor anyone else, owned the production rights to "Hair." Taking his father's advice to heart, he met with the authors and quickly arranged to buy the necessary options to produce "Hair." He then made plans to take the show to Broadway.

One of the many things Michael noticed about "Hair" was that it was sort of autobiographical. Up to this point Jim Rado had not played the part of Claude in the show. Michael thought the show would be uplifted if Jim would actually play the part he created. After convincing Jim to play the role of Claude and Gerry to play Berger again, Michael then very wisely took the advice of both Jim and Gerry, and chose Tom O'Horgan to direct and restage the new show for its big debut on Broadway.

Tom O'Horgan brought to "Hair" many years of experience with off-off-Broadway productions. He had become an expert of sorts in improvisational techniques, vigorous ensemble playing, a more physical style of acting, and greater use of dance, music and pop-camp comedy.

With "Hair," Tom's original idea was to use the whole theatre as much as possible. He wanted the audience to be able to move and to see what was going on all around them. Michael gave Tom virtual free rein with "Hair" with only a few limitations. Tom wanted the ushers to be hippies as well, but because that presented other problems he settled with having the cast mingle in the isles with the ushers. Tom also thought it would be great if some of the actors would actually live in the theatre. That notion was dropped for obvious reasons.

It was O'Horgan who first brought total nudity to the Broadway stage with "Hair." Its inclusion in Hair" was inspired by a production of "The Emperors New Clothes" that had played in Central Park. Although a nude scene was considered in the original script, it didn't appear until the Broadway production. The nude scene expressed the real sex attitudes of this generation of kids and Tom understood them completely. The nude scene, although very brief and clandestine in its presentation, became a powerful statement in "Hair." It also attracted the curiosity of the world which inevitably helped to sell tickets. The ultimate effects of adding the nude scene to the show was totally uncalculated and unexpected. The controversy it created was ultimately a Godsend for the show.

THE ORIGINAL BROADWAY COMPANY,
Opening Night April 29, 1968 at The Biltmore Theatre

The Manitou Tribe

Michael Butler, Producer
Bertrand Castelli, Executive Producer
Tom O'Horgan, Director
Julie Arenal, Dance Director
Nancy Potts, Costumes
Robin Wagner, Scenery
Jules Fisher, Lighting
Robert Kiernan, Sound

The Cast

Donnie Burks
Steve Curry
Lori Davis
Ronald Dyson
Sally Eaton
Leata Galloway
Steve Gamet
Walter Michael Harris
Robert I. Rubinsky
Paul Jabara
Diane Keaton
Lamont Washington

Lynn Kellogg
Jonathan Kramer
Marjorie LiPari
Emmaretta Marks
Melba Moore
Natalie Mosco
Suzannah Norstrand
Shelley Plimpton
James Rado
Gerome Ragni
Hiram Keller

Musicians

Galt MacDermot, Alan Fontaine, Steve Gillette, Jimmy Lewis,
Zane Paul Zacharoff, Donald Leight, Eddie Williams,
Warren Chaisson, Leo Morris, Neil Tate

Next, I've included excerpts from Clive Barnes second review of "Hair." Compared to the first review, one could see that Clive had been moved deeply by the show since its move to Broadway. Contrary to what some people may think, Tom O'Horgan's contributions brought much life to the show. The show was now alive and bursting with a new energy.

Clive wrote, "What is so likeable about "Hair," that tribal-rock musical that last night completed its trek from downtown, via a discotheque, and landed, positively panting with love and smelling of sweat and flowers, at the Biltmore theatre? I think it is simply that it is so likeable. So new, so fresh, and so unassuming, even in its pretensions."

Clive went on to say, "Hair" is now a musical with a theme, not with a story. Nor is this all that has been done in this totally new, all lit-up, gas-fired, speed-marketed Broadway version. For one thing it has been made a great deal franker. In fact it has been made into the frankest show in town—and this has been a season not noticeable for its verbal or visual reticence."

He also wrote, "The American flag is not desecrated—that would be a Federal offense, wouldn't it?—But it is used in a manner that not everyone would call respectful."

"The show is the first Broadway musical in some time to have the authentic voice of today rather than the day before yesterday." "But the essential likeability of the show is to be found in its attitudes and in its cast."

Unfortunately, "Hair" suffered its first tragedy August 10th of 1968. Critically acclaimed actor, Lamont Washington, passed away after jumping out of a window to escape a fire. Lamont, who was starring as "Hud" in "Hair," was critically injured in a fire at his apartment on West 15th Street.

Lamont was only 24 years old and suffered burns to over 50 per cent of his body as well as internal injuries when he jumped out of a window to the roof of an adjacent building to escape the blaze. The fire apparently started in a mattress in his bedroom. After this terrible tragedy, Donnie Burks took over the role of "Hud."

On August 25th, 1968, Lamont Washington died in St. Vincent's Hospital from injuries he sustained in the accident. Lamont had preformed more than 100 performances as Hud for "Hair" on Broadway.

Frederick O'Neal, president of Actor's Equity Association, said, "Mr. Washington had one of the greatest potentials for the musical theater I'd seen in a long time."

A native of New York, Lamont Washington had understudied Sammy Davis, Jr. during the Broadway run of the hit musical "Golden Boy." He also went on for the star several times when Mr. Davis was out because of injuries suffered on the stage.

In the September 1968 issue of Playbill Magazine, Colette Dowling wrote some of the following. *"Hair*, the American Tribal Love-Rock Musical that opened on Broadway last April and went on to become the season's biggest hit, came as a surprise to everyone. No one expected the rebellious stuff off off-Broadway theatre to hit Broadway quite yet. And when it did in the form of *Hair*, no one expected it to pack the audiences in—a thousand a night—night after night after night. For *Hair* is vehemently antiwar, anti big business and by extension, anti the whole, older, theatre-going generation."

She went on to say, "*Hair* is not just a "message musical." It entertains—so much so that even while those bare-chested bodies are creeping down on you from all sides, writhing down the center isle, wriggling over your lap and up onto the stage (which is the way *Hair* begins), even as you're thinking, "My God! They're taking over!" a larger part of you is wishing you were flying forty feet through the air on a rope, flowers stuck behind your ear, like that guy with the hairy armpits."

About Michael Butler she said, "All he takes credit for in the overhaul *Hair* got before it moved into the Biltmore is "instilling some discipline" in the production. He could have attempted to impose total discipline. Instead, he allowed *Hair* to become a sort of ensemble or group effort that dismissed the usual hierarchy of professional status (from producer, to playwright, and on down to the least significant chorus boy) and ideas poured in from everyone. No one was insignificant."

"The challenge of harnessing the power of a conglomerate of individuals, channeling it into the kind of ordered anarchy that occurs onstage and which is perhaps the play's most distinguished quality, fell to director Tom O'Horgan. It was not a problem with which he was unfamiliar, having worked out rigorously, as he had, in the "new theatre" experiments at the Café La Mama workshop."

"No one in the cast, as it happened, was as emotionally liberated as a play about hippie life called for. To put them in touch with one another and with the play itself, O'Horgan used a series of techniques, devices, if one will, culled from projects as far-flung as Esalen Institute for Human Potential in San Francisco and the Polish Lab Theatre. In order to establish a very basic "gut level" trust, Tom O'Horgan had each actor stand arms down and eyes closed, in the center of a circle of the others, and allow his body to fall, be caught, and then be passed around. The kids were also encouraged to take turns touching one another's bodies all over, to break down bodily inhibitions and to help them "get inside of" or *experience* one another as persons. Exercises in extreme slow motion promoted a kind of self-hypnotism. "We'd do something like put on a shoe very slowly." O'Horgan said. "What happens is that your sense of gravity gets shifted around and you become aware of things you hadn't been aware of before."

In Paris Hair had advance sales twice that of any previous show in Paris history. ~ From "Hair" publicity notes, 8/7/69.

3

Give Me A Head With Hair

By the spring of 1968 I decided I was no longer going to wet down my hair with water and stuff it in my collar while at school. I was tired of kids saying I was a greaser and decided to take a bold step and "let it fly in the breeze." As I walked through the halls the first day, all the other students were shocked to see how long my hair actually was, some even asked if I was wearing a wig. Word was spreading fast and it only took about 45 minutes for Mr. Zemick (the Dean of Students) to find and expel me.

My parents were not too pleased about the situation but not so much with me. Even though they didn't like my long hair they despised the school for telling me how to wear it even worse. This became a constant battle and the only compromise we could reach with the school was for me to continue hiding it by wetting it back.

Because of this I decided I would ask to move in with my grandmother, as the Seattle school district was more liberal in that they allowed the boys to wear their hair long.

THE LONDON COMPANY,
The Shaftesbury Theatre, *Opened September 1968*

Robert Stigwood, Producer
Michael Butler, Producer
David Conyers, Producer
John Nasht, Producer

Bertrand Castelli, Executive Producer
Tom O'Horgan, Director
Julie Arenal, Dance Director
Derek Wadsworth, Musical Director
David Toguri, Assistant to the Director
Nancy Potts, Costumes
Herbert Sidon, Costume Re-Design
Robin Wagner, Scenery
Jules Fisher, Lighting
Robert Calder, Sound

Known Cast History

Gary Aflalo

Steve Alder

Paul Barber

Beverly Baxter

Perry Bedden

Floella Benjamin

Jonathan Bergman

Peter Blake

Miquel Brown

Angela Bruce

Paul Burns

Luie Caballero

Ena Cabayo

Carl Cambell

Cher Cameron

Helen Chappell

David Charkham

Demetrius

Chistopholus

Lucy Fenwick

Andy Forray

Brett Forrest

Kim Fortune

Kate Garrett

Dee Garvin

John Gulliver

Gary Hamilton

Murray Head

Patricia Hodge

Marsha Hunt

Derek James

Linzi Jennings

Colette Kelly

Linda Kendrick

Junior Kerr

Paul Korda

Sonja Kristina

Diane Langton

Ethel Coley

Glenn Conway

Tim Curry

Delano Davis

Pamela Douglas

Helen Downing

Kookie Eaton

Vince Edward

Michael Feast

Christopher Neil

Peter Newton

Paul Nicholas

Maxine Nightingale

Richard O'Brien

Peter Oliver

Elaine Paige

William Parker

Jimmie Payne

Kathy Preston

Marianne Price

Colin Prowell

Joyce Rae

Clare Rees

Leighton Robinson

Adam Russell-Owen

Sherine Savan

Vicky Silva

Belinda Sinclair

Joshua Smith

Cindy Ann Lee

Anabel Leventon

Annabel Littledale

Judy Loe

Caroline Lyndon

Rohan McCullough

Rory McDonald

Amanda Moore

Mike Mulloy

Linbert Spencer

Kirk St James

Michael Staniforth

Gloria Stewart

Peter Straker

Catherine Sydee

Jeannette Tavernier

Oliver Tobias

Edwin Van Wyk

Mike Wade

Trevor Ward

Jacki Whelan

Bruce White

Joanne White

Liz White

Sheila Wilkinson

Jimmy Winston

Lucy Winters

Kimi Wong

David Yip

A "Hair" Highlight

After the finale of "Let the Sunshine In," the cast goes out into the theatre and encourages the audience to come up on the stage with them to dance and sing. Although this is a seemingly integral part of the show in all productions of "Hair," it was not always so.

Beginning with the London premier of "Hair," the audience was so moved by the performance, that after the finale they spontaneously rushed the stage to join the cast, completely uninvited.

This was a natural phenomenon that continued on in London and was later added as an "invite" to all other shows. Only in the other shows, it was not a spontaneous reaction. ~ Story relayed by former London cast member, Annabel Leventon

---

After long arguments and much debate, my request to move in with my grandmother was granted. I moved to Queen Anne Hill as soon as my junior year ended. After moving in with my Grandmother I started spending a great deal of time with my old friend David, whose mom ran The Door coffee-house. He told me about a guitarist friend of his named Sarge who was also going to Queen Anne High. During my first week at the school I ran into Sarge and we became quick friends. Sarge was very tall and had long, straight dark hair that went about half way down his back. I was amazed the school did not care about such things. Life was going to be great here, no more greasing back the hair!

Sarge and I started hanging out a great deal and jamming. He lived right around the corner from the school in an old Victorian house. It was a large house, which was not only shared by Sarge, his mother and sister, but also by any number of boarders. The house had a great little tower room that was Sarge's bedroom. We used to crawl out of the tower window at lunch to sit and enjoy the view. While on the roof, we would often relax and smoke a little weed.

One day after school I stopped off at another friend's house on the way home to my Grandmas. We listened to some records at his house and before I left he gave me a couple of joints. When I arrived home my grandma had just started cooking dinner. So I went upstairs to my room, put a record on the turntable, closed the door, opened the window and proceeded to smoke both joints all by myself. Since I was hanging out the window, I expected no one would know of my evil doings.

After finishing off both joints I was pretty well lit and decided to take my very happy self downstairs to see how grandma was doing with dinner. As I got about half way down the stairs, the thick smoke in the hall distinctly reminded me of grandma's previous illusions to pot smoking when it was only cigarettes.

Panic set in as I feverishly ran to open every door and window I could find! I madly fanned the smoke with an old poster or something of that size and shape. I finally did manage to clear the air and although my grandma never new better, my little trip was certainly cut short. The irony of it all was thicker than the smoke and even to this day, it never fails to give me a good laugh.

Even though David was living in the north end of Seattle with his mom, he came by to jam with Sarge and me more often. The three of us decided to start a band together that was to play original music only. We all agreed that being from Seattle our name should be "RAIN."

It was basically David's band as he wrote most of the music we played. We all sang, which was something I had always been looking for in a group. I no longer wanted the pressure of being the lead and only singer. Besides, harmonies were an important aspect of the music I liked.

Since all three of us played the guitar we were in need of a bass player. With my previous experience in playing the bass I was delegated to handle the job. I didn't have a bass so I went to a local music store on Queen Anne hill, talked my grandmother into co-signing for a loan, and bought an 8-string Hagstrom bass guitar on time.

Somewhere around this time, David and I were goofing around downtown Seattle when we ran into Robin Ball and her friend Vicky. The four of us were talking and walking through a department store together. After awhile it appeared Vicky was coming on to me quite strongly, but I was only interested in Robin. I was hoping she was no longer with Dan but was too shy to ask. Before I could get the nerve to ask her about Dan, Robin gave me a firm little pinch on my backside as we were walking through a department store. I quickly turned around, saw that twinkle in her eye and knew we were meant to be together from that moment on. She giggled and said, "Sorry, I just couldn't resist." As it turns out, while I had always had a crush on her, she had one on me as well.

Later that week I drove to visit Robin in Renton. Robin dropped a bombshell on me. She told me she had gotten pregnant a month before with another guy's baby and had just had an abortion a few days earlier. She was visibly upset about having to give up a baby and was also worried it would make a difference to me. It made no difference in my feelings towards her. There was something special about Robin and I was completely sincere in my compassion for her situation. We really bonded that night. There was no sex involved, simply a meeting of mind and spirit. We were two kids falling in love with one another. From that day forward we were pretty much inseparable.

Although living with my grandma was not a bad thing, it was difficult to have my friends over to visit. Not to mention it was getting difficult traveling back and forth from Sarge's house each night for practice. All things considered, I asked if I could move in with Sarge. More than anything I wanted the freedom to spend more time with Robin.

Life at Sarge's house allowed me to pursue my talents and spiritual quests without hindrance or prejudice. God forbid my grandmother ever were to find out I frequently visited the hippie house up the street and even participated in some Buddhist ceremonies there.

Even though I loved the company and long chats I had with my grandmother while living at her house, I was always on guard; worried I might offend or disappoint her in some way. My grandma was a little saddened by my departure, but I made every effort to stop by to visit her often and on occasion I would use her home as a refuge to crash for the night.

One pill for Rabbi Schultz...one pill for The Rockefeller Foundation...Two pills for...

Here's a little story where my timing might be somewhat off. I remember this was the night Elvis Presley had his big special on TV. Everyone at the house was geared to watch it. It was a rainy night and I was cooking some fried rice and veggies for us that evening. We all took turns with cooking, cleaning, etc. in the house. Anyway, while I was in the kitchen someone knocked at the back door which was in the kitchen. I answered it and there stood a couple of guys who wanted to speak with Paul, one of the boarders. I asked them to wait and called for Paul to come to the door. I then went back to the stove to finish cooking.

Paul was a tall, lanky, geeky looking guy with dark horned rimmed glasses and greased back, jet black hair. He wanted so desperately to be cool but just couldn't quite cut the mustard. The guys at the door were friends of Paul who had some acid he was interested in buying. Paul smoked a little pot but didn't do any other drugs, so he turned and asked me if I would be willing to take some of the acid. He wanted me to see if it was any good. I said I would and promptly swallowed the 2 tablets of Peach Ozley acid he handed to me. The guys at the door smiled and said that normally one should be way more than enough, as they were each double hits. They said "good luck" and left.

I continued cooking dinner and when the rice dish was finished I stepped into the living room, sat on a couch and began watching the Mod Squad on a small black and white TV. Although I was eating, it appeared I was making no headway at all on the bowl of rice. The more I ate, the less it went away. As I was watching the TV, the show was now in color, fantastic colors! I heard some babbling across the room and was taken back at an old, over stuffed chair that was talking to me. "Oh my God," I thought, "what the hell did I just do?"

By this time Paul had told Sarge and David about my trip. They all desired to keep me quiet as Sarge's mom was expected home anytime now. So I went upstairs for a while to watch Elvis in Mary's room. Mary had a great room with a color TV and a great collection of records. Sarge came in to see me after awhile and kept asking me if I was having a bad trip. I kept answering no, but as he persisted in this line of questioning, I started believing that maybe I was having a bad trip. David finally came around and convinced me I was just fine.

Sarge's mom came home and also wanted to watch Elvis, so I was escorted up to the tower to trip alone. They all wanted to conceal my behavior from her. When I got up to the attic room I proceeded to lie back on a bed and stare at the ceiling. On the ceiling there was a collage of pictures pasted that were cut out from magazines. Nothing special on any normal occasion, but I was not normal this evening. As I lay back on the bed, staring at the ceiling, all the people, animals and characters in the collage started moving and racing around. I started tuning into the sound of the rain hitting the roof and as I did the pictures then started dripping. It was as if the rain was coming through the roof. This was all an incredible experience and I was digging every minute of it.

Later on in the evening after the rain had stopped, David and Sarge came up and asked me if I wanted to go out for a ride. After saying I would, they took me for a ride in the back of a pickup truck. I laid on my back again, but this time I was staring at the stars in the sky. By the time the morning came around I was still high but starting to come down. I went for a walk on Highland Drive to a park where you can look out over the city. As the sun was rising I was looking west over the horizon. The Earth appeared small, like a little tennis ball, and I felt so, so small. I had a tremendous feeling and awareness of God. It was as though I heard an inner voice saying God was within me and I didn't need drugs to find him.

Robin and I were still as tight as could be. Although she never knew it, I was a virgin before we got together. More than sex though, Robin gave me something I had never before experienced in my life. She had an unconditional love for me. We both gave one another great freedom to go and do as we pleased and our loyalty to one another was never questioned. My band wasn't working as yet only rehearsing, so we were able to spend a great deal of time with one another. Because we were both dirt poor, most of our time was spent walking about town, playing in and exploring Seattle's many parks. There were also many free concerts outdoors, be-ins and events to keep us busy.

Robin still lived in Renton, sometimes staying with her dad but mostly with her mom. Her mom was really great to the two of us. Somehow she knew we were right for each other and did everything within her means to help us enjoy our love. She would loan Robin her car many times each week and Robin would drive the 20 plus miles north to Seattle to be with me. Her mom would usually even spring for the gas. My car was completely dead by this time, so I abandoned it on a street corner by my grandma's house. It remained there for over a year before the city finally towed it away.

The two of us spent a great deal of time going for rides in her mom's car. Since neither of us had a private residence to be alone together in, the car served as our private place. Like most kids our age we would try to find romantic places to sit in the car and neck or just talk and stare at one another. Many times we would just park in the driveway of the Lee Street house. Very seldom was the house ever empty of people so the car was our little hideaway.

One night Robin took me over to her dad's house so she could pick up something. She had been trying to avoid my meeting him and thought the coast was clear this one particular night for me to meet her brother. Robin's brother Bobby (who was a few years younger) was there. As the two of us were visiting with Bobby, Robin's dad came home. He was a large man with a stone cold face that couldn't possibly smile. He walked in, looked directly at me and within seconds, all hell broke loose. He started screaming obscenities, directing them at me, and told me to get out or he was going to kill me!

Before I could even get a grip on what was happening, Robin and I were outside, running to the car with Bobby following, shouting for us to leave for our safety. Both Robin and Bobby were exchanging curses with their dad who was obviously very drunk. We sped off into the rainy night while her dad was still screaming at us from the porch.

Here I thought I had such a bad childhood experience. I felt very bad for Robin as hers was obviously much worse than I could imagine. Her mom and dad divorced because of her dad's drinking and abuse to her mom as well as to the kids. The physical abuse was very severe and Robin told me that on at least one occasion a gun had been fired in the house. The kids really did love their dad though, in spite of his drinking problems.

I remember one time the two of us drove back down to Renton. We had been visiting our friend Brenda there and were on our way to see my mom who lived nearby. There was about six inches of snow on the ground that day and it was causing quite a lot of trouble on the roads. We had noticed before pulling into Brenda's that many cars had already skidded into the ditches on ahead. Robin felt very uncomfortable about driving her mom's car in the ice and snow for fear of getting into a wreck, so I happily volunteered to drive when we left Brenda's place. Of course I thought I was a much better driver than she and I could drive great under any circumstance.

In any case, we only got about one half a mile up the road before the ice suddenly propelled us into the ditch. There were no injuries except for the car's right front fender. We were enormously happy we were safe but also sad about her mother's car. Luckily enough, because I had turned with the slide correctly and was only going about 20 mph, we were able to move out of the ditch without assistance. Because I didn't have insurance and really wasn't supposed to be driving her mom's car, Robin took the heat which wasn't much. Her mom, being equally thankful for our safety, let it go with a hearty "oh well." Much later when we finally told her mom the truth about this story, her mom told us she had figured out as much.

In the pages of the Los Angeles "Hair" program, Jay Thompson wrote the following about Tom O'Horgan's Sensitivity Exercises.

"Early in the rehearsals for "Hair," an individual member of the cast is led, blindfolded, into the center of the huge rehearsal hall by the director Tom O'Horgan."

"There is a deadly silence."

"Suddenly a burst of sound as the other 20-odd members of the cast rush the blindfolded one, whistling, touching, whispering, yelling."

"He is hoisted aloft, whirled in a canvas, whisked across the floor. He hears vices whispering beautiful things in his ear; then they begin to call his name, louder and louder, crowding around him. At the peak of sound, his blindfold is slipped off and a mirror is held inches in front of his face."

"He is scared, but everyone else is, too, at what they have put him through. Hostilities have been shown, but also love. He relaxes; they hug him and laugh with him. Rapport has been born."

"On another day the cast, eyes closed, move to the center of the hall until they touch another person. Eyes still closed, they gently explore each other's faces with their hands until they *really* feel each other. Then they open their eyes and look, *really* look, at each other. It is difficult to be other than loving and understanding after this kind of communication."

"O'Horgan's "sensitivity exercises" were done nearly every day. By the middle of the rehearsal period, the cast had become not a group of actors rehearsing, but a group of human beings who liked and understood each other, who had been *through* things together. Instead of caring about themselves as individual egos and performers, they cared about relating to each other and "doing their thing," individually and collectively, for the audience."

"O'Horgan's way generates this kind of feeling: At the end of an exhausting day of rehearsal, he ran the cast through the finale of the show for the first time. Just as the final note was played, the doors opened and co-authors Gerome Ragni and James Rado walked in, dead tired from a cross-country flight. The entire cast, most of whom had never seen them before, fell upon them, kissing, laughing, and embracing. Everyone, cast and crew, locked arms, joined in a huge circle and sang "This Is The Dawning of the Age of Aquarius" at the top of their lungs. It was a loving moment. And you will, hopefully, feel it and be a part of it as you experience "Hair.""

THE LOS ANGELES COMPANY,
The Aquarius Theatre
Premiere Opening December 3, 1968

The Chumash Tribe

Michael Butler, Producer
Ken Kragen, Producer
Tom Smothers, Producer
Ken Fritz, Producer
Bertrand Castelli, Executive Producer
Tom O'Horgan, Director
Julie Arenal, Dance Director
Danny Hurd, Musical Director
Nancy Potts, Costumes
Robin Wagner, Scenery
Jules Fisher, Lighting
Guy Costa, Sound

Known Cast History

Christine Adams	Abigale Hanes
Greg Arlin	Gina Harding
Leni Ashmore	John Herzog
Lynn Baker	Carolyn Hill
Richard Baskin	Elaine Hill
Teda Bracci	David (Pappy) Hunt
Alan Braunstein	Gloria Jones
Corinne Broskette	Frankie Karl
Genie Brown	Gregory Karliss
Jim Carroza	Randy Keys

Joel Christie

Kay Cole

Jerry Combs

Zenobia Conkerite

Robert Corff

Denise Delapenha

Leo Elmore

Patrick Elmore

Tom Eure

Linda Faust-Press

Randy Brooks Fredericks

Tadg Galleran

Dobie Gray

Albert Greenberg

Delores Hall

Carol Miller

Lee Montgomery

Susan Morse

Joe Morton

Buddy Mullaney

Holly Near

Ted Neeley

Allan Nicholls

Cecelia Norfleet

Rhonda (Coulet) Oglesby

Helen Pollack

James Rado

Bennett Raffer

Gerome Ragni

Joey Richards

Lee King

Jessica Kluger

Cheri Kohler

Gene Krischer

Llewellyn Lafford

Karen Lippolt

Clifford Lipson

Gar MacRae

Heather MacRae

Bruce Maltby

Alan Martin

John McKinnis

Meat Loaf

Mary Mendum

Richard (Kim) Milford

Jobriath Salisbury

Melody Santangelo

Tyrone Scott

Rhoda Seven

Stan Shaw

Red Shepard

Bert Sommer

Avery Sommers

Oatis Stephens

Greta Stewart

Ray Uhler

Tata Vega

Ben Vereen

(Lady) Helena Walquer

Jennifer Warnes

Erik Robinson	Willie Weatherly
Barbara Robison	Tom Westerman
Robert Rothman	Tammy Winters

On February 5th, 1969, Clive Barnes wrote his 3rd review of "Hair," the second for the Broadway adaptation.

"Hair" is beautiful," wrote Clive. "Now, nearly a year after the opening, the cast at the Biltmore Theatre is almost entirely new, and "Hair" tribes are playing in London, Los Angeles, Copenhagen and probably elsewhere. Also, nearly a year after the opening, the show has a kind of radiant freshness. It still seems as thought the whole thing is swiftly, deftly and dazzlingly being improvised before your very eyes."

"Seeing "Hair" again did raise a few questions. Its success stems from two things. First its perfect reflection of a generation that seems in no mood to lower its voice—it knows what whispering can do to people. Second, the music by Galt MacDermot and the lyrics by Ragni and Rado. This is pop-pop, or commercial pop, with little aspirations to art—a clever and honest dilution of what is happening in pop music. Fundamentally it is pure Broadway—but Broadway 1969 rather than Broadway 1949."

"Then I found myself thinking about so many of the misconceptions about "Hair," which seem to have risen among that great section of the public who have never seen the show."

"People say that it attracts only middle-aged suburbanites (although they never go on to explain what is so wicked about being a middle-aged suburbanite) and has no appeal to youth. This is a lie. At last Wednesday's matinee in a packed orchestra, I myself, at 41, was among the oldest, two dozen in the audience. I felt like a senior citizen."

"Also, people say the show is dirty. Rubbish. It is as clean as Tide and not half so chemical. Members of the cast do occasionally use naughty words, but in a quite childlike fashion. They do—for one moment of social and esthetic revolt—take off their clothes if they wish to. But this is not obscene. It is also totally asexual. If you are proposing to go to "Hair" for sexual stimulation you don't need a theatre ticket, you need treatment."

"So go and see "Hair." If you have just one show to see on Broadway try and make it this one. If you hate it, I cannot promise to give you your money back. But I rather doubt if we could ever become friends."

"According to its publicists, there is by now no hour of the day or night when somewhere in the world the Ragni-Rado-MacDermot assault on the Establishment is not playing to some Establishment audience." ~ From Opera News—12/20/69.

4

Going Down

Our band, RAIN, was getting better since David had asked Brian, an old friend of his to join us on the drums. David came up with some money for studio time so we began to rehearse some of his songs to record. During the sessions we submitted a tape to an A&R person at Elektra Records. They liked what they heard and asked us to come to Los Angeles for further consideration. Brian couldn't make the trip so just three of us planned on going. We arranged to stay with Sarge's sister at her boyfriend's house in El Monte. We only had planned on staying for a couple of weeks unless we were signed to a record company.

When we arrived in LA, Mary and her boyfriend Frank picked up the three of us at the airport and drove us out to their place in El Monte. Frank was an entrepreneur and owned his own business. The business was a vending machine company that specialized in the rides for kids that you see at grocery stores. At his shop he had a small studio apartment which he also used as an office. That is where Sarge, David and I stayed. It was in an industrial area and only about a mile away from Frank's apartment.

Frank seemed like a really nice guy who appeared excited to help us enjoy our stay in Los Angeles. He drove a classy little red Corvette Stingray and he also had an older company pickup truck that was used to transport the machines around. While we were staying there, Frank invited us to use his truck anytime if we needed it. Also in the shop, Frank had a great looking, customized Harley tricycle. While we were admiring it, a conversation came up that he was planning on giving it to a commune of hippies he said he was friends with. He told us they lived up on an old movie set where we could ride horses for free. He also made mention there were many pretty girls at the ranch who were willing to do anything we pleased. The girls didn't excite me too much but riding horses sounded fun. So we made plans to go visit this place later in the week.

The next day we visited our A&R contact at Elektra Records. We were given a bunch of LP's from their stable and told that although they were still considering signing us, they hadn't made up their minds as yet. They also told us of a cabin in the mountains the studio sometimes had available. The cabin was in Paxton and they said they would consider sending us there for a month or two so we could get a little tighter with our music. We were a little let down as we were of course hoping to get signed to a record deal. In any case, we decided to at least enjoy our visit to LA before returning to Seattle.

We spent the next couple of days visiting all the tourist spots in Hollywood, one of which was a trip to the Aquarius Theatre. "Hair" (which was extremely popular at the time) had just opened there in December 1968. We wanted to see the incredible artwork the "Fool" had painted on the building. We also wanted to check out the ticket prices as we planned to see the show before returning to Seattle.

Later on Frank drove the three of us out to the Spahn Movie Ranch in the pickup. It was a long cold drive for those of us riding in the back of the truck from El Monte out past Topanga Canyon. We arrived at the ranch in the afternoon. As we were pulling up, a bakery truck was leaving and Frank pointed out they had probably dropped off a load of donated bread goods. Frank explained that lots of people donated stuff to Charlie's clan, even Dennis Wilson of the Beach Boys.

Frank wanted to introduce us to Charlie, but this Charlie person was busy in a meeting with some of his folks about something. I could see Charlie sitting in a chair outside in the distance playing with what appeared to be a hunting knife, while a group was gathered around him. I have no idea what was going on or being said, but it seemed a little strange. None of us were disappointed in not meeting Charlie as we were only interested in riding the horses.

Even though we came to the ranch to ride horses we were not dressed for the occasion. We were dressed in our rock star wanna-be attire, hardly suitable for hanging out on a ranch. The girls at the camp immediately started referring to us as "pretty boys from the city." As we were getting ready to hop on some horses, David mentioned he wished he had some boots to wear instead of his tennis shoes. He had no more than gotten the statement out of his mouth that a tall young man took off his own boots and said, "Here, they're yours." We were thinking, "What's the catch? Does this mean we have to give everything of ours to you?" It was very strange.

The horse ride on the ranch was very memorable for me. I could recognize much of the landscape from many of the old western movies and television programs I used to watch as a child. When we returned, we were invited into an old gutted out mobile home to smoke some weed. It was very dirty inside, really disgusting to say the least. The back of the trailer was completely gone and it faced out to a pasture with some horses, cows and assorted farm animals. They had a couple of guitars and an amp or two, so we decided to jam a little. As we were sitting there I mentioned I wished I had a bass guitar to play. A guy got up and left, and within about ten minutes he returned with a bass guitar that looked as though it had been buried under six feet of dirt. As we were playing our music we noticed out the back of the trailer that all the farm animals had their asses pointing towards us, as if we were being mooned by them. The more we smoked and played, the worse the vibes got. Although the folks seemed nice enough, there were some real strong negative vibes going on so we were past ready to leave.

It was getting dark by now and we were soon invited to sit around the campfire. Charlie was still not around. We were asked to sing again and some of the girls started to sing with us. Shortly thereafter one of the girls suggested we stop because Charlie might get real jealous if it appeared that the group was enjoying someone else's music other than his. We thought this was a very weird request. Also, Frank never mentioned even once about Charlie being a musician. Just as we were having this conversation, a helicopter started flying overhead. Immediately the group panicked, doused out the fire and began scrambling towards the bushes. They were grabbing our arms and telling us to run and hide. Being guests, we complied with their wishes but couldn't figure out what the purpose of all this was.

As the copter was circling overhead I heard a strange noise next to me. I looked down and one of the girls was squatting next to me, taking a leak. I was totally disgusted and couldn't imagine how anyone could even think about being with one of these girls. I missed Robin more than ever and really just wanted to go back home to Seattle.

The copter soon left and it was really never explained to us why they were so paranoid about being seen by it. As we were getting ready to head back to Franks Apartment, a couple of folks in the camp told us of their plans to move out to the desert. They said we could come if we wanted to. We politely declined, said our thanks for the days visit and drove off on down the road back towards El Monte.

That night when we got back to Frank's apartment, he mentioned he had recently received a shipment of about 29 kilo's of pot. Frank said he had to go out for a business meeting and would be back a little later. He said we should use the truck to go back to the shop when we were ready to crash for the night. We visited with Mary for a little while and then decided to go back to our place as we were tired from the long day at the ranch. Sarge decided to spend the night at Franks to visit more with his sister.

As David and I were driving home I noticed some flashing lights off in the distance over by Franks shop. I also saw what appeared to be Franks Vette. Without hesitation I just knew he was getting busted. I said so to David, while at the same time making a sharp U-turn back to Frank's apartment. We quickly ran up the stairs to tell Mary and Sarge. Within minutes after we arrived the phone rang and it was Frank confirming he had been arrested.

After Frank hung up, we immediately took stock of all the pot that was in the house and flushed it down the toilet. There was approximately 4 kilos of it. David couldn't stand the thought of it and stashed a few joints outside under a trash container to retrieve at a later time. We scoured the house for any other damaging evidence and when we were sure it had all been removed, we went to bed.

The next thing I remember was a very loud boom at around 6:00am as the door of the apartment came crashing in. Mary was in the bedroom and the three of us were sleeping on a sofa bed in the living room. At first I thought it was an earthquake until I looked up and saw a couple of El Monte's best with their guns cocked and pointed towards our heads. They were shouting,

"POLICE, DON'T MOVE!! PUT YOUR HANDS UP ABOVE YOUR HEADS!"

We were still half asleep, but of course did as they asked. They told us to get up and one of us started putting on our pants. They yelled again,

"WHAT ARE YOU DOING? WE TOLD YOU NOT TO MOVE!!"

"We were just going to put on our pants," one of us said.

After a few minutes of this confusion they told us we were under arrest and began to handcuff us all. When we asked what for, they said,

"For paraphernalia."

Knowing we had gotten rid of everything, we asked, "What paraphernalia?"

One of them pointed up to a bookshelf, at a pristine, never used water pipe. Frank's mother had gotten it for him while on a trip to India. He then said,

"That's an opium pipe if I ever saw one."

So away we went in handcuffs and chains, even Mary. If we asked any questions they would just yell at us to shut up. About one minute into the drive, David put his handcuffs on the back of the seat and said, "They're too tight. Can someone please loosen them?"

With that, one of them shouted back, "I thought we told you to shut up!"

During the drive to jail the officer in the front passenger seat asked which one of us owned the Hofner bass guitar. I was immediately concerned, as my Hofner had been at the shop and the case had been locked, so how did he know what it was?

"It's mine," I said, "Is it okay?"

"Yeah, it's fine," he said, "What a bitchin' guitar."

I asked how he got it open and he said they broke the locks on our cases looking for drugs. The conversation soon ended and with the silence came fear. We were all scared shitless, not knowing what was about to happen. We could only imagine the worse.

First they took us to the LA County drunk tank. We told them we were only 17 years old but they didn't believe us. They interrogated each of us separately hoping to glean what they believed might be the real truth. They could not or would not believe that we had nothing to do with Frank's drug deal. As I sat down for my initial interrogation the officer yelled at me and said, "Don't touch that coffee, that's mine!"

I then looked at the styrofoam cup on the desk next to me and softly replied, "I wasn't planning on drinking anything sir, besides, I don't drink coffee."

"Oh, just smoke a little pot here and there, huh?" he replied.

I smirked, trying to hold back my thoughts of laughter and figured I was better off not saying anything to these jerks from this point on.

After the interrogations were finished we were promptly thrown into a fingerprinting and a photo session, after which they marched the three of us off into a common cell and gave us only one blanket and one pillow. Thinking this was just an oversight one of us said, "There's only one blanket and one pillow here, can we get two more?"

They responded with a quick, "That's all you get, fight over them!"

We were really starting to see the humor in the whole process and decided to not let them get us down. We began to sing songs together and got some of the other guests to encourage us in our endeavors. The guards were not happy with us. This was not a happy place and we were acting otherwise. In their eyes we were being very disrespectful, but we were simply trying to maintain a sense of sanity in a very, very crazy situation. We weren't about to fight with anyone, most especially with one another.

After spending several hours in the drunk-tank they discovered we were telling the truth about our age and transferred us to a juvenile detention center across town. That had to be one of the most depressing situations I have yet to experience in my life. From the moment we arrived until the moment we left, you could hear boys crying all over the place and grown men shouting and corralling them around. The first night we didn't get any sleep. Just as we would start to sleep someone would move us to a different bed in a different place. Sometimes a bed wasn't even available and a bench, a mat or a chair was our resting spot. We felt like animals, like we were worthless. I couldn't believe it was happening at all.

In the morning they split the three of us up in different directions. All the kids were making fun of our long hair. One little boy kept coming up to me with a pair of scissors insisting the guards gave him permission to cut my hair. He would not leave me alone and was determined to complete the deed. I'm not a violent person but after several polite attempts to make him quit failed, I finally totally lost my temper. I then screamed a warning out that I would stab anyone who tried to cut my hair with the scissors. They all must have believed me because within a short period of time I was put in solitary confinement. Solitary was a relief and a blessing to me and I stayed there until we were released 2 days later.

While in solitary confinement I volunteered to make some cartoon drawings and signs for some of the bulletin boards they had throughout the facility. This kept me busy and I felt like I was able to bring a little joy into the lives of some of these forgotten children.

When I finally heard we were going to be released I was humiliated to find out that the police had called our parents and would only release us into their custody. All three of our mothers came along with David's stepfather. Here I had been completely independent and now had to have my mother's help. I was not a happy camper. All charges had been dropped as there really weren't any that would have stuck, yet they had the nerve to tell us to leave California and never return.

We all drove back to Washington State in David's mom's station wagon. Throughout the trip back my mother was trying to convince me to return home with her, but I refused to consider it. On the way back to Seattle we passed through San Francisco and managed to talk our parents into visiting the Haight Ashbury district. It wasn't anything like we expected, as the magic of the summer of 1967 had long since passed. Although there were plenty of hippies to be seen, they all appeared to be drug cases from the lower class of life. It seemed more like the skid road district in Seattle. When we finally returned to Seattle, I continued to make my home the Lee Street house.

The Mexico Fiasco

There were some strange scenarios surrounding "Hair" in Mexico. The ill-fated company was a collaborative effort between Michael Butler, Alfredo Calles and Bertrand Castelli. The cast members were from Mexico, the U.S., England and South America.

Rehearsals were held in Mexico City for the first few weeks in late 1968. From the start, the cast had to keep a low profile as several hundred students had been wounded and killed in the same area the previous spring for protesting the Vietnam War. While in Mexico City a full show album was recorded. Unfortunately only about 500 copies were printed so this is a very rare 3-album set done in Spanglish.

Soon the cast was moved to Acapulco where an old open-air movie theatre had been prepared and renovated for the show. In Acapulco the cast and crew were routinely harassed throughout the city. Several of the band members were accosted on the beach and had their heads shaved, after which the cast bought them some wigs.

The American cast members had applied for working visas and there was no indication that they would not be approved by opening night, January 3, 1969. They soon learned the approvals were stalled and were then told to use their own discretion in performing the nude scene on opening night. At this point everyone presumed the show would be shut down so the cast did the nude scene as planned.

After the first performance, in the dark of night the Government padlocked the Theatre. In addition all the equipment was seized (which Mexican Producer Alfredo Calles had paid thousands of dollars in escrow to bring in from the States) and the Producer's Private Club "Theatro Aquario," was shut down as well.

Surprised they had not been detained; the cast partied the next night. At about 4:00 a.m. they were rudely awakened, arrested, and taken to Immigration for deportation. After hours of negotiation the cast signed legal documents saying they would leave the country within 24 hours or be sent to prison. Unfortunately those documents were dated the day before and they were forced to go into hiding until the Producer's could arrange air transportation for them.

Gerry Ragni and Jim Rado had come to Acapulco for the opening. Luckily, they had hid under the bed in Danny Hurd's apartment (the Musical Director) and were not included in the cast round up. Gerry, afraid they would cut his hair, stuffed his mane under one of Danny's hats. Both Gerry and Jim then went into hiding with the rest of the cast. Three mini buses were driven to a closed resort in the mountains near Mexico City, where they all stayed for 3 days. While waiting, Gerry and Jim put the others through all kinds of acting exercises and taught them songs that did not make the final cut of the show.

Finally, to a big media fan fare, they left Mexico City on January 10, 1969, flying into Los Angeles. There they were met with a big party put on by the Los Angeles Cast. ~ Story relayed by Mexico cast member, Corinne Broskette

Doors Locked

While I had been having this great adventure on the west coast, there had been a great deal of press concerning a feud between Michael Butler (the producer of "Hair") and the author's (Gerome Ragni and James Rado). The big secret the press never learned about was what this altercation was really about. In reading the press clippings, one might have been inclined to believe the authors were being treated unfairly. That they were simply making changes to their own creative work, something authors are entitled to do.

In realty and fact, I believe Michael Butler was really saving the show and protecting the authors from themselves. Rather than getting angry they should have eventually thanked him. The issue revolved around changes Gerome Ragni improvised in the show. The specific changes that caused Michael to have the authors locked out were definitely distasteful enough to get the show closed down.

Fortunately for all parties concerned, Michael's reaction was quick and the changes went unnoticed by the authorities. Without getting into detail, Gerry decided to perform a scene in the nude. In addition to the added nudity, he had a feather sticking out of his ass. Needless to say, although Gerry was a brilliantly creative person, he was also often out of control. It's important to also understand that "Hair" was always under the constant watch of the authorities. There were those who were looking for any excuse to shut it down. ~ Story relayed by Michael Butler

---

In April of 1969 the press got a hold of the fact that producer Michael Butler had barred the authors of "Hair" from the Biltmore Theatre. The authors, James Rado and Gerome Ragni, had been playing the lead roles in the show.

Management sources (unidentified) said that the authors had been improvising their performances and not adhering to the script since their recent return to the show after a five-month absence, during which they worked in the Los Angeles Company.

Jim and Gerry denied they had been departing from the script. They also said they would be willing to eliminate anything that the management found "objectionable."

Since they were banned from performing they decided to watch the show with the regular audience. However someone in the lobby had told them that they could not go in.

Their lawyer soon appeared and told them they were dismissed from the cast but management would pay their contract as actors. He also said because they were authors they could sit in as such to see the rehearsal.

So they entered the theatre and sat in the orchestra section. They were soon approached and told that they were "not to come into the theatre." They were upset but followed their lawyer's advice to leave.

"How dare he throw us out, treating us like garbage!" Gerry Ragni was quoted as saying.

Outside, Jim Rado was quoted as saying, "They asked us to come back from Los Angeles to take up our parts. I came back on Monday, Gerry on last Wednesday. Last night, I called Mr. Butler in Chicago but he wouldn't talk to us."

"I wish it would close, it doesn't belong here," said Gerry, while waving at an armored truck that had come to pick up receipts from the box office.

Galt MacDermot, composer of "Hair," joined the actor-authors outside the theatre. He said he wanted to find out more about what was at issue. "This is not reality," he told the author's. Mr. Rado and Mr. Ragni suddenly smiled.

"We're not angry, we have a sense of humor," Gerry said "but it's a very bizarre trial."

The feud between the authors and producer Michael Butler only lasted about a week. Michael Butler had charged that Gerry and Jim were making unauthorized revisions and that Gerry in particular, as an actor, had strayed from the script with improvisations.

To make amends Michael invited the author's and composer Galt Mac-Dermot to meet with him at the home of a friend, Peter Yarrow, of Peter, Paul and Mary, the folk singers.

Gerry and Jim suggested to Michael they meet at the Sheep Meadow in Central Park near the zoo. So they met there in the late afternoon and resolved their differences. [Ellen Stewart, of La Mama ETC fame, was the person who suggested this meeting location to the authors. She also participated and mediated during the meeting.]

5

Come To The Be-In

Soon it was spring in Seattle. The ice and snow had disappeared and people were beginning to come out of their winter isolation. I can vividly remember a day Robin and I spent together at Seward Park in south Seattle. She had brought a camera and the two of us were taking pictures of each other. We were holding hands, laughing and running along the shores of Lake Washington. We were two young people, madly in love, not a care in the world.

After a short time Robin's camera ran out of film but she continued to take pictures anyway. It was as if she were preserving photo memories in her mind. She was even taking pictures of total strangers and having them take pictures of us, all without film. It was all very typical of Robin's sense of humor and I soaked up every minute of it. She was a natural comic, fun to be around and a beautiful free spirit.

She was also more of a true hippie than I was. Unlike most girls her age she wasn't at all into the vain issues of style and dress of the times, like most of the girls I had known. A t-shirt, jeans and minimal makeup suited her just fine. When she was not with me, she was off participating in as many demonstrations, be-ins, concerts and events she could muster a ride too. If there was something happening around town, she was there.

With spring came many more outdoor events for Robin and myself to attend. This was still the sixties and there were many free concerts in the parks. We made it a point to attend as many as possible. Although we both indulged in the communal social events of "getting high," we were also very moderate. It was after all, "the thing to do."

One weekend Robin and I went to a free outdoor concert and be-in at Volunteer Park. I remember two of the bands that played that day because they were both very good. One was "Easy Chair" and the other was a band called "Juggernaut." The lead guitar player for "Easy Chair" was Burke Wallace, who eventually became a cast member in the Seattle production of "Hair." Jeff Simmons, their bass player, later went on to join Frank Zappa and the Mothers of Invention. Pernell Alexander, the lead guitarist for "Juggernaut," also joined the "Hair" band at the Moore Theatre.

It was at this be-in, on this sunny Seattle day, when Robin convinced me we should have a child. We were both sitting down with some friends and were admiring a beautiful little girl with long dark hair. The little girl looked a lot like Robin and I fell in love with the idea of having a child with her. Here we were just two kids ourselves, no real jobs and planning a family. We were truly blinded by our love which we thought could conquer all.

Later in June Robin invited me to go camping for the weekend with her grandparents to Spirit Lake. We went and after visiting with the older folks for a while, we got bored and decided to take a rowboat out onto the lake. It was while we were rowing out on the lake that Robin told me she was with child. I couldn't have been happier. We rowed the boat to the other side of the lake, hiked up a short distance into the woods and made love.

Even British royalty took notice of the excitement of "Hair."

In London, April 15th 1969, Princess Anne paid a surprise visit to "Hair" and wound up dancing on stage with the cast. "The audience sat up and cheered as the 18-year-old Princess broke into a hip swinging routine, flinging her arms in abandon."

In May of 1969, Clarence Petersen wrote a lengthy article about "Hair's" famous producer, Michael Butler. He wrote,

"Michael Butler was introduced to the assembled press agents who constitute the Publicity Club of Chicago as the world's hippiest millionaire. And there he sat, waiting to begin his speech, in his long hair and bushy mustache and love beads and his kind of hippie-looking, cocoa-colored suit. But the suit, you see, was not bought at one of those second-hand thrift stores or anything like that—it was pure suede."

"Michael Butler is a name you might remember no matter which sections of the newspapers you read most. He has been on the main news pages as an adviser to President Kennedy on Indian and middle eastern affairs, as a special projects man for Gov. Otto Kerner, as an unsuccessful Democratic candidate for state senator from Du Page county [where he was something of a phenomenon even as a loser because no Democratic has won a state office in that county since the Civil war and Butler at least had his Republican opponent worried]."

"The entertainment columns are talking about Butler as the producer of "Hair," which is most often described either as "America's tribal love-rock musical" or as "that play where they dance nude on the stage." "Hair," which will open soon in Chicago, was the reason for Butler's appearance before the publicity club."

"Many members of the audience expected Butler to talk about "Hair," even though his speech was titled "The New Communication." That's his term for what "Hair" is trying to do—to bridge the gap between the young idealists [and that's what they are, most of them, even if they don't always proceed in an ideal way] and what Butler calls "the great uncommitted semi-establishment people."

"The new generation accepts the state of constant change as a way of life. Much of the rest, Butler says, is "word games, so they investigate love: Spiritual love as an imperative and physical love as a fact of life."

All that, he said, is the message of "Hair."

The draft was becoming an issue now because I was soon to be 18 years old. Robin and I talked a great deal about it and we were both scared I would get called up. Pretty much anyone who was drafted at that time was sent to the front lines in Vietnam, unless you had a specialized skill or knew someone important. Kids were dying left and right for a war in a far away land that none of us understood. Hell, we couldn't even vote back then!

Friends suggested I apply to become a minister with The Universal Life Church. The notion was widely accepted that you could get a conscientious objector deferment if you were a minister. This church offered a membership through the mail and if you so desired, ordination as an official minister. It was a long shot but we felt it was worth it. I applied and like thousands of others was of course accepted. My pastoral credentials arrived within a few weeks. But even with my certificate in hand I still didn't feel safe.

Later in July both Robin and I attended a three-day music festival in the town of Duval, Washington. David's mom was the promoter and all of us again helped her without any pay. We designed the poster for the event and helped to make sure all the bands got on and off the stage on time. The day before the festival it had rained, but on the first day the sun came out and it was beautiful. This three-day weekend away was to be real special for the two of us. She was pregnant and we were both very excited about it.

Music blared while people were playing naked in the mud holes that the rain had left. Akin to Woodstock, there was around the clock music, too many drugs, too much booze and not enough security. The concert promoters made little if any money because most of the people just climbed over the fences and let themselves in. The place was also rampant with bikers who immediately declared themselves to be the law. If you didn't obey them you got your head bashed in. It was a mess.

I made a grievous error on the afternoon of the first day. Robin had gone off to help the promoters by watching the fences for people who were getting in for free. What a pregnant girl could do to stop them I haven't a clue. I on the other hand was working at the bandstand, shuffling the many acts on and off the stage. It had been awfully hot out and to quench my thirst I innocently accepted a glass of Kool-Aid from a young lady. I quickly drank the entire glass of Kool-Aid and set out to find Robin.

I found her and quickly persuaded her to come back with me to listen to the music. She was not feeling well because she had been standing out in the sun for quite some time. On the way back to the bandstand Robin told me she had heard that someone was passing out some real bad LSD in Kool-Aid. "Oh that's just great," I said, "I might have drank some." That was about the last rational thought I was to have that day.

I spent the rest of the day and night in a tent totally zoned out. It was awful. There was not one redeeming factor or value to this experience, not a one. I remember Robin coming in and out of the tent, bringing me water and comforting me. The next day she confided she had a miscarriage. We were both devastated. The weekend was a total disaster. By coincidence, a picture of the two of us appeared in a Seattle newspaper from the first day of the festival. My mother cut it out and saved it for us. Luckily it was the before picture, not the after.

One of the performers at the festival was a guy Robin had seen before and she was really excited for me to hear him play. He played very funky folk and blues on the acoustic guitar as well as harmonica. His name was Don Copeland and he was indeed very fun to listen to. Don would later on become a cast member of the Seattle and Miami productions of "Hair," and a very dear friend of mine.

Within a month Robin was pregnant again and this time we both told our families. You can imagine the response we got and deservedly so. From our point of view we were in love, we were "soul mates," and nothing else mattered. We could and would make it work. From their point of view we were too young, unstable and just weren't thinking. They were of course right but supported our decisions regardless. It was after all too late to change the circumstances. Having an abortion or giving our child up for adoption was not an option for the two of us.

The pressure was on. Although Robin and I were content to raise our child outside of marriage, that idea did not please our families. We were easily convinced by them to get married. I had just turned eighteen at the time and Robin was about 2 weeks shy of seventeen. Our families of course led the way with the plans. There was so much to prepare for and to be honest; it was beginning to scare the crap out of me. I started to avoid any and all conversations related to "the wedding." The one thing I did enjoy about this time was the joy and exuberance that emanated from Robin. This was in many ways, one of the happiest moments of her life and to a point I relished in her happiness.

While our parents were all gleefully making our wedding plans, the two of us rented our first apartment together. It was very close to my parent's house in Renton. Up to this time Robin and I had never really lived with one another. Oh sure we spent lots of days and nights with each other, but we had never actually lived together.

So when we actually got our first apartment together, Leo the lion and Cancer the crab finally met their match. I mean we argued about the stupidest things! Things like; what kind of toothpaste to buy; what kind of vegetables to buy, canned, fresh or frozen; who sleeps on what side of the bed, the list went on and on. This was new ground for us because we had never fought at all before. I was beginning to think our families were right in the first place. Maybe we were too young for this. I was ready to explode and so was she. Fear and uncertainty were taking over all my sense of reason. I began to question everything, including my love for Robin.

One night during this time Robin and I were at my mother's house and Robin was talking to her sister on the phone. I can't for the life of me remember what was said to Robin and relayed to me, but whatever it was I used it as an excuse to cancel the wedding.

Deep inside I was immensely frightened of the uncertainties of marriage and was looking for any excuse possible to get out. I was a coward, a cad and a jerk. No one believed me when I said it was over, least of all Robin. On the petty side, our families were grossly concerned with the fact we would now have to return all the wedding shower gifts and the embarrassment of it all. Robin was crushed and I on the other hand, only thinking of myself, was terribly relieved.

For Lack Of Bread

Robin and I both left the apartment and went our separate ways. She went to stay with her mom and I went back to live at Sarge's house. David was planning a trip back to Los Angeles and I decided to go along with him. So sometime in September David and I flew down to Los Angeles.

David had a few contacts he wanted to present our tapes to, but this time around we had no idea where we were going to stay. All we had was faith and about twenty dollars. We hitched a ride from the airport to Hollywood and just sort of bummed around from there. "Hair" was still playing to large crowds at the Aquarius Theatre. We had missed out on seeing it before and we were determined to get in to see it this time while we were in town. It never occurred to me to see if I could audition for the show.

We managed to meet some people the first day and we were invited to crash at their house on Tamarind Street, not too far from the Aquarius Theatre. It was a nice group of people and we felt very fortunate to have found a place to stay and so quickly.

Bob, one of the guys who lived at the Tamarind house, was an avid surfer and introduced us to the wild and wacky ways of Venice Beach. Our first trip to Venice Beach was bizarre story in and of itself. Bob went over to a light post in the sand, dug a hole and pulled out a pack of cigarettes he had buried on a previous visit. Inside the pack of cigarettes he had kept several hits of acid. He very joyfully offered to share his buried treasure with us. Being the young immortal that I believed I was at the time, I readily agreed. We spent the day body surfing, tripping and playing in the sand. It took a sober trip back to Venice days later to realize that the strange carnival of body builders and freaks on Venice Beach were real and not hallucinations of mine.

One night for free entertainment we stood in line to see if we could get into the Steve Allen show. We did and it was great fun. We sat in the front row and at the beginning of the show Steve looked at us and said, "You guys look like you could use a free meal." He then threw us two pieces of fruit. Little did Steve know just how correct his assumption was.

Our money ran out very quickly and since David was busy shopping our tapes, I decided to get a job. I went to work right away with a neighbor on Tamarind Street who worked at a car wash. It was a crap job but it paid enough for us to keep buying groceries. Also, I was able to get a free ride with him back and forth to work.

Bob had a puppy named Roach. He was a scrawny little brown rat dog but cute as can be. Roach was still untrained so we were always keeping a close eye on him while he was in the house. One night we had a party and Roach was allowed in. He was walking around the room going from person to person, getting love and treats. This was one happy dog.

As we were all watching this dog, someone walked through the living room and dropped some guacamole dip on the floor. We all saw it, except for Bob. Just as the food dropped and Roach had gone over to check it out, Bob came in, looked at Roach and the mess. Before any of us had time to react, Bob grabbed the dog by the scruff of the neck, rubbed his nose in the guacamole dip and promptly threw him out the door. We were all hysterical with laughter. We told Bob what really happened after he stepped back in the house. He was embarrassed and felt bad for the dog. Roach was brought back in and spent the rest of the night doing whatever he pleased.

After only a couple of weeks, David decided to make a quick trip back to Seattle to see his girlfriend. He planned on coming back to Hollywood and thought I should stay on by myself. I didn't really want to stay alone but relented and agreed to stay for a while. I lasted about one week then abruptly changed my mind and decided to go home also. I left my luggage with a girl I had recently met and told her I would be returning soon. I never did though, and that was the last I saw of the girl or the luggage.

David and his longtime girlfriend picked me up at the airport. It was in the dark of night and raining profusely as it often does in Seattle. David and Ellen had been estranged for quite sometime and had just gotten back together. They had a little boy together named Kevin, whose name they later changed to David. They were very happy to be back together again and told me they planned on getting married. Within a few weeks they did indeed get married. They chose Halloween night for the date and I was David's best man. I was very happy for them, but at the same time it only made me long more for Robin.

The Door Coffeehouse had long since closed and David's mom opened a new club at a different location in downtown Seattle. She called it the Apricot Orange and both David and I spent many hours working to help with its success. I never got paid for any of my efforts although I believe David did. It was operated similar to The Door in that no alcohol was served. Many well known bands as well as local bands played this club during the relative short time it was open. One night a local band named "Annie" played the club and they had a great lead singer who also played keyboards and flute. His name was Charlie Irwin and I was real impressed with his work. Later I would work with Charlie in several casts of "Hair."

Winter was well on its way and my band was pretty much non-existent as was my love life. I borrowed a white Gibson SG guitar from David and decided to see if I could play solo in some of Seattle's local clubs. The guitar had no case so I carried it under my large, knee length coat. I had no car so I took buses and walked from bar to bar. I was only eighteen but because of my mustache and long hair I never got carded for identification. I generally plugged in and played while the bands were on their breaks. The pay never amounted to anything more than all the popcorn and beer I could consume. It did however; give me some needed experience with playing my own music to crowds.

David was now living with his family on Alki Beach and my living arrangements were as close to homeless as possible. I knew I was more than welcome to stay with many different friends and relatives so I was relatively secure. I also knew I could always live with either my mother in Renton or my father in Lynnwood. At eighteen however, I was out to show my parents I could succeed and live on my own.

It was around this time we had heard the news that the people responsible for the Tate murders in LA were caught. We were absolutely freaked out! The Manson Family was the same group of hippies Frank had taken us to visit months before! We began to realize just how lucky we were to get out of that weird situation unscathed!

The end of 1969 was coming fast and I was desperately seeking a change. I had been reading more about the success of the Broadway musical "Hair" and decided to buy a copy of the paperback to see what the play was all about since

I hadn't seen it when I was in Hollywood. It didn't take long to read the book because it was primarily a script.

I found I could really relate to the show. After all, in real life I had myself heard similar lines spoken to me and around me many times. Although many people had said there wasn't much of a plot, to me it was very clear. Each of the characters reminded me of either myself, someone I knew, or someone I had heard of. I was clearly moved and I soon began to wonder if it might be possible to start a production of "Hair" in Seattle. I started talking to different friends about my idea but I was at a loss to figure out how to get the show to Seattle. I had absolutely no contacts in theatre.

In January of 1970 a crowd of 21,000 gathered at Madison Square Garden to see a "Winter Carnival For Peace," a benefit for the Vietnam Moratorium Committee.

Besides the cast of "Hair," there was a wide range of performers including Harry Belafonte, Richie Havens, Dave Brubeck, Judy Collins, the Rascals, Blood, Sweat and Tears, Peter, Paul and Mary, Jimi Hendrix, the Voices of East Harlem, and Mother Earth.

The show was likened to "an over sized revival meeting. It shouted approval of an array of peace-oriented songs, clapped, stamped and sang along."

6

The Hair Cut

After the New Year had begun I started hanging out a lot in the university district in Seattle. There were lots of bars in and around the avenue, so we did a lot of bar hopping, played a lot of pool, and drank lots of beer.

One afternoon when I was walking up University Avenue I was paying particular attention to all the "head shops" and other capital adventures that were cluttering the up avenue. At that time I really considered myself a "flower child of the sixties." All these commercial ventures, along with the end of the sixties, to me became symbolic of the end of an era. I truly did not want to see the sixties end. I had immense hope that the sixties were only the beginning of a transformed world of peace. To me it wasn't a fad to be a hippie, it was a lifestyle that I loved and purposely chose.

There was an underground newspaper called the "Helix" in Seattle. It was a free paper that I had at one time enjoyed reading very much. It had also become a venture of capitalism in that they had started to print many commercial ads in it. As I was walking up the avenue, very depressed, there appeared before me on the ground a torn and ragged copy of the Helix. Without hesitation I kicked the paper as I was walking. When it landed back on the ground, it had completely opened up to somewhere in the middle of the paper. I slightly glanced at my grand accomplishment when the words "Auditions for the Broadway Musical Hair, Equity only," appeared before me. I quickly picked the paper up to read it. The auditions were to begin on Monday, February 23rd.

My spirits were immediately lifted to the greatest heights! "Hair" was actually coming to Seattle and I had a chance to be in it! I didn't know what "Equity Only" meant, but I was convinced I was going to be in this show. I quickly

56

started prowling the town to see if I could find someone with a copy of the cast album so I could study the material.

My friend John told me about a girl he knew who had the cast album and a stereo to play it on as well. He took me over to meet her. She and her roommate were both students at the University of Washington and had an apartment near by. John told them with much excitement that I needed to listen to and learn the songs in "Hair'" because I was going to audition for the show soon. They were both very sweet and let me use their apartment for a day or two to practice while they were off in classes.

In March of 1970 John Zichmanis wrote a review of the Toronto production of "Hair" for the Toronto Daily Star Sunday Magazine.

Among other things, John wrote, "The driving force behind "Hair" is a message, an appeal for human change, and appeal to break down the barriers between people." "To get the message across, "Hair" discards the conventions of the theatre. It communicates not so much through words as through the mood and feelings created by the cast. It preaches revolution, but it is a revolution of energy, a desire to live."

"Hair" invariably incites the audience through a spectrum of reactions: boredom, disgust, and inspiration. But in the tangle of opinions, only two things remain graphically certain. First, "Hair" can break down the inhibitions, which separate people. Second, the cast themselves live in hope, not despair of the future, and are genuinely immersed in "Hair's" tribal ideal."

The auditions for the Seattle Company of "Hair" were on the horizon and I felt the need to focus on a specific role for me to play. I decided I would like to play the roles of either Claude or Woof in the play. I was hesitant about playing the role of Woof because he seemed to be a bisexual which didn't appeal to me. I did like the fact he was a flower child though. That was a role I could relate to in real life. Claude was the role I really desired and he made believe he was from Manchester England! So I mainly practiced his songs along with a few Beatle songs.

One of the first auditions (there were many to follow) was held at one of my favorite places, the Seattle Center. I was amazed at the amount of people who showed up to audition. They began in the morning and lasted all day long. I sat and listened to what seemed like hundreds of performers. My stomach began to turn as I thought of my chances of landing a role. When it was my turn I decided to sing the song "She's A Woman," by Lennon and McCartney. I was more comfortable with the Beatles than with the new "Hair" songs I had learned. Besides, it was the only song I could find the sheet music for which was required for the audition.

At the end of the day the casting crew labored through calling out a long list of names of those performers they had chosen. My friend John and I were ecstatic to hear my name as one of those chosen. I was in! They asked for our group to stay while the people who weren't chosen were graciously thanked and escorted out. My heart sank to my knees as they told us all we had made it through the first audition. There were to be a few more auditions over the next few weeks and we would have to participate in them all to be hired. I was both disappointed and elated. A change was coming my way and I could feel it.

The whole audition process itself took a few agonizing weeks and somehow I managed to pass them all. After the last audition was held I was invited to attend a gathering at the Moore Theatre, which was undergoing a million dollar restoration by the shows producer. I took John with me as a guest. I wasn't sure what the purpose of this gathering was for but I had assumed we would be told who made the final cut. I was surprised to see about 70 or more people who had been at the auditions. I was thinking, "What on earth do they need so many cast members for?"

After we had all settled in our seats they told us they were going to change our seating arrangements. They had designated one side of the theatre to be side A, and the other side B. They then began to call each of us out by name, after which, they would say, go to side A, or go to side B. I don't recall which side I was on, but after everyone was seated they said the side I was sitting on was the new Seattle cast of "Hair!" The other side would be called upon should future cast members be needed at a later date. My world was about to change completely after that night.

Promptly after those who weren't chosen were thanked and left, a party began. Champagne was flowing and I began to meet my fellow cast members, producers, directors, choreographers, stage managers, and the list went on. They still hadn't told us the roles we would play. They were saving that news for later on.

I felt like I was on top of a mountain. Needless to say, John and I got extremely polluted on the champagne. In the wee hours of the night we both staggered off into the streets of Seattle.

Look at the Moon

In the middle of March we had our first official rehearsal. It was held at the ACT theatre at the foot of Queen Anne Hill and we would continue to rehearse there until the renovation at the Moore Theatre was complete. I don't recall any formal introductions of the cast members to one another. It was as if we were all students reporting for the first day at school. The first concept we were introduced to was that we were all tribe members, not cast members. Even though there were lead roles in "Hair," there were no stars. We were all to be equals.

For the first few days we were put through a series of sensitivity exercises which at first made every homophobic hair on my neck stand up. We were asked to pair up and sit informally on the floor across from one another. Next we would be asked to do things such as closing our eyes and touching the persons face across from you. We moved on to exploring other parts of each other, nothing sexual though. Boys were with girls, boys with boys and girls with girls. We were also asked to split up into small groups where one person would stand in the center and purposely fall forward or backwards. The purpose of this exercise (along with many others) was for us to earn a strong trust in one another. The overall purpose of these bonds would become more evident later on as we learned more about the show.

During this period we also had to deal with contracts and union issues as well learning the show. None of us knew up front which roles if any, we were going to be asked to perform. None of us had ever belonged to Actors Equity, few of us had any money, and it was somewhere around $300 to join the union which was mandatory to be in the show. The producers made an arrangement with Equity to pay our dues in small installments that were to be taken out of our checks over a few weeks.

I had been toying with the idea for quite some time to change my name as I always hated it so much. I figured now was as good a time as any to do just that. On the day we were finding out which roles we were to play an announcement was made saying two people were going to have to change their names because another member of Actors Equity already had their name. Before they could say who had to change their names I knew without a doubt I was one of those two people. It was destiny and really solidified my feelings I had always had about my name. To me this was more than a coincidence, it was an omen and to think I just knew it!

I had already decided I would name myself after John Maack, my grandfather. John was a kind and gentle soul. Although he was actually my dad's stepfather, he had come into my dad's life when dad was really young. He couldn't have loved my father and uncle more if he had been their biological father. Although I was prepared to change my first name, because of a childhood promise I had made to my father I decided to keep my last name as Johnson. From this point on I would be known as Jonathon Johnson. There was no turning back.

Here's a fact for all you numerology buffs out there. A few years after changing my name I had a numerology study done on both my given birth name and my new name. If you take all the letters in the name Glen Arthur Johnson, they equal the number 3. Likewise if you take all the letters in the name Jonathon Johnson, they also add up to the number 3. Had I spelled my new name any differently, the numerology scores would have been different.

Number III, "The Artist" ~ You are a colorful person—bold, imaginative, exciting, vibrant, and the life of any party. Your success is based on your talent, charm and luck. You are carefree and confident and have the ability to see life clearly and wholly. Versatility is one of your outstanding traits, but you may have so many talents that you have difficulty choosing a single one.

~ *A Numerology profile from the pages of a Los Angeles "Hair" program.* Copyright 1969, 2004.

When they finally called me up to sign my contract they said they would like to offer me the role of Woof. They offered me $250 a week and asked if I was interested. I said yes without any hesitations or reservations. It wasn't Claude but hell it was one of the lead roles, which most certainly boosted up my confidence another level. Now I could more than afford a place of my own and a car.

On April 10th 1970, a small article appeared in the Seattle Post-Intelligencer, "206 Magazine." There was a picture of the cast of "Hair" during rehearsals, which described us as "reverently forming a human cathedral during the first act."

The article also noted the fact that our gala premiere on April 18th was a benefit for the American Indian Youth Foundation.

By the time we moved rehearsals over to the Moore Theatre the show really began to take on a life of its own. I was personally having difficulty with acting out the scenes as I hadn't any previous experience with acting. I must have been awful as our director Joe Donovan appeared at times to be exasperated with coaching me. He was constantly interrupting me, asking me to project more and also to say the lines as I would say them myself. I remember explaining back to him that I wouldn't be saying these lines. I mean, how can you say you love Mick Jagger and mean it?

When what Joe was trying to teach me finally sank in, it was like a revelation. After our first pre-opening performance (a week prior to opening) Joe came into my dressing room telling me how dynamite my performance was. He also revealed he had nearly lost faith in me several times along the way. I will forever appreciate Joe's teaching as well as his patience with me. He was a great director.

Also with the move to the Moore Theatre, we were beginning to see the big picture of the show as it pieced together. Just looking at the tall scaffoldings and knowing some of us would have to dive off of them into awaiting arms below, the importance of Tom O'Horgan's sensitivity exercises began to become clearer in our minds. Developing a sense of trust in one another would be essential for our safety if nothing else.

On April 17th 1970, the Seattle Post-Intelligencer, "206 Magazine," again wrote a small note on the Seattle cast of "Hair."

"Hair" finally opens tomorrow night at the refurbished Moore Theatre. The cast is made up almost entirely of non-professionals from the Pacific Northwest who have had little theatre experience but the production team itself is composed of seasoned veterans who have been involved in other presentations of the show."

They go on to write, "This "Hair" had the shortest preparation and rehearsal time of any of the productions now playing (the "company astrologer" decides the opening day) and this is the first such show for Seattle."

THE SEATTLE COMPANY, The Moore Theatre
Opening Night April 18, 1970

The Chinook Tribe

Michael Butler, Producer
Bertrand Castelli, Executive Producer
Joe Donovan, Director
Rhonda Oglesby, Dance Director
Celttoras, Assistant Director
Steve Gillette, Musical Director
Nancy Potts, Costumes
Robin Wagner, Scenery
Jules Fisher, Lighting
Abe Jacob, Sound

Cast

Raul C. Arellano
Rose Marie Barbee
Bob Bingham
Skip Bowe
Alice Campbell
Les (Claude) Carlsen
Otis K. Carr
Catherine Chamberlain
Don Copeland
Debbie Cotton-Walker
Joan Daniels
Arthur L. Dillingham
Janice M. Dobbs
Rooth Dye
Karen Gardner
Janis Gotti

Jo Ann Harris
Barbara J. Hempleman
Jeffrey S. Hillock
Charles W. Irwin
Stephanie Janecke
Jonathon Johnson
Tony Lake
Kevin Mason
Linda Marie Milburn
Tyrone Miles
Eric Miller
Marcus K. Mukai
Michael Rhone
Todd Tressler
Robin Turrill
Burke W. Wallace

Musicians

Norm Durkey, Piano	Joe Brazil, Sax, Flute
John Day, Guitar	Steve Cole, Trumpets
Pernell Alexander, Guitar	Ed Lee, Trumpets
Doug Demeerlerr, Bass	Norm Durkey, Conductor
James Williams, Drums	Dennis Smith, Conductor and
Dick Jenson, Percussion	Assistant Musical Director

Unbeknownst to many, including some of the cast and crew of "Hair," there was serious trouble brewing in Seattle concerning the show. An extremely radical group called The Weathermen threatened the opening of "Hair' by demanding $100,000 or they would blow up the Moore Theatre. The threat was real and was of great concern. At this time the Weathermen were known to have been responsible for several bombings around the country, including banks.

The Weathermen were an extremely violent group. Their known enemy was the establishment, big business and the government. The group was a faction that was a split off from another radical group, the SDS. The Students for a Democratic Society was also a leftist group that organized many student protests against ROTC on campus, against the draft and the war.

Michael Butler was put in a very perplexing situation. There was no way he was going to give in to their extortion demands. If he did other groups would follow suit and the threats would never end. On the other hand the threats were real and he needed to consider the lives and safety of people. But what could he do? The Seattle police were willing to offer protection but that would lead to paranoia, possible hysteria and very bad press. Here you have a show about love and peace with armed police walking all about the theatre. That would not have been a good scene.

As Michael pondered the unfolding events his trusted friend and bodyguard, Teru Kawaoka, came up with a plan. He was a Japanese gentleman who was an extremely gifted Marshall Arts expert. Teru said to Michael, "Let me take care of this." Having great trust in his friend Michael said okay. So the plan was put into action.

Teru went to nearly every Marshall Arts studio in the Seattle area and hired dozens of the best experts available. They were all outfitted with black slacks, white shirts and black ties. The plan also included contingencies for a safe evacuation of the theatre should it be deemed necessary. At the opening of "Hair" in Seattle this clandestine security force was stationed throughout the theater, in the isles, the lobby, the balconies and the perimeter as well as back-stage. To the audience and cast members it only seemed like an excess of ushers. As it turns out the gamble paid off. After their demands were spurned The Weathermen backed down and did not bother Michael again.

Over 5,350,000 people have seen Hair ~ From the "Hair" press kit—1/1/70.

7

Tribal Awakenings

The show in Seattle was a phenomenal smash hit! I think we were all pretty amazed at what we were able to accomplish in such a short period of time. It was apparently the shortest rehearsal time ever for any cast of "Hair."

Michael Butler, who remained in town for our opening night performance, hosted an incredible celebration after the show. For this party he chartered a very large boat. If my memory serves me correctly this boat was about as large as a ferry; in fact, it may well have been a ferry. We cruised out on to the waters of Elliott Bay. Eventually we made our way out to an island where an incredible salmon bake cookout on the beach was waiting for us. It was a fantastic party and as expected, many of us over partied a little. There were even rumors that someone almost fell overboard.

Very early in the morning of April 19th, the day after "Hair's" opening night in Seattle, I was awakened by a phone call from my mother. My daughter Melissa was born. Both Robin and Melissa were in great condition at University Hospital. I was elated! I was now a father!

On the way to the hospital, I bought some flowers and the biggest stuffed animal I could find. I then quickly drove over to make my unannounced visit. Robin seemed real surprised yet happy I showed up. She also said she had seen one of the previews of "Hair" and was very proud of me. She said it was very hard not to come up and see me after the show but she wanted to give me my space.

This was the Robin I had fell in love with. Here she was with child, scared and alone, yet thinking of me. Looking at her lying there in the hospital bed with Melissa made me want her all the more. I wanted to win her back but at the same time I was feeling I had blown it so bad with her that it was all far too late. Like the foolish child I was, I didn't even have the guts to ask if she still cared and would take me back. Instead I did promise her I would be there for her and Melissa whenever they needed me and left it at that. I left the hospital and went home glowing with the excitement of being a new father.

After opening night, Wayne Johnson of the Seattle Times wrote one of the first reviews of the Seattle cast of "Hair." Some of what he wrote was,

"One of the happiest surprises I've had in the theatre in some time was the joyous success of "Hair" at its opening performance Saturday night at the Moore Theatre."

"The kids in "Hair's" new "Chinook tribe" at the Moore Saturday night had such freshness and openness and delight—in themselves and in the show. The Seattle "Hair" is basically a carbon copy of the New York "Hair," but it's a much different—and better—show."

"Hair" expresses the freshness and exuberance of today's youth. It also expresses their positive interests—in love, sex, fun, the feeling of community—and their negative hangups—with the war, the draft and other societal evils."

"The kids in the "Chinook tribe" on the Moore stage are so engaging and likeable—to say nothing of their energy or talent—that it's entirely possible to be fully entertained and charmed by them."

"The biggest Theatrical success of modern times (first year gross some $18 million) and unquestioningly the biggest outlet for black actors in the history of American theater is Hair, a free-for-all musical about peace, pot, freedom, and love. " ~ From Ebony Magazine, May 1970.

Some Personal Reflections on "HAIR"

There are undoubtedly a myriad of reasons why "Hair" was able to touch so many people and continues to do so throughout the years. That not withstanding, I believe the main reason is because "Hair" embodies the truth of the times. Or as Clive Barnes said on numerous occasions, it is the "frankness" of the show. And it's exactly that core of honesty and truth in "Hair" that is able to transcend time and effect people today just as strongly as it did the audiences of the sixties and seventies. I am personally convinced the love for this show will continue in perpetuity.

With "Hair" it is not impossible to find a little resemblance to someone you knew, know, or even with yourself, in nearly every character. Not a word sung or said was ever really new, just the presentation. "Hair" was and remains a means for society to gaze at itself into a mirror as it reflects the truths of an age, as it is still being lived. Although there are some who might think the show is only a period piece, it is not. The show is about youth, is flexible, free spirited, and continues to adapt well to the changes in society.

For some the show is like being slapped in the face with a backhanded dose of reality. For others however it can be an awakening of sorts. Although you may have heard all the issues before it was not with the sense of urgency and love that "Hair" projects. It cries out to the depths of your soul for compassion and understanding.

"Hair" was and is a powerful piece and much of its success is in its believability. It is believable not only in the content of the dialog and its remarkable score, but ultimately in the conviction of the cast members themselves. To say that many of the young cast members had "been there and done that" would be an understatement. In most cases we love the show because it speaks to our hearts and had the ability to make our voices heard. Where maybe no one was willing to listen within our individual lives, the mass was now willing to pay to hear what our particular generation had to say.

"Hair" puts all the major issues out on the line, right up front and in your face. Racism, freedom of speech, the sexual revolution, drugs, love, war, peace, the draft, life, death, gay rights and women's rights. I could go on but in a nutshell, if you can name it "Hair" has it. It confronts society's unabashed curiosity along with its greatest fears and takes no prisoners while doing so. From the beginning of the show when Berger flies out over the audience and sits in an audience member's lap to ask for spare change, to the finale after Claude dies and the audience is invited on the stage to sing and dance, it is an explosion of life. You have to be comatose not to be moved.

Woof was an interesting character to play. There are some actors who choose to play Woof as openly gay or bisexual. I chose not to see him that way and therefore didn't project him as such. To me Woof is the consummate flower child of the sixties. Although you can easily guess he has tried anything and everything, he also glows with innocence. From his love of planting his seeds or gazing at the moon, to his obsession with Mick Jagger, it is evident he is bursting full of life and love, and in love with life. He may not be the brightest light in the chandelier but he is a loving friend to all in the tribe. That I could definitely relate to.

I saw Berger as the wild, rebellious, say what you feel, do what you feel, radical and impertinent guy that many people can only imagine being in their dreams. Berger is a self-described "psychedelic Teddy Bear." He is a dichotomy in that he is not only a capricious free spirit, he is also amiable, charismatic, sweet and could probably charm an old lady out of her pension with little or no trouble at all. Bursting with an unbridled cosmic energy he is the unmistakable leader of this exuberant, restless and life-happy tribe of kids. A high school drop-out blatantly urging the rest of us to join in with him, looking for Donna.

Sheila is quite likely the only non-dropout in the tribe. Sheila is a weekend hippie, a supporter of the cause and a voice of change, but she is still clinging on to a higher social class. Sheila is smart, pretty, educated, and the chief organizer of all the protesting activities. She believes herself to be Berger's girlfriend and Berger's girlfriend alone, even though at times it seems as though Berger could often care less. She is madly in love with Berger while Claude is madly in love with Sheila. This all provides for an interesting dynamic as this gangly group of young people struggle with peace and harmony from within as well as without. Just listen to her painful cries in the song "Easy To Be Hard" after Berger has torn a shirt Sheila brought him as a gift.

"How can people be so heartless? How can people be so cruel? Easy to be hard, easy to be cold."

Claude was the easiest character for me personally to relate to. He is greatly misunderstood by his family as well as the tribe and is constantly being lectured on what he wants to do with his life. On one hand the pressure from his family to be a man, get a job, join the service and go to war, is enormous. On the other hand his extended family, the kids in the tribe are exerting equal pressure on him to reject what his family is telling him. They are urging him to drop out, tune in, turn on and burn his draft card.

Claude is so confused and desperately wants to do what's right, but it is never clear to him just what that is. To avoid the confusion and pain he creates a pseudo alter ego to escape the darkness of the decisions he is grappling with. He almost convinces himself he is from Manchester England and not from Flushing New York. Claude even pretends to be invisible but in reality there is no escape. His confusion is very clear at the end of the first act with the song "Where Do I Go?"

"Where do I go? Follow the river. Where do I go? Follow the gulls. Where is the something? Where is the someone? That tells me why I live and die?"

In retrospect, these were questions I had been asking myself.

Then there is Hud, the ultimate soul brother. At first impression you think you are meeting a leader of the Black Panthers, a militant, honky hating, white boy beating, mean, bad-assed, son-of-a-bitch. He comes on hard to stir up any and every prejudice thought one might be inclined to have. Hoping to scare the shit out of you and perhaps any bigotry he can find. Nothing's held back here as he stares you down with the haunting, confrontational, yet tongue and cheek, "Colored Spade."

"I am a Colored Spade, a Nigra, a Black Nigger, a Jungle Bunny, Jigaboo, Coon, Pickaniny, Mau Mau, Uncle Tom, Aunt Jemima, Little Black Sambo, cotton picker, fuzzy wuzzy, junk man, shoeshine boy, elevator operator, table cleaner at Horn and Hardarts, slave, voodoo zombie, Ubangi-lipped, flat nosed, tap dancer, resident of Harlem, and president, of the United States of Love."

Throughout the show as you get to know Hud, what you begin to see is a warm-hearted human being, tired of being put down and demanding only the equal rights his race so rightfully deserves. If Berger is the light of the tribe, Woof the spirit and Sheila the heart, then Hud is most definitely the soul. We want what we want and we want it now!

On April 26, 1970 the cast of "Hair" on Broadway celebrated their second anniversary to a crowd of approximately 10,000 people in the Central Park Mall by putting on a two and a half hour, free concert performance. Songs were performed not only by the cast and musicians from "Hair" but guest singers like "Oliver," who had a successful recording of "Good Morning Starshine."

The Seattle cast of "Hair" was invited to perform at an outdoor rock festival in Canada. It was billed as the Strawberry Mountain Fair. Management arranged this event with the understanding that those who went would be back in time for our evening performance. About half of the cast agreed to go but to get there on schedule we would have to leave very early in the morning. A few of the cast members decided to rent a limo while the rest of us carpooled for the trip. Otis Carr from the cast needed a ride so I suggested he come home with me, stay the night at my place and then the two of us would leave bright and early.

Now Otis Carr was a tall, slender, good-looking young man who also happened to be black. By the time we got back to my sisters house it was long after midnight. My car was acting up so after parking in the garage I proceeded to open the hood to take a look. I invited Otis to let himself in and I would be right in after him in a minute. I figured my sister would be asleep but what I didn't know is she had invited my elderly aunt over to spend the night. I also didn't know my aunt was still up watching TV in the family room which was on the other side of the garage door.

At this time I was only about three feet behind Otis when I heard a blood-curdling scream. It was my aunt, who being a bit on the prejudice side, assumed Otis was breaking in to rob, pillage and rape. I think she scared Otis more than Otis scared her though. I quickly jumped in the doorway, got her to calm down and introduced her to my friend. I then apologized to Otis and he understood. Otis and I always got a good chuckle over the situation.

In the morning we headed off to the festival. The border crossing we had to use was not a well-traveled one. It was the crossing far east of Blaine. We got almost all the way to the border before my MG died. Here we were out in the middle of redneck heaven, two young guys, one black and one with hair down past his shoulders. We started hitchhiking but didn't have much hope we were going to get a ride from this place. Actually, we were more than a little concerned for our safety.

Within about a half hour of trying our luck at hitching, a huge limo appeared and pulled over in front of the MG. It was our company manager,

David Hedges and a few other cast members. We rode the rest of the way in luxury. Just before we got to the border David Hedges asked the driver to pull to the side of the road. When the car stopped, David got out and hid a couple of joints just in case we were to be searched at the border. We would pick them up later on the way back.

We had no idea what to expect when we arrived at Strawberry Mountain. We were surprised to see thousands of people in attendance. So many people that it was very difficult for the limo to maneuver its way up to the back stage area. We were only here to sing a few songs from "Hair" so we started right into it. After finishing our first song the reception from the crowd was subdued and much different from what we were accustomed to.

To get the crowd in a better mood I recall suggesting we perform a group Om, a sort of mantra, and ask the audience to join along with us. When we performed our show each night in Seattle the tribe would always gather together in a circle before the show started, lock in a big hug and center ourselves by holding a group Om. It was sort of a prayer ritual that I personally enjoyed immensely. I don't know if the other tribe members felt the same way or not but it worked for me.

Anyway, the tribe agreed to do an Om. So as we stood on the stage, arm over shoulder facing the audience, I explained to the people what we were about to do. I asked the audience to put their arms around one another and join in with us. For me the feeling was absolutely the greatest. My eyes were closed and I was focusing into the mantra. As the drone of the crowd got louder I opened my eyes to see an ocean of life, a sea of people rocking gently back and forth and enjoying a special moment with their brothers and sisters. It was a fantastic feeling which climaxed in a passionate rendition of "Let the Sunshine In," to which the crowd joined in.

When we got off the stage we heard some of the tribe had been turned away at the border. Apparently they asked to search a few folks. Everyone complied and no one felt they had anything to hide. Unfortunately when Cathy Chamberlain emptied out her pockets, one very lonely pot seed went bouncing across the table. It wasn't enough to arrest anyone on, in fact I don't believe anyone in the world has ever gotten high off a seed, but, no, no. Those Canadians did not want her type in their country so they promptly sent her back. I still think it's quite funny to picture Cathy emptying her pockets and being shocked to see one lonely pot seed bouncing across the table.

We headed back and picked up the pot on the other side of the border. David asked if I wanted some but I declined saying I had a show to do. I told him after the brownie incident, I was not interested in performing "Hair" stoned. One night before the show started some of the girls had made some brownies and had left them out to share with the tribe. They looked great and without even thinking about it, I ate one or two. I had no idea they were hash brownies! Although I was able to perform I remember asking what my lines were before every entrance. By the end of the evening my mouth was sore from constantly smiling. After telling David this story he just laughed and insisted I would be just fine.

Well it was just like the line in the show where Claude wakes up from his bad trip and exclaims,

"What was in that joint Berger?"

Whatever it was I was down for the count! I guess some other folks in the limo were as well because none of us were able to do the show. We all sat in the audience with David and watched a very small cast of less than 20 people doing the show. I thought it was great! It was actually the first time I had seen "Hair!" Then again, I was so stoned anything would have been great.

I was thoroughly enjoying all the recognition being a part of "Hair" was bringing. I was amazed to be receiving fan mail and packages with gifts from local fans. Some were even bold enough to send me joints and odd assortments of pills. Of course my first instinct was always to quickly discard any apparently illegal substances, but I was flattered none-the-less. A few of the other cast members used to tease me about the mail and gifts.

One of my all-time favorite groups The Kinks came to town and the "Hair" cast was invited to perform with them. We were to be bused over to the arena where they were playing immediately following our evening performance. I was very excited about meeting and performing with them and because we were going to be up so late, I decided to take some uppers. Not a good idea at all in that besides staying alert, I was very grumpy and anxious to say the least.

The excitement of playing with the Kinks continued as we all got off the bus. Not knowing what to expect however, the Kinks ran well over their time into ours. They did put on a great show and consequently returned for many encores. By the time we finally got a chance to go on, we only had time for one song.

After the show I was disappointed and not knowing what to do with my very awake self, I stopped over to see some friends who were artists. They needed to get to bed but understood my inability to sleep due to the speed. So they very happily set me up with some canvas and paints, and I spent a large portion of the night creating a very ugly painting. That was the last time I ever took speed. It just wasn't for me.

The Silver Indian

Ever wonder why Michael Butler is referred to as "Hair's" Silver Indian?

At a rehearsal, Tom O'Horgan turned to Michael and said in front of everyone, "We have something we want you to do," thereby putting Michael on the spot. So at the beginning of Act 2, he was to be revolved on stage (The Aquarius Theatre had a revolving platform), painted in silver, with only a war bonnet and loincloth. He was standing on a 50-gallon drum, painted in silver. His arms were akimbo and as he was revolved in and out, he opened his arms and gave the peace sign. In Michael's own words,

"No lines—they would not have been heard over the noise made by the shaking of my legs."

This night (during the first act) Michael was in the private producer's booth with friend Minnie and under the influence. He was going to chicken out but Minnie told him he had to do it. Tommy Smothers (his co-producer) was asked and did cop out. Michael said,

"This act was far more frightening to me than the times I did the nude scene. But I got my Equity card." ~ Story relayed by Michael Butler, "Hair's" worldwide producer.

KENT STATE MASSACRE

On May 4th, 1970, a very sad event occurred that I personally hope will never be forgotten. Four students of Kent State University were killed and nine others were wounded when members of the Ohio National Guard fired nearly 70 shots into a crowd of unarmed students during an anti-war demonstration.

The dead students were: Jeffrey Miller, Allison Krause, Bill Schroeder and Sandy Scheuer. The nine other Kent students who were wounded were: Alan Canfora, John Cleary, Tom Grace, Dean Kahler, Joe Lewis, Scott Mackenzie, Jim Russell, Robby Stamps and Doug Wrentmore.

All 13 of the Kent State massacre victims were full-time students, but only 2 the students were active protesters—not that it should have mattered. Forever will the events of that horrible day be a reminder of how one group's presumed liberties can greatly impinge upon and or destroy another's if not put in check.

This tragedy epitomized the prevailing attitude and mentality of the federal government towards youth during the late sixties and early seventies. On one side you had a group of students exercising their constitutional rights to protest and in a non-violent fashion. On the other side, you had a tyrannical, radical, right wing government seeking to silence the youth by force. Their philosophy was "the end justifies the means." Their actions were completely contrary to the very foundations of this great country.

Fighting this attitude was what "Hair" was really all about. In a completely non-violent fashion, "Hair" took its anti-war message to the world. Yes, "Hair" was indeed a musical with lovely song and dance, but its message was strong and clear to those who saw it. Its message was so on target that the show and those involved with it would continue to receive violent threats for many years on. Unfortunately, some of these threats were acted upon.

Wayne Johnson wrote his second review of the Seattle cast of "Hair" a month later. Here are some excerpts from the review he wrote,

"I'm happy to report that this exuberantly theatrical piece has not only held up but actually improved during its run." "The show has improved partly because the young actors have become more secure in their roles, but primarily because they have managed to get closer to the polemical, satirical core of the show."

"Hair" is a celebration of youthful life and love, but it's also a sharp attack on the individual and collective hang-ups, which prevent that life and love from being appreciated to the fullest."

"Hair's" thrusts at the adult "establishment"—at the war, the draft, pollution, and other examples of societal insanity and uptight, phony rectitude—now have more point and bite than they had on opening night. The show is tougher, harder—and better."

"The considerable energy level of the show has not been diminished a whit by the routine of repeated performances, and the kids' joy in making the stage come alive together and in making a life statement together is still clear, engaging and altogether contagious."

I went to work early one night thinking I would have some time before the show to walk down to Pike Place Market and shop a little. There were several great little antique shops and head shops in the market that were interesting. So I parked at the Moore Theatre and headed down towards the market.

It was a rare sunny day and I was in an exceptionally good mood. Just after I had turned off Second Avenue and on to Pike Street, an old man hit me in the face without warning as I was walking by him. He hit me hard enough to knock me down and caused my wire-framed glasses to cut next to my eye. It really took me by surprise and by the time I stood back up he had already disappeared.

Several people stopped to assist me while others went after the man. In particular there was one couple that showed me a great deal of concern. The husband had gone after the man while his wife had called the police to the scene. Within a short amount of time the police drove up with the suspect in their back seat. The police then asked me if I would like to file assault charges against the man. I said I would first like to speak with him before I decided what to do. I was thinking maybe there was some mistake on his behalf, that maybe he thought I was someone else. I mean why else would he hit me, I was thinking? I don't know him, didn't say anything to him, I was minding my own business, etc.

So the police officers opened the back door and I said to the man, "Sir, why did you hit me?"

He then replied with much hate and anger, "If I had of had a gun I would have shot you!"

I was stunned, turned to the cops and said, "Lock him up and throw away the key."

As the police car was driving off this wonderful couple was still hanging out to make sure everything was okay. I thanked them and told them I was in "Hair" and would be happy to get them into the show if they were interested. They were, so I took their names and told them tickets would be at the window for them.

Tyrone Miles, who played Hud, was going to be married soon and he came up with a plan to do it on stage at the Moore Theatre. He was telling us about his plans during one of our rehearsals. He definitely wanted to have the whole cast involved and thought it would be even greater if one of us were a minister. Somehow it was mentioned I was a minister and although I was very reluctant, Tyrone talked me into performing their wedding ceremony.

This had to be one of the most unique weddings ever. The ceremony started out sort of like "Hair" starts, with all the cast members gathering on the stage in a circle to music. I believe it was Aquarius the band was playing but I can't be sure. For the vows, the couple and I were in the center of the circle while the cast then sat down around us in a circle. The theatre was full of relatives, family members and media. It was an event.

I think I was as nervous as Tyrone and his wife Suzy because I had never performed a wedding ceremony before. In some ways I felt responsible for them both and I do believe it brought Tyrone and me closer as friends. Their marriage was also going to be more difficult than most because it was interracial. Although interracial marriages are very common nowadays, they weren't back then.

A Strand of Hair

"Hair" ran into trouble before its opening in Boston. A District Attorney tried to shut the show down due to questionable content. The claim was that "Hair" desecrated the American Flag and was lewd and lascivious. The show was due to open at the Wilbur Theater on February 20, 1970 but the DA's office was determined to get it cancelled. One of the lawyers for "Hair's" producers went to the State Supreme Court to allow the production to open in the midst of the court proceedings.

The case went to the Supreme Judicial Court of Massachusetts. The Court ruled the show was protected under the First Amendment and should be allowed to continue if certain conditions were met: The Courts conditions were that each cast member should be clothed to a reasonable extent at all times and that all simulation of sexual intercourse or deviation be removed. The Court made no ruling on the flag issue.

All involved in the production were unwilling to alter the content of the show. Consequently to protest the Courts ruling, "Hair" closed on April 10, 1970. The cast would have also faced arrest if they appeared on stage nude.

During the whole time off the cast and crew remained on full salary. Those expenses as well as the enormous legal fees busted the productions budget. Even with advanced ticket sales of a million dollars they lost money, but upheld a principle.

The producer's and cast of "Hair" received notes of support from Actors' Equity Association as well as many others. Although the Court's decision was appealed to the U.S. Supreme Court, the Court did not clear the way for "Hair" to reopen without threat of criminal action until May 22, 1970.

THE BOSTON COMPANY, The Wilbur Theatre
Eventually Opened in May1970
The Wampanoags Tribe

Michael Butler, Producer
Bertrand Castelli, Executive Producer
James Sharman, Director
Natalie Mosco, Dances Restaged
Joe Donovan, Assistant Director
Steve Gillette, Musical Director
Nancy Potts, Costumes
Robin Wagner, Scenery
Jules Fisher, Lighting
Abe Jacob, Sound

Known Cast History

Jonathan Ames	Carolyn (Coco) Kallis
Bill Anstatt	Marlena Langston
Karen Benson	Ben Lautman
Michael Berz	Doug Lee
Bobiel	Sandra Renee Lee
Karyl Britt	William Lindner
Kim Brodey	Joyce Macek

John Contardo
Dell Cunningham
Carol De Carter
Cecilia Eaves
Dick Evans
Paul Fitzgerald
Andrea Gaines
Linda Gaines
Tressa Gilliland Jr.
Emanuel Johnson

Steve Menkin
Francine Mills
Kathy Nixon
Vicky Nunis
Charles Robinson
Troy Robinson
Bryan Spencer
Richard Spiegel
Toby Stone

8

Aquarius

As "Hair" begins, the tribe members start making their way up to the stage from various locations in the theatre. They are moving in slow motion to the very strange and cosmic sounds emanating from an old truck sitting to the side of the stage. As the tribe begins to reach the stage, they gather in a circle, arm over shoulders and move counterclockwise in sequence to the rhythm of Aquarius. One night as I find myself moving within the circle, a new yet very familiar tribe member finds his way into the circle and puts his arms around me. His stoic smile and lion locks give him away. It is Gerry Ragni, one of the authors of "Hair" joining in the celebration, unannounced with no fanfare.

Gerry and I became friends right off. The day following his first night in Seattle he asked me to show him around the city, so I did. After exploring downtown he asked to see where I lived. So we started the drive out east to Bellevue.

He asked about my family and I then told him about Robin and Melissa as well as my girlfriend. That's when I first found out Gerry was married and had a young son. He told me all about how wonderful his son was, how much he missed him and he also spoke very highly of his wife.

When we got to my house my sister was asleep. She was working as a cock-tail waitress at the time and would generally sleep in late. Not wanting to be disappointed, Gerry insisted on meeting her anyway so into her bedroom he marched. With a big smile on his face he woke her up by introducing himself as my friend. She recognized who Gerry was from pictures and exclaimed, "Oh my God!" as she hid under the pillow. She was very embarrassed to be seen while still in bed by anyone, especially a celebrity of sorts. After talking with her for a while we made our way up north to visit my dad. It was a very enjoyable day. I always enjoyed Gerry's free spirit and was intrigued by his creativity.

While in Seattle, Gerry also played Berger on a few occasions. Not that Eric wasn't good in his interpretation of Berger but it was great to see the original Berger in action and much different. As I got to know Gerry it became evident in many ways that much of the character came from him personally. Many of the best Berger's who I eventually worked with closely emulated Gerry's Berger. Oh hell I'll just say it; Gerry was Berger on stage and off. At least at times it appeared so to me.

Around this time I was starting to think "Hair" was just a means to an end for my career and maybe I should leave to pursue my own music. The money was great, the show was fantastic, but I was impatient and wanted to make my own music. The topic came up in a conversation with Gerry and he proceeded to convince me otherwise. He asked that Earl Scott and I to go with him on a visit to see the San Francisco show and off we went. I told management I would be gone for a couple days, and without any airline reservations we all hopped in a cab to the airport.

When we arrived at the Seattle airport the plane was already boarding. Gerry handed them his American Express card to pay for three first class tickets but had no other identification. The airline personnel looked at the card and then back at Gerry. They looked at me and they looked at Earl. No way were they about to let three hippies on a plane—American Express card or not.

There we stood at an impasse, the three of us desperately trying to convince the attendants that Gerry was Gerome Ragni, one of the authors of "Hair" while they were holding the plane for us. Finally Earl Scott came up with an idea. Earl had a "Hair" souvenir program with him. He retrieved it out of his bag, found a picture of Gerry in it, and showed it to the attendants. They were very pleased and a little embarrassed. They quickly processed the tickets and ushered us onto the waiting plane.

We arrived at the theatre just before show time. Back stage Gerry introduced me to several tribe members before we went to sit in the audience. The San Francisco production was wonderful! There was one tribe member who stood out the most to me this evening. He was not playing a lead this night, just bit parts. Yet every time this young black man stepped up for a line he mesmerized the audience and stole the show. I remember turning to Gerry and Earl with the statement, "That man is going to be a big star, he's just amazing"

His talent was overwhelming and after the show I made a point of introducing myself to him to say how much I enjoyed his performance. His name was Ben Vereen and he was both appreciative and kind. We talked for a while and found we had much in common spiritually. He was actually from the Los Angeles production and was heading back to his home the next day. Ben left the party early, saying his goodbyes with his travel bag in hand. I remember him saying how much he missed his kids and that he couldn't wait to get home to see them.

THE SAN FRANCISCO COMPANY,
The Geary and Orpheum Theatres
The Ohlone Tribe

Michael Butler, Producer
Marshall Naify, Producer
The American Conservatory Theatre, Producer
Bertrand Castelli, Executive Producer
Tom O'Horgan, Director
Jules Fisher, Lighting
Julie Arenal, Dance Director
Nancy Potts, Costumes
Jerry Combs, Assistant Director
Steve Gillette, Musical Director
Robin Wagner, Scenery
Guy Costa, Sound

Known Cast History

Toad Attell	Reggie Mack
Arsenio Avizado	Susan Madley
Nancy Blossom	Robert Marcum
Roscoe Blount	Soni Moreno
Light Brown	Kenny Ortega
Michael Brown	Michael Owen
Tom Bullock	Bruce Paine
Robert Castro	Lydia Phillips
Elizabeth Caveness	Shezwae Powell
Maria-Elena Cordero	Joey Richards
Roger Cruz	Karl Richey
Star Donaldson	Merria Ross
Debi Dye	Annie Sampson
Candice (Candi) Earley	Rhoda Seven
Marsha Faye	Michael Sorafine
Gayle Hayden	Dale Soules
Bruce Hyde	Eron Tabor
Jonathon Johnson	Philip Michael Thomas
Paulette Ellen Jones	Ben Vereen
Jolie Kanat	Charles Weldon
Johnnie Keyes	James Wigfall
Ted Lange	Willie Windsor
Danny Lawyer	Jeannie (Jurgun) Wood
Jennifer Lee	Winston Yong

The following day was spent goofing off in and around the city. Gerry went into a store to purchase a stereo cassette recorder. He most generously bought one for me as well. I was a little uneasy about accepting such a gift but was thankful none-the-less. It seemed as though money and fame did not mean much to Gerry. In many ways he was just happy to be goofing off with anyone. There was nothing in his attire or mannerisms that would lead you to believe he was a very successful human being. He was a very giving and unpretentious person in that way.

During the trip and on the way back home, Gerry and I talked quite a bit about writing songs. When we returned I shared some of mine with him and he also showed me some new material he was working on. He wanted us to go into a studio and record some stuff so we booked time at Kaye-Smith Studio's where Norm Durkey ("Hair's" piano player and conductor) worked part time.

My tracks were easy enough as I recorded a couple of original tunes which were pretty straight forward, with just me and my acoustic guitar. Gerry on the other hand declined to use the professional recording equipment and instead placed his new cassette recorder on top of the piano and spent about 2 hours of studio time playing into it. The engineer explained the cost was the same but Gerry didn't seem to care. I can still remember part of the song he recorded, the chorus repeated "Paranoia Parade" over and over.

There was always something going on nearly every night after the show. If we weren't having a party at a cast member's house we were having one at the theatre. The Moore Theatre had a full bar downstairs under the lobby which we used on many occasions after hours. One of the things management would do for us was to invite whatever famous rock band was in town to stop by for a visit after our shows were over. These parties were private and closed off to the public. On one such occasion The Doors were invited to come over, which they did.

The Doors were another all-time favorite act of mine so I was looking forward to meeting them. Downstairs in the lounge my girlfriend and I spent a little time visiting with Ray Manzarek and his wife. They seemed to be extremely nice people and very down to earth. After a short time someone suggested a jam session, so nearly everyone went upstairs to the stage. Members of the "Hair" band and a couple members of The Doors plugged in and started playing together.

Meanwhile Gerry Ragni is out on the street inviting all kinds of folks into this private party. Some of the people he invited in had seen "Hair" that night, but still others had just been passing by. In typical Gerry fashion there were even a few derelicts in the house. The theatre was filling up with people of all sorts. It was beginning to look like a carnival, classic Gerry Ragni style.

I was standing close to the band when I noticed Jim Morrison was sort of aloof on the other side of the stage. Jim had a full beard at this time, a big pot-belly, and was wearing a dark blue t-shirt and jeans. He was standing off by himself and appeared a little downhearted. I thought it was strange that no one was speaking to him and mentioned it to my girlfriend. I then said that we should go over and introduce ourselves.

So we walked over to Jim, introduced ourselves to him, and told him I was in the cast. He was very nice and although polite, reserved and apparently—more than a little drunk. During our conversation I told Jim I thought he looked a bit down and if he wanted someone to talk to we would be around. He said thanks and we went back to the other side of the stage to listen to the band.

Within a few minutes someone came from behind me, put their arms around me and gave me a big bear hug. I actually thought it was Gerry Ragni at first but turned to see that it was Jim Morrison.

"Jonathon, how the hell are you?" Jim exclaimed, as if had been years since we last saw each other.

"Just fine Jim," I replied. "How the hell are you?"

Still hugging me even closer he then asks,

"Jonathon, who the fuck runs this place?"

I then asked, "Why?" and with a grin continued, "What do you need Jim?"

Jim then showed me a microphone in his hand which had been separated from the cord. He said, "This fucking thing doesn't work" as he was banging it against his hand.

I guessed he thought it was a wireless microphone. Anyway, with a smile I told him I'd take care of it and proceeded to plug it in. Jim thanked me, happily took the microphone, sat on the stairs at the front of stage and started to sing. Unfortunately after having just finished his show in combination with being drunk, his normally incredible voice was none too pleasant to hear.

Sometime later we decided to leave the party. On our way out we couldn't help but notice one of the girls that Gerry let in. She walked by Jim Morrison on the stairs and paused to give him a pathetic little pat on the head. We found it sort of sad and could still hear his awful singing out on the street as we were walking to the car. I was starting to see the effects drugs and alcohol could have on even a great talent.

Although he was no longer a political candidate, Michael Butler was still very active in politics. At this time the United Nations was sponsoring a new organization entitled "The World Youth Assembly." The idea was to appoint and gather together young representatives from every country in the world. They would then meet and discuss issues of world concern from the viewpoint of the youth. To fund this gallant project every country in the world was encouraged to contribute money. Sadly both the United States and the Soviet Union chose not to donate any money.

Flabbergasted and yet determined, Michael decided "Hair" would come through where our government did not. So "Hair" chipped in to help the World Youth Assembly Fund. For about a week cast members from every production of "Hair" throughout the world gathered and collected donations before and after each show as well as during intermission. It felt a little strange when we all stood in the lobby and in the isles holding buckets for people to drop money in. Not surprisingly though, people gave a lot. I think the final donation from "Hair" worldwide was somewhere around $250,000. We showed up the two world superpowers!

> Hair was the principal financier of the UN Youth Assembly

On one of these afternoons the results from the official draft lottery was going to be announced, so many of us were anxiously awaiting the news. The war in Vietnam was still going on and there was still much opposition, especially to the draft. In the past the government randomly chose boys to draft, pretty much anybody who could walk and carry a gun. This year they were holding a lottery where all 365 days in a year (each representing a birthday) were put into a drawing. The first date they pulled would signify that people with that particular birth date would be drafted sooner than those with birth dates drawn later. The word was the draft was soon to end and this lottery might be the last of its kind.

When the results were finally in I heard my birth date was almost drawn last and I was extremely elated! Others were not so lucky. But on a humorous note, I remember Michael Rhone loudly exclaiming in a very boisterous, yet effeminate voice, "Shit, no way I'm going!" Up to now I hadn't ran across very many people who were openly gay and Michael didn't just come out of the closet, with this news he burst out! I still find humor in Michael's response. I think his number was 3.

We also held a free benefit concert at Moore Theatre around this time and if I remember correctly, this benefit was also for the *World Youth Assembly Fund*. Besides the cast of "Hair" performing some of the ensemble show tunes, many of us performed individually as well. I put together a short solo set of my original material and it went over pretty well.

> ## *Lost In The Folds Of The Flag*
>
> I'm remembering when the astronauts came to the show and there was an air of excitement about the cast. The show seemed to be on a high energy that night. But what happened was that the astronauts became furious with the way we were using the flag and left—but not until they saw the nude scene, which as you know, came much later. I thought that summed it up nicely.
>
> ~ Story relayed by Broadway cast member, Larry Marshall.

In June of 1970 a well-publicized event occurred at the Biltmore Theatre in New York. Two of the Apollo 13 astronauts, Capt. James A. Lovell Jr. and John L. Swigert Jr., both walked out of a performance of "Hair" at the Biltmore Theater along with their entourage. They said they were offended by how the American flag was treated in the show.

Having left sometime after the first act they were approached by Mrs. Michael Gifford, who was in charge of "Hair's" publicity. As they walked to a taxi Mrs. Gifford asked why they were leaving.

"I don't like what you're doing to the flag." Mr. Swigert answered. "I don't like the way they wrapped the flag around that guy."

Mrs. Michael Gifford replied: "If they can wrap the flag around dead men, I don't see why they can't wrap it around a living one. It doesn't touch the ground and it's not abused."

In the scene, three characters are onstage with an American flag. One of them has the flag gently draped over him, then all three slowly and carefully fold it, military style, and with great affection. While doing so the three sing the song called: "Don't Put It Down" which is actually a tribute to the flag.

There had been many rumors and articles written attesting that "Hair" was going to stay in Seattle for a long time. Tickets were selling out and we had also developed a large following of folks who repeatedly came to the show. We were all starting to believe it was true until one of the musicians in the band got fired from the show.

This person had not been consistent in showing up for work, was often late, and was not playing very well when he did show up. After he was fired he put up quite a protest and made public claims his firing was racially motivated. The charges stunned us all because "Hair" was a very integrated and diverse show. The charges were both false and outrageous, and we all knew it. Shortly thereafter management made the decision for "Hair" to leave Seattle altogether rather than put up with a protracted lawsuit.

For a while the entire cast was in limbo in regards to having a job. Before too long it was announced we were going to be the new Miami production of "Hair." That was the good news. The bad news was not all of us would be going and we might not have the same roles. Some of the cast members had families and therefore made a decision not to go to Miami at all. When the news was finally announced, I was relieved to find I still would be playing Woof. I was lucky as a couple of the other leads were to be recast. I've got to hand it to those folks though because they still chose to continue with the show in Miami as tribe members, understudying the roles they once had held in Seattle.

It was a sad day in Seattle when "Hair" had its final performance. The theatre was packed way beyond standing room only. There were people sitting cross-legged in the isles. Many had been regulars to the show and the emotions were running high. We were all leaving our home and our tribe was changing. It didn't really feel right, at least not to me. The Miami tribe ended up with a very strong cast because of it.

THE CHICAGO COMPANY,
The Shubert and Blackstone Theatres
The Pottawatomie Tribe

Michael Butler, Producer
Paul Butler, Producer
Bertrand Castelli, Executive Producer
Clint Spencer, Regional Director
Tom O'Horgan, Director
Julie Arenal, Dance Director
Jerry Combs, Assistant Director
Steve Gillette, Musical Director

Nancy Potts, Costumes
Robin Wagner, Scenery
Jules Fisher, Lighting
Dan Dugan, Sound

Known Cast History

Richard Almack

Blake Anderson

Ferne Bork

Tom Bowden

Julienne Ciukowski

Isaac Clay

Dennis Cooley

Ellen Crawford

Crosley Crosby

Charlotte Crossley

Carolyn Cunningham

Stephen De Ghelder

Geraldine DeHaas

Andre De Sheilds

Michael Delano

Michael Deluca

John Dickson

Dylan Dunbar

Leo Elmore

Patrick Elmore

Michael Federal

Robert Golden

Steven Klatch

Danny Lawyer

Jennifer Lee

Rosemary Llanes

Betty Lloyd

Billy Love

Joe Mantegna

James McCloden

Chuck McKinney

Michael Meadows

Mary Mendum

David Molina (Kalani)

Cecelia Norfleet

Eamon O'Neil

Carol Penner

Helen Pollack

Alaina (Tiny) Reed

Linda Rees

Linda Rios

Carol Ruth

Stephen Scharf

Stan Shaw

Kenneth Griffin	Lana Silva
Edmund Handy	Rita Simonini
Ula Hedwig	Michael Smartt
Sylvia James	Arlene Vrhel
Jonathon Johnson	Freida Williams
Kathleen Johnson	Valerie Williams
Ursuline Kairson	Willie Windsor
Danny Kantner	Tony Zito
Gary Keyes	

In the morning we were to all meet in front of the "Hair" business office down the street from the theatre. Management had chartered a bus to take us to the airport. I arrived early as did a few others. I remember Bob Bingham gave me a good laugh because he had dyed his beard, red, white and blue. He looked a little like a circus clown. We were all very anxious as the bus took off, anticipating something new and exciting. On the way to Miami we were all invited to stop and spend a couple of days in Chicago as guests of Michael Butler.

On the plane flight to Chicago we were all quite wild. We didn't charter a plane; we just sort of took over a commercial flight. If you can imagine being on a plane with about 40 good friends, it was more than that. A better description would be a "flying be-in," packed full of longhaired, wildly dressed hippies. We were loud, obnoxious, and basically took control of the cabin. Back then smoking was allowed on planes, so there was no notice to the fact that many of us were slipping away into the bathrooms for a little pot. People were probably wondering why, how and for what reason two people would go into the can together. Hell, it's difficult for one person to fit in an airplane lavatory! The plane personnel were very friendly though and just sort of played the game with us. No one seemed to complain.

While in Chicago we stayed at the Lincoln Hotel right across from the park. The hotel was a little bit on the funky side. I think most of us were expecting the accommodations to be a little nicer than they were. The elevators had cages instead of doors, the air conditioning wasn't working in some of our rooms and it was very hot and humid in Chicago.

Soon after arriving I stepped outside to the corner drugstore to get a news-paper. As I was going up to the counter with the paper, a large man gave me a dirty look, then purposely bumped into me yelling, "Watch it faggot!"

Immediately knowing where he was coming from and remembering my run-in with the bum in Seattle, I politely said, "excuse me," as if it were me who ran into him. He then sneered at me, mumbled some other comment, and we both went our separate ways. I remember chuckling to myself all the way back up to my room.

That evening we all went to see the Chicago Company of "Hair" perform. We were amazed at the many differences between our show and theirs, yet it was still "Hair." I always enjoyed seeing the different interpretations people had to offer. The Chicago cast was just as fantastic as the ones I had seen in Seattle or San Francisco.

The next day we were all bused out to Michael Butler's home in Oak Brook for a polo match and an ensuing party afterwards. Michael was going to par-ticipate in the polo match and we were all going to watch. I think we were all blown away to find out when we got there, the polo field was on his property! It was a huge estate and a completely amazing day.

The party after the polo match was very interesting. As could be expected there was a lot of booze, pot and also live music. Michael spared no expense and hired Muddy Waters to play at poolside. Within an hour or so several cast members began to take over on the instruments and play. Things only grew more interesting throughout the evening with the staunch polo-playing crowd, mingling and partying down with the wild hippies.

The only problem with this party was the food was late. Michael had spe-cial ordered some vegetarian food to be flown in from Hawaii and it hadn't arrived on time. By the time the food was finally served it was no longer day-light. The natives were pretty restless by then and very rowdy. Regardless, all had fun and partied hard, well into the night.

Coconut Grove

Come morning we packed our bags again and headed out for Miami. We were actually playing outside of Miami proper at the Coconut Grove Playhouse. The weather in Coconut Grove thoroughly impressed me. It was hot and humid but unlike Chicago, it was bearable. It seemed to rain at least once a day but when it wasn't raining the skies were blue. The water was incredible as well. It was crystal clear with a hint of azure, paradise compared to what I was used to.

After spending the first couple of days in hotel rooms some of us decided to rent an apartment together rather than get individual rooms. To save money on transportation several of us also rented bikes to get to the theatre.

Soon after settling in to our respective digs we were all to report to the Coconut Grove Playhouse for a rehearsal. As Tyrone and a few others were walking into the front doors of the theatre, a carload of guys drove buy shouting "Nigger!" and other racial obscenities, obviously directed at Tyrone. It was very disturbing to all of us and I said something to the effect that they were just a bunch of idiots and should be ignored. Tyrone especially was noticeably and understandably upset.

After the rehearsal was over we all started heading back to our rooms. Being one of those who had chosen to rent a bike, I was beginning to get on it for the ride home when Tyrone stopped me. Tyrone said, "Jonathon, give me a ride."

Now Tyrone is a very large man and I'm 5' 7" and weighed about 130 lbs. wet and with all my clothes on at this time. I said, "You're joking of course?"

He then said, "No I ain't joking. Give me a ride."

I said, "No way Tyrone. The bike's not big enough for both of us to ride. The rental place is right across the street if you need one."

Tyrone then exclaimed, "Fuck it then honky!" and walked off.

I was livid! I couldn't believe he would talk to me that way, and he called me a honky to boot! I rode my bike on back to the apartment, fuming all the way. I was very upset and when I got back to the theatre before show time I made a point to track Tyrone down. Tyrone was talking to a group of people in the lobby when I walked up to him, stuck my finger into his big old chest and said, "Why did you call me a honky?"

Tyrone smiled and said, "Because you are a honky and I'm a nigger."

I said, "No you aren't, don't say that! Nigger and Honky are crappy, derogatory words that are thrown out by jerks and idiots, not us."

Tyrone grinned at me, chuckled a little and said, "Okay, I'm sorry. I was only kidding and didn't mean to get you so upset."

Looking back I guess he was just venting out his own hurt and frustration over the remarks made by the guys in the car earlier in the day. That was the kind of crap "Hair" was standing up against though.

The make up of the Miami cast was a good mix. Oatis Stephens came down from the Broadway production to play Berger along with his then girlfriend, Heather MacRae who played Sheila. Tyrone Miles retained the role of Hud; I continued to play Woof, while Charlie Irwin stepped up into the role of Claude.

THE MIAMI COMPANY, COCONUT GROVE PLAYHOUSE,
August 1970
The Chinook Tribe

Michael Butler, Producer
Bertrand Castelli, Executive Producer
Armand Coullet, Director
Rhonda Oglesby, Dance Director
Fred Waring Jr., Musical Director
Nancy Potts, Costumes
Robin Wagner, Scenery
Jules Fisher, Lighting
Abe Jacob, Sound

Cast

Raul C. Arellano
Rose Marie Barbee
Bob Bingham
Skip Bowe
Alice Campbell
Joan Daniels
Arthur L. Dillingham
Janice M. Dobbs
Rooth Dye
Janis Gotti
Jo Ann Harris

Les (Claude) Carlsen
Otis K. Carr
Catherine Chamberlain
Don Copeland
Debbie Cotton-Walker
Kevin Mason
Heather MacRae
Linda Marie Milburn
Tyrone Miles
Eric Miller
Marcus K. Mukai

Jeffrey S. Hillock
Charles W. Irwin
Stephanie Janecke
Jonathon Johnson
Tony Lake

Michael Rhone
Oatis Stephens
Robin Turrill
Burke W. Wallace

During the opening night performance there were many local dignitaries among the audience along with the media. Sitting about 3 rows from front center stage was a woman and her husband who were well known political figures. I will not mention any names here to avoid any embarrassment for them. Anyway, the woman had a political column in one of Miami's papers and was intent on slamming "Hair" in it. She frantically took notes throughout the entire first act while her husband sat quietly by her side, intently watching the show. She was obviously disgusted with each and every one of us and was especially offended by Berger crawling out over the seats, asking for spare change and swinging out over the audience on a rope nearly naked. She was getting some awfully good dirt on us.

When intermission came she and her husband went into the lobby for a drink. She wanted to leave but her husband insisted on seeing "Hair" in its entirety. Reluctantly she returned with her husband to see the rest of the show. Somehow during the second act this woman allowed herself to get caught up in the story and by the shows finale; she was up on her feet and in tears.

She and her husband came up on stage when the audience was invited after the end of "Let the Sunshine In," introduced themselves and thanked us profusely. She was so moved by the "Hair" experience that she also invited us all to come over to her home for lunch the following day. She said she wanted to ask us for some advice having to do with her own children. She seemed so sincere that many of us accepted her invitation.

The next day the woman sent a couple of limo's over to pick up those of us who were going to lunch at her house. Their home was a modest one considering their stature within the Miami community. There was of course a pool and guesthouse, but the home itself was not a gigantic mansion by any means. There were casual pictures of United States Presidents along with famous dignitaries plastered on nearly every wall. We were all out of our comfort zone to say the least.

Her story was this; she had a falling out with her 2 oldest children. I don't remember the details but they were both between 18 and 20 years old and the mom had kicked them both out of the house. Seeing "Hair" helped her to see what her own children might have been going through and she was feeling really bad about it all. She wanted to apologize to her children, tell them she was wrong and ask them back into her life. She wanted our advice on how to approach them. As we all talked over lunch, our basic consensus was for her was to be honest with her kids. That she should talk to her children like she was talking to us. It was really an emotional experience for her.

After our discussion and lunch, the party moved poolside. One cast member got a little too loose and lit up a joint. Luckily our hosts didn't notice. Her youngest son, who was around 12 years old, showed up and started conversing with some of us. I overheard him saying he couldn't wait to turn 18 so he could get out of the house. Hopefully there was a change in the atmosphere in his home that would change his feelings. I thought his mom had a lot of guts and heart to realize and admit she may have been wrong in how she related to her children. Anyway it was all very moving and we had much to reflect on after we were driven back to our rooms later in the afternoon.

Dade County was not the friendliest spot in the nation at that time, especially if you weren't white or if you were a guy with long hair. People were always shouting obscenities and things like "Faggot" at me as I walked through town. Les Carlsen and I went for an extended bike ride one day to see how the regular folks lived. We thought we would avoid the rednecks by riding through a black residential section of town. Well, my guess is they didn't like us either as I was shot in the ass by a pellet gun! It stung a little but we continued our ride regardless.

The road we were on started to turn into a sparsely populated country road. We stopped to talk to a young teenage boy who wanted to know if we had a cigarette. He said, "You guys are pretty cool but I'd turn around and go back if I were you. You might not ever come back if you don't." Wise enough words for us after what had just happened. We took the boys advice and rode back to town.

At the show one night I was told someone from the Robert Stigwood Organization had seen my performance and wanted to meet with me about a possible record deal. Gerry had just come into town so I mentioned it to him. Gerry warned me not to get involved with the Robert Stigwood Organization.

He convinced me I should go to New York instead to join the Broadway Company of "Hair." Gerry said he would arrange everything and would pay for my stay until I got settled. He also told me he would finance a record for me so I didn't need their help.

I did indeed have a meeting with someone from the Stigwood Organization during a photo shoot at the theatre. They were looking for someone who could be promoted for the teen audience, which looking back would have been an excellent opportunity for me. I was rather cocky though and expressed little or no interest in their ideas. I told them I was going to New York and had already made arrangements to record an album. I most likely blew off an opportunity of a lifetime that day. It wouldn't be the last time though.

> 726 recordings have been made from the score of Hair, making it the most recorded show in Broadway history. The cast album was number one, and 4 songs recorded from the show have reached number one on the charts: Aquarius/Let the Sunshine In by the 5th Dimension, Hair by the Cowsills, and Good Morning Starshine by Oliver. ~ From the July 1970 "Hair" press kit.

9

Where Do I Go?

I soon quit the show in Miami thinking I was going to be in the New York cast. In New York I stayed at the Chelsea Hotel compliments of Gerry Ragni. Gerry had spoken very highly of the Chelsea and said it was where he lived whenever in New York and was sure I would like it there as well.

Located on West 23rd Street in Manhattan between Seventh and Eighth Avenues, the Chelsea was often referred to as the "Hippie Plaza" because so many young, famous artists either lived there or stayed there. The hotel, Victorian Gothic in design, was built in 1884. Some of its noted residents have been, Thomas Wolfe, Dylan Thomas, Arthur C. Clarke, Andy Warhol, Arthur Miller, Jimi Hendrix, Janis Joplin, Tiny Tim, and of course, Gerome Ragni and James Rado.

I was excited to be in New York and went over to the Biltmore the day after we arrived. Before I left Miami Heather MacRae and Oatis Stephens had suggested I introduce myself to Allan Nicholls who was a close friend of theirs. Allan was playing Claude in the Broadway production at the time, although he also played Berger often. They thought it would be nice for me to know someone who was in the show, as all the cast were strangers to me. They were right of course, as Allan welcomed me with open arms and introduced me to several others in the cast.

The following day I went back to the Biltmore in the afternoon. Ted Rado, who was the Artistic Director for all the "Hair" companies, was at the theatre and asked me what I was doing there and why I wasn't in Miami. I said Gerry had sent me to be in the show. Ted then shocked me by saying there were no openings in show. He did say I was welcome to audition if I like though, just in case something were to open up in the future.

I was devastated and hurt, not to mention pissed off! More than anything else I was mad at myself for allowing this to happen. After very little thought I made the decision not to audition at all. Even so, during my stay in New York I continued to hang out at the Biltmore with the tribe and on occasion I would join in the show without being paid. The management didn't seem to mind as they always needed extra bodies.

Not long after I arrived in New York trouble came to some of my friends in the Miami cast. The article below appeared in many newspapers around the country. The complete story is told by Kevin Mason in "The Voices of the Tribe" section near the back of this book.

In September of 1970, several members of the Miami cast of "Hair" were arrested and charged with disorderly conduct. There was a police photograph printed in the paper showing Marcus K. Mukai, Oatis Stephens and Heather MacRae, daughter of Gordon and Sheila MacRae.

The police said the incident stemmed from a confrontation with plainclothes officers. The policemen had been watching two narcotics suspects in a park where the group was gathered, the police said.

Several days after I settled in Gerry Ragni showed up. He then introduced me to Rick (a friend of his) and the three of us hung out in New York for a couple of days. One of the first places Gerry took us to was Sammy's in the Bowery. Sammy's Bowery Follies, known for songs and dances of the gay 90's, was a very weird cabaret which had a 19th century vaudeville atmosphere to it. There were strange fat ladies dressed up in bustled dresses along with a few dwarfs. It was a circus atmosphere and Gerry seemed to know everyone there. I was a little uncomfortable but tagged along with our wild and crazy host, never knowing what may happen next. Life was always an adventure with Gerry to be sure.

At around 4 am we were finally able to pry Gerry away from Sammy's. Ever try to catch a cab in New York? Here are three long hairs at four o'clock in the morning, trying to hail a cab, but none are stopping. It was looking pretty bad so we stepped back into the club and called for one. Soon after calling a cab one showed up, took a look at us and then sped off like the others had. So Gerry went back inside to call for another.

While we were waiting for the next cab a low rider pulled over to the side of the road and two young thugs, apparently gang members, got out of their car and slowly started walking towards us. They produced some chains and a few knives. Gerry was still in the club calling a cab so it was just Rick and me. They were calling us names in Spanish and we were quite sure they were going to have a little fun with the hippies.

Rick was quick to call their bluff by putting his jacket over his arm (acting like he had a concealed gun) and calmly provoked them to come on. They stopped in their tracks, looked at each other and then back at us. Once again Rick asked them to come on. They looked at each other again, this time motioning to get back in the car. While their tires were still spinning and screeching Gerry returned, having missed out on all the action. We started telling him the story as we were all getting into the cab for the ride home.

Over the next few days Gerry took me to a few of the off-off-Broadway shows that were going on at the time. Trying to give me a feel for "Hair's" roots, we also went to the La Mama Experimental Theatre. While we were there Gerry introduced me to Ellen Stewart who ran La Mama. She then invited us to stay for the performance.

While staying at the Chelsea Gerry also introduced me to Bert Sommer who was once in the New York cast of "Hair." Bert seemed to be a real nice person and we got along nicely. Since we were both singer-songwriters we got together a few times at the Chelsea with our acoustic guitars and jammed a little. I was impressed with Bert's talents and also that he had a recording contract.

Gerry also set up a meeting for me with his publisher, Nat Shapiro, in hopes that Nat might be able to help me get some of my songs published. Nat's offices were on the upper east side of New York. He was a very nice man and gladly listened to my tapes. Although he said he liked my material he was also very honest and said it was not something his company would publish. We then talked at great lengths about "Hair" and its history. Although I had already heard similar stories on the history of "Hair" from Gerry and others, it was very educational to hear it in detail from Nat's perspective.

Nat described his initial shock at seeing Gerry and Jim's first lyrics and script to "Hair." He said Gerry and Jim walked into his office carrying a briefcase filled with notes and drawings on napkins, brown paper bags and old envelopes. They basically spread it all out on his desk and when it was all pieced together it made up the first draft for the lyrics and script for "Hair." They still hadn't found a suitable composer for their project though. Nat was however impressed enough to forge ahead. He soon introduced them to Galt MacDermot, a straight looking Staten Island resident who seemed to understand and also loved the kind of music they were looking for. After the three first met it took Galt a relatively short time to complete the score for the show. All they needed was a producer.

"Hair" was then shopped around town but no one knew what to do with a free style show having 25 characters, about a tribe of loveable kids who have free sex, burn draft cards and smoke pot. Finally, "Hair" came to the attention of Joseph Papp and the rest was history. Even though Nat said he could not help me, I felt very honored and privileged to have met him and was thankful for his stories.

A Tangled Hair Story

In Munich Germany, the city objected to the nude scene. They informed Bertrand Castelli, producer of the Munich show, "We just don't go around with our clothes off." Bertrand informed the city fathers that he had personal friends who'd been marched to the German gas chambers with their clothes off.

The following night at the theatre, the nude scene was blocked from the show. On a banner were printed the names of every concentration camp during the World War II. The following day, the city had a sudden change of heart. "Hair" was permitted to reinstate the nude scene.

Having no job and having to rely on Gerry for assistance was really starting to get me down. I was very unhappy and on top of everything else I was missing Robin immensely. Realizing I wanted her back in my life, I thought of writing her a letter to tell her how I felt. Although I was still unsure as to whether or not she would ever have me back, I went ahead and wrote to her anyway.

One of my favorite things to do at the Chelsea was to hang out in the lobby and watch all the famous people go in and out the door. There were always lots of rock stars and actors, and many times they would hang out and chat as well, either in the lobby or in the El Quijote restaurant and bar downstairs.

The El Quijote restaurant and bar was attached to the hotel and had become a happening place all of its own. Both places had an incredible aura about them. One could spend hours just hanging out, chatting with both the famous and the not so famous, or just watching the passers by.

I found most of the employees at the Chelsea to be very friendly and always willing to tell a story or two about the hotel and its many patrons. There was one lobby assistant in particular who always had lots of stories and dirt to tell about the many goings on in the hotel. I heard stories from him about Janis Joplin, Jimi Hendrix and Andy Warhol, just to name a few. On one of those nights in the lobby I ran into an old acquaintance from Seattle, Jon Keliehor, former drummer for The Daily Flash.

Jon had just returned from London. He had been playing over there until his work visa had expired, forcing him to return to the USA for a while. It was great to see a familiar face and the two of us started spending time together in New York. Jon introduced me to Tommy Bolin and his band Zephyr, who were also staying at the Chelsea. Tommy, who was very young at the time, was already a killer guitar player. He was also a very nice person and was pretty laid back. Zephyr was in town to record a new album and they invited Jon and me to their recording sessions. The sessions were held at Electric Ladyland, Jimi Hendrix's new studios in the Village.

Electric Ladyland was really pretty amazing for its time. It had a real relaxing atmosphere designed to enhance artistic creativity and that it did. Even the bathroom was decorated for the times. All the walls and the ceiling of the bathroom were covered with a decoupage collage of psychedelic images and beautiful naked women. I can also recall seeing one of Jimi's guitars sitting on a guitar stand in a corner. It was a right-handed Stratocaster that had been strung backwards. It was all an incredible experience for me and the Zephyr recording sessions were eventually released as their "Going Back to Colorado" LP.

Back at the Chelsea one night Tommy was telling us how beautiful Boulder Colorado was. He was sitting back on the bed, strumming an acoustic guitar and describing the snow capped mountains and blue skies of the town he thought of as his adopted home. In contrast to what I was experiencing in New York City, his description impressed me for years. So much so, I eventually moved to Boulder myself in 1976. I was also very saddened to hear Tommy Bolin had died of an apparent drug overdose that very same year.

One night when I was alone in my room at the Chelsea sitting on the bed and playing a new song on my guitar, I could faintly hear someone playing in the room beside me. I would stop playing so I could listen to the music I was hearing but whenever I would stop, so would the music next door. This went on like this, back and forth, until I finally opened the door to see if the sound I was hearing was coming from the hall. As I opened the door to look down the hall to the right, my next-door neighbor opened his door to look down the hall to his left. The both of us smiled, said hello and went back into our rooms. I found out later from Rick, the guy staying in the room next door to me was Leonard Cohen.

I soon received a long letter back from Robin in which she basically said she would always love me and also wanted us to get back together. She told me how beautiful Melissa was, how fast she was growing up and that she couldn't wait to see me again. I really needed to hear this as I was beginning to fall into a deep depression living in New York without a job. To make matters worse, while in the Chelsea lobby I overheard that Jimi Hendrix had just died while in London. So strange since I was just in his recording studio. Here I was hoping I might even get to meet him. What a tremendous waste of talent!

In a few days I called Robin on the phone and the two of us talked for quite awhile. I told her about all my New York adventures and she updated me on Melissa. The news and shock of Hendrix came up as she proceeded to tell me she had attended Jimi Hendrix's funeral in Renton. She said it was a real big event with many fans and was a very sad occasion for all. She asked when I was coming home and I said I didn't know but it could possibly be very soon.

Not even a few weeks had passed when I was riding in a Chelsea elevator and overheard the news that Janis Joplin had also died of an overdose. The vibe at the Chelsea was now getting very dark. Within a month's time two of the Chelsea's most famous residents had passed on. With no job and no prospects, I decided to go back home to Seattle to be with Robin and Melissa. I broke the news to Irene Ragni who arranged with Gerry to buy my ticket home. Irene, my fairy God Mother, once again came through to help me again and I will always be eternally grateful to her.

Now more excitement was happening with "Hair." This time the problems were on the west coast. Some of the Los Angeles cast members found themselves in a little trouble to say the least.

Busted

In October 1970, 12 members of the Los Angeles cast of "Hair" were arrested on drug charges.

A couple of the percussionists in the band, Maurice Miller and Melvin Telford were picked up in West L.A. and were also charged with suspicion of robbery but were subsequently discharged as wrongly identified. Others arrested were, Teddy Neely, Delores Hall, Kay Cole, Joe Morton, Jerry Combs, Albert Greenberg, Cecilia Norfleet, Tadg Galleran, Peter Kunkle and Norman Glenn. They were all at a party in Torrance.

According to the police they received a call about too much noise coming from an apartment at about two in the morning. After arriving to issue a warning, they smelled marijuana. They claimed that other pills were also confiscated. The cast was subsequently released on bail without missing any performances.

The Lovers

This was one of the best homecomings I had ever experienced. Robin, Melissa and my mom were waiting for me at the airport and I could have gotten lost in Robins embrace forever. It was as if some strange force had separated us and we were now reunited. This is where I belonged. Feeling like I'd aged and grown ten years over my recent experiences, I was now ready to settle down with my family. On the ride back home from the airport we couldn't keep our eyes off one another.

Robin and Melissa were now living in her dad's basement apartment. Robin assured me her dad had changed and he was looking forward to having me stay with them. She said he had stopped drinking and wasn't even around much. I was recalling my last encounter with her father and was therefore a little uncomfortable, not to mention skeptical about the situation. We both agreed it would be best to get our own place so we were immediately discussing our living arrangements. First though, I needed to get work quick. I started exploring band options and solo options as well as local theatre.

Robin and I were trying to sleep in one morning as we had been up with Melissa most of the night because she was beginning to teeth. We had just made love and were lying in bed talking and enjoying each other's company. Suddenly the front door opened and there stood her dad looking in our bedroom door. My heart sunk to my feet looking up at this very large man. Here I am, lying in bed with his daughter and I'm wondering what he's going to do? Before I could say anything, he gave us a cheerful "Good Morning Kids," threw us a joint and said, "Have a great day, I gotta go now."

Before we knew it he was already headed back out the door. I was dumbfounded and at the same time highly amused. I turned to look at Robin and she laughed and said, "See, I told you he changed."

We soon found a little apartment on Capitol Hill in Seattle. It was an older Victorian style apartment complex that even had a small lobby in the center. We were up on the second floor and had a slight view of the city. Although there was much potential in the place, it seemed to be held together with thumbtacks and cockroaches. Not the kind of atmosphere either of us were accustomed to or wanted to bring a baby up in. Although we were happy to have our own place, we fully expected to move on up as soon as I could find work. My dad drove down with his pickup and helped us move into our new place.

The three of us went up north to visit my dad. When I went to Miami I had left my VW camper bus at their house. We wanted to pick it up so we wouldn't have to borrow cars all the time. I was a few months behind on my payments and had also stopped my insurance, so that was definitely a big concern. We had a great visit with my family. It was wonderful as they had not spent anytime before with Robin or Melissa.

We ended up staying with them for a few days while I busied myself trying to figure out what we were going to do next. I still hadn't found work and was thinking of going down to San Francisco to see if I could get into "Hair" there. To hell with pride, I would audition and do what ever it takes. I just needed to have a steady income to take care of my family.

I didn't want to ruin my credit but the VW bus payment was just too much of albatross, so I was thinking I would let it be repossessed. One of my brother-in-laws suggested I first drive it to San Francisco. That way I would at least get a free trip out of it and who knows; maybe I could get a job right away and catch up on my payments.

Robin and I decided it was a good idea. No matter if we stayed or left, the bus was probably going to be repossessed, so we decided our best bet was to go to San Francisco. Besides, we were really starting to hate our apartment even though we had just moved in. Once we made the decision we told our families. They were all none too pleased as they were enjoying that we were together again. But they understood our reasoning and stood behind us.

On our way to San Francisco, we stopped in Kelso Washington to visit for a few days with Robin's grandparents. Robin's mom showed up as well and we all had a good time. Robin's mom and grandparents also made us an unusual offer. They said if we got married before we left they would give us $400 to help with the trip. Since we had already decided we were going to get married anyway, we took them up on their offer. So on November 2nd 1970 we got married at the Kelso courthouse with Melissa smiling and cooing in her grandma's arms. No big fancy wedding, but a fairytale come true for the three of us. After the ceremony we had a small reception back at her grandparent's house. We couldn't have been happier.

The trip to San Francisco was pretty much uneventful. Because it was November we didn't have the luxury of taking our time. We were concerned about the amount of snow that may be in the pass between Oregon and California. So we drove straight through to San Francisco from Kelso, only taking meal and rest stop breaks. Robin had never traveled outside of Washington State so she was thoroughly enjoying this trip. Melissa was also being a great baby, with little or no fussing. After many hours of driving we stopped in Berkley and spent our first night in a hotel there.

In the morning we had breakfast at a local coffee shop on Telegraph Canyon road and then drove over the Bay Bridge into San Francisco. It was very exciting for the two of us as we came into the city. We made our way over to the Golden Gate Bridge as all tourists do. We parked the bus at the foot of the bridge and the three of us cuddled together admiring its beauty. As we were standing there, an Asian couple came over to us with a camera. They didn't speak any English and were motioning to us. We thought they wanted us to take their picture, but what they really wanted was a picture of us by the bridge. We both broke up in laughter when we figured out they were trying to get pictures of "San Francisco Hippies!" It made me think of the Margaret Mead scene in "Hair" where the cast lines up for pictures for the tourist couple.

Knowing we didn't have enough money to waste on hotel rooms, we grabbed a newspaper and began calling for apartments. We spent the entire day driving around looking for rental signs and calling ads. There was not much of anything available. We finally found a cheesy little apartment off Market Street on 15th. It was just as bad if not worse than the one we bailed on in Seattle, but we needed a place quick and took it. It was also pretty close to the theatre where "Hair" was playing.

Not long after settling in I wrote a letter to the bank to tell them where we were staying and that I hoped to catch up on my payments for the bus. We had spent most of our money getting into the apartment, so I went to a pawnshop on Market Street and pawned some of my musical equipment.

I then made my way over to the theatre where "Hair" was playing only to find out the show was due to close soon. After visiting with some of the tribe I also learned there was going to be a new National Touring company of "Hair." The show's new director was also going to direct and cast the tour. So all hope was not lost. The director was not around this evening but he was holding a meeting concerning the tour on the following day. It was suggested I come to this meeting to see if I could audition.

When I got back home to our apartment Robin was distressed in that there were cockroaches galore. She had spent most of the evening stomping on them. Needless to say she was very excited that I might be able to land a job in the touring company of "Hair."

In the morning I thought I heard the unmistakable sound of a Volkswagen starting. I looked out the window in time to witness the repo man driving my bus away! No knock at the door, no asking for keys, just gone! The bank must have just jumped at the opportunity upon receipt of my letter.

Later I walked down to the meeting concerning the tour and was more than surprised to learn Joe Donovan was the mystery director of the tour. After giving me a big hug Joe said, "Where have you been? I've been asking all over about you." He then said he wanted me to play Woof in the tour. I said I would love to without any hesitation. A tremendous burden had just been lifted from my shoulders.

I got more than I could have ever asked for and without an audition. Things were beginning to look up. The only problem was the tour wasn't going to start for at least a month. The plan was to shut down the San Francisco show in a few weeks, move to Chicago for that company's last few weeks and then the tour would officially begin.

After explaining our financial situation to Joe, he said he could hire me now as a tribe member for the San Francisco Company and then for the Chicago Company until the tour began. His only stipulation was I wasn't to tell anyone what role I was to be playing in the tour. Some cast members were not going to be asked to join the tour and he didn't want any bad feelings, which was understandable.

One of the nicest people Robin and I met in the San Francisco Company was Kenny Ortega. After hearing about how miserable our accommodations were, Kenny invited the three of us to stay with him at his apartment until we were to leave for Chicago. Compared to where we were staying, Kenny's home was extremely luxurious. So we moved out of our crappy little apartment and over to Kenny's.

Kenny was a great host, fun to be with, and the three of us became good friends. I was impressed to find out Kenny had already enjoyed much success as a choreographer. I remember him showing me his credits on a cast album of a play he had choreographed at the Redwood City Playhouse when he was only 15 years old. Kenny is just another example of the tremendous talent that flowed through "Hair."

When "Hair" in San Francisco closed out, Kenny decided not to go. He offered to store some of our stuff at his place. As a token of friendship, Kenny and I traded leather jackets. Mine was a custom made, red white and blue suede jacket, calf length with stars and stripes. His was a soft, shiny calfskin coat, which was about knee length on me. We soon said our good-byes and moved on to Chicago.

The Chicago cast welcomed us with open arms. Ursula Szlagowski (later to be Ula Hedwig) and Danny Kantner invited us to stay at their house somewhere in the suburbs of Chicago. It was Christmas time, snowing and very cold in Chicago. Both Robin and I missed our families, so it was good to spend time with Ula and Danny. Their house was decorated for Christmas and the whole atmosphere was so much better than staying in a hotel, especially with a baby. Knowing we were shortly going to be in hotel rooms across the country, it was very good to be around friends in a home.

The only incident I can recall in Chicago was on my first night in the Chicago production of "Hair." It concerned my first meeting with David (Kalani) Molina. Kalani was a very large and handsome Hawaiian. He had a great head of frizzed out hair shaped into an Afro style. Kalani was also very feminine and very obviously gay. This didn't bother me at all as some of the nicest, kindest and endearing people I had met in my life had been gay. I respect choice and all I ask in return is that my choice is respected as well.

In the choreography staging of this show there was a scene in the first act where one person would be at the foot of the stage, laying on their back with their head facing the audience, while another person would be straddled on top of them, facing the same direction and flinging their hair from side to side. It might have been during the song, "Hair," but I can't be sure. Two other cast members on the other side of the stage also mirrored what we were doing. It must be said that this staging also happened directly in front of two foot-mikes at the front of the stage.

Okay, you get the picture. Lucky me, I'm the person on the bottom that night and Kalani is on top of me. While this scene is happening, Kalani decides to plant a big old kiss on me, right on the lips. Hello! I was taken by surprise and because of the foot mikes; I couldn't say a thing without the audience hearing. My immediate reaction was to give a small bite to Kalani on the cheek. I don't know why, I just did it without thinking! Not the preferred method of telling someone to stop but in this case it was very effective. The scene ended as fast as it started as most scenes in "Hair" did. As we both walked off the stage, Kalani was holding his cheek and said, "Damn, why'd you bite me?"

I replied, "Why the hell did you kiss me? Don't ever do that again!"

Kalani then said, "Okay. God, you're so butch." An accusation I heard quite often from my gay friends. That along with, "When are you going to come out of your closet?" Both Robin and I soon became good friends with Kalani. He was a warm and kind soul, and the incident was soon forgotten.

Another Strand of Hair

"Hair" also ran into trouble in Chattanooga Tennessee. The board of the city municipal theater opposed bringing the show to town. They rejected the show on the grounds it would not be, "in the best interest of the community." The producers of "Hair" stated that rejecting the show would be a violation of the First Amendment rights to free speech. The board then claimed they did not feel the "Hair's" producers were entitled to any First Amendment protections seeing the show contained what they termed as "obscene" content.

The case was eventually brought to the U.S. Supreme Court. The U.S. Supreme Court refused to address whether the show was obscene or not. Instead, they only considered the procedures used by the board for rejecting the show, in addition to some of their subsequent actions. In the end, the show was allowed to go on.

10

Mercury Rising, The Tours Begin

Just before the Chicago show closed; announcements were made as to the final lineup of the Mercury Tour. The New Year had just begun and as with previous "Hair" flights, this one was not chartered, it was a commercial flight. The tour didn't start off on a good foot as there was a blizzard in Chicago and we were stranded at the Midway airport for about 9 hours. After such a long wait many of us were not too anxious to get on this flight. The first stop on the wild circus ride ahead was going to be Louisville Kentucky.

After a harrowing flight through heavy winter storms we finally reached our first stop on the Mercury tour in Louisville. As we were driving to our hotel I was impressed by the immensity of the landscape surrounding Louisville. The rolling hills with few trees were a stark contrast to what I was used to in the Pacific Northwest. There seemed to be so much beautiful farmland and even the city seemed down home, quiet and lazy compared to the other places I'd traveled to.

It was in Louisville that people started referring to the Mercury tour as the "Super Tribe." That's because management had pulled the best performers from the other companies as they closed. We had tribe from Detroit, Chicago, San Francisco, Seattle, Las Vegas, New York, Boston, Indianapolis, Cincinnati, Montreal and other cities.

A local Catholic layman who organized a sidewalk demonstration to protest "Hair" orchestrated the most memorable event. He had gathered around 40 demonstrators, who carried signs and showed up to parade in front of the Brown Theatre before each performance

They called themselves "The Christians for Decency," a new organization put together just to protest "Hair." They had hoped to become a permanent organization though. They wanted to protect the community from similar disgusting events in the future.

The Christians for Decency claimed "Hair" was lewd, anti-American, blasphemous, and an attack on both the Catholic Church and religion. In their minds they were taking a stand for Christ. Funny, but the leader of the Christians for Decency had never personally seen "Hair."

City policemen were stationed at the front of the theatre to intervene should there be any trouble. The only incident was when a young man shouted at a marcher, asking if they had seen the play. He asked how they could picket if they haven't seen it.

All of the cast members took the news of the protesting and demonstrations with a grain of salt.

Kalani was quoted as saying, "We're great believers in everyone doing his own thing. If picketing is what makes you happy, then you should do it. Even in Las Vegas we had trouble with the sheriff and the county attorney. In Las Vegas—where they have nudes in every club!"

Although there was quite a bit of excitement surrounding the show in Louisville, it went on without a hitch and the overall public reception was very positive.

There was a strange occurrence I personally had at one of the matinees concerning two elderly ladies. They were sitting about three rows back from the stage on the center aisle. Throughout the entire show they seemed to be all smiles and thoroughly enjoying themselves. For some reason both of them seemed to be looking my direction quite a bit. It made me feel a bit awkward, like my great aunts were watching over me the whole time.

At the end of the show when the audience is invited to come up on stage, the two ladies approached me. Looking me over with twinkles in their eyes, one of them said something to the effect of, "You're the one you know."

The other lady nodded in agreement, echoing, "Yes, you are."

This statement caught me off guard and before I could ask them what they were talking about, one of them spoke again.

"You're a special spiritual leader. We know it, we were told so."

Again, they were both nodding in agreement, standing serenely in front of me, eyes just twinkling away.

I was caught by surprise and totally blown away. I was wondering what their minister had put in their Sunday wafers! If someone really gave them this message they certainly got wrong directions! Must have been some other theatre! Wanting to laugh but not wanting to be rude, I stammered out,

"No, I think you're mistaken. I'm just an Actor. I'm really glad you liked my performance though. It's a real compliment. Thanks a lot."

Once again, this time in nearly perfect unison, they said, "No, you are the one, we know it."

Now I was beginning to feel a little creepy, hair standing on the back of my neck and all. For God sakes I was not playing the role of Jesus in Superstar here! I was playing freaking "Woof" and singing about Sodomy! Where on earth were they coming from?

Once again I reiterated, "Really ladies, I'm flattered but I'm not good enough to be what you are saying. I'm just an actor." With that, I gave them hugs, thanked them again and left the stage.

This was a very strange encounter indeed. I was used to having young men approach me on occasion after shows saying things like, "I'm bi-sexual too" or "I'm gay too." After which I would say I was not gay, I was just an actor, playing a role. That all made more sense to me as it followed the tone of the role. The two ladies assertions made no sense to me at all.

The other thing that happened in Louisville was I decided to take up photography as a hobby. With Melissa growing up so fast and so many great things to see, I went out and bought a 35mm camera. I took many pictures from this point on.

William Mootz of the Louisville Courier-Journal gave a long, yet excellent review of "Hair" after it opened. Some of what he wrote was,

"Hair" is a beautiful, wonderful, eye-dazzling, ear-opening show. Everybody in the house was rising to his feet in what was the most spontaneous standing ovation I have ever seen in a theater. People clapped their hands raw. People raised their arms in the peace sign. People cheered themselves hoarse. And finally, people rushed up on the stage to throw their arms around this marvelous tribe of youngsters who had just given the best of themselves in the cause of "Hair" and the message it is spreading around the world."

"Hair" is unlike any other musical ever conceived. What you don't know, unless you've experienced it, is that "Hair" gradually takes possession of you, body and soul. It seeps into your bloodstream; makes you grab on to a reality that you didn't suspect existed. You see these kids live out a vision of the world that is original. By the time the second act is rising to its heart-stopping climax, that vision is also absolutely fine and pure and honest."

"If ever there was a show that celebrates the beauty of man as he has been created in God's image, "Hair" is it. At its core it preaches a sermon of brotherly love, preaches it with a certain naiveté and obviousness. But preaches it with an emotional fervor that lifts the heart. If it mocks false idols in the process, more power to it for its freshness and it's daring."

"The cast bringing "Hair" to Louisville performs it with an energy that is almost frightening. Last night's performance made the one I saw in New York look as tame as a second-rate road show of "Naughty Marietta." There are new songs in this version, too, as well as different inventive touches in the staging."

There was another interesting article in the local paper while we were in town. Sally Bly of The Courier-Journal interviewed Robin, Jennifer Lee and me. I don't recall when we started giving Melissa the nickname of "Mo," but by this time we must have used it a lot because it showed up in the article. The article included a great picture of the 3 of us sitting on some stairs with our daughter Melissa.

In the interview we talked about "Hair" being like a revival in that it has the power to change people, both the cast and the audience. We also expressed how the show had personally changed us. Because of our shared "Hair" experiences we were more sensitive, were able to touch people easier, and were able to love people easier.

We went on to say that "Hair" had brought a lot of people together. Even off-stage, the cast was very much as it was on stage. We all truly believed in; peace and love, and the closeness was also the same off-stage. I specifically commented that it was as if our daughter had 40 other parents.

We went on to say that although the show may be outdated to some of the younger generation, it was not outdated to the people who need to be more sensitive. The topic will never be outdated—that people should get together; love; live in peace and stop the war. Maybe when war is outdated, "Hair" will be outdated.

There was much truth in my comments that Melissa had 40 other parents in the show. While we were traveling with her it seemed everyone was always willing to help out with her needs. Whether it was feeding, changing a diaper or just entertaining her. Even though the tribe hadn't known each other for very long there was something about being in "Hair" that made you an instant family member. It was easy and very spiritually rewarding to be a member of the tribe.

The Mercury Production of Hair," like the other two National Tours, Venus and Jupiter, was a real hybrid. I was like a melting pot in that the cast members were drawn from several different casts around the country that had recently closed or were about to be shut down. The cast was therefore the cream of the crop as far as talent goes. On a few occasions we would audition and pick up new tribe members while on the road, but in most cases we were all seasoned "Hair" tribe members.

Our next stop was Milwaukee. The main thing I remember about Milwaukee is it was so damn cold there. Snow was everywhere and the wind chill factor was averaging somewhere around zero. Robin and I were just not prepared for such cold weather. Oh we had gloves, scarves and warm jackets but the wind in Milwaukee just cut right through it all. We tended to stay in our room an awful lot during our stay there.

On one of our ventures out, the three of us were walking down to the theatre for a rehearsal. I almost always took Robin and Melissa to both the rehearsals and the shows. Just as we were about to get to the theatre, a man came running out of a shop holding a bag with a lady chasing and shouting after him, "Stop! Thief! Help! Please someone help! We've been robbed!" It was a scene just like you would see in the movies or television.

Without thinking for a second about the ramifications, I began to chase this person. While Robin and Melissa stayed with the woman, I ran down the street after this man. He then darted into an alley and I pursued. About 20 feet into the alley this guy stops and turns to face me. I felt a tremendously angry vibe from him and I knew he was ready to confront me. Call it a little voice inside or whatever, but something told me I didn't really want to catch this guy and I should walk away. After staring at him for a few seconds, I turned away and walked back up the street. When I got back to Robin, Melissa and the woman, I simply said he got away. On the way to the theatre I told Robin the real story. She was very glad I had let it go.

More Personal Reflections on "HAIR," Act I

The first Earth Day was celebrated in April of 1970, but "Hair" had since its inception brought the cause of ecology to the attention of the masses. Jeanie, popping up from a trap door in the stage wearing a gas mask and obviously pregnant, sings and coughs her way into your heart with the song, "Air."

"Welcome sulfur dioxide, Hello, carbon monoxide, the air, the air is everywhere. Breathe deep, while you sleep, breathe deep."

To me Jeanie is also the consummate hippie, who hangs out with whomever, living day to day and loving everyone. She's not even sure who the father of her baby is. She's really in love with Claude and desperately wishes her baby were his. Persistent in her determination to get Claude to love her as well, you almost hope she will eventually succeed. She is sweet, loving and caring, but certainly not innocent.

The innocent character in "Hair" is Crissy. With one song, "Frank Mills," Crissy easily and consistently steals your heart away. Standing alone, vicariously under the Waverly Theatre sign, she pleads for assistance in finding the possible love of her life. Hearing her words you can't believe she is a day over 14-years old.

"I met a boy called Frank Mills, on September 12th right here in front of the Waverly, but unfortunately, I lost his address."

A not so innocent scene but one of my all time favorites, is where the tourist couple comes in just before the title song Hair" is performed. It is known as the Margaret Mead scene. Two male members of the cast play Margaret and her husband Hubert, auspiciously. The role of Margaret is played in full drag and goes over much better if it is delivered with all the sincerity of someone's great aunt. In some of the productions I was in, if we were short on someone to play Hubert, one of the girls would step in and dress as a man. That was also fun, especially if a penciled-in mustache was used.

The surprise comes at the end of the scene, after the song "Hair," when one of the cast members compliments Margaret on her dress. To the full view of the audience she opens her cloak exclaiming,

"Oh, but I'm not wearing a dress."

At this time she has exposed herself or should I say, himself—jockey shorts and all. She then crosses the stage, pauses to the audiences laughter, and then says,

"Why, thank you."

As the audience erupts in more laughter she turns again to the audience, hushing them with her index finger to her mouth and says,

"Shhh.... he doesn't know,"

while pointing to her husband Hubert with her other hand. The Margaret Meade Scene is a great, classic scene.

Many people thought "Hair" was disrespectful of the American Flag but nothing could have been farther from the truth. This is evident in the song "Don't Put It Down." Always one of my favorite songs to sing in the show, three of us very carefully folded and handled a flag to military specifications while singing the song.

"Don't put it down, best one around. Crazy for the red, blue and white. Crazy for the red, blue and white. You look at me, what do you see? Crazy for the white, red and blue. Crazy for the white, red and blue. 'Cause I look different you think I'm subversive. Crazy for the blue, white and red. Crazy for the blue, white and red.
My heart beats true for the red, white and blue.
Crazy for the blue, white and red.
Crazy for the blue, white and red, and yellow fringe."

I feel this song is important to the message of "Hair" because back then if you hated or questioned the war, or our countries objectives, it was automatically assumed you didn't love America. The big saying we always heard was, "America, love it or leave it." Well we loved it and surely did not want to leave it. We only wanted to make it better.

Okay, for over 30 years people have been fixated on the nude scene. Whenever someone finds out I was in the musical "Hair" the jokes about the nudity start rolling in. For those who never saw the stage presentation the general belief is we spent the whole show running about in the buff. The truth of the matter is, the nude scene was at the very end of the first act and so short that many did not see it at all! At times it could be and was an expression of the freedom we all had experienced. Many other times however, it appeared irrelevant and totally unnecessary to get the real messages of "Hair" across.

Another aspect of the nude scene from an actor's point of view was it was voluntary. You only performed it if you felt up to it. Actors Equity had also arranged for extra pay if you did participate. In fact, there were many times when only a few cast members exposed themselves in the nude scene. The stage managers were often trying to find out who was willing to go on and do it, minutes before show time. Just waiting or undressing under the huge parachute while Claude was singing, "Where Do I Go?" wasn't very pleasant either and was often embarrassing. You really had to be in the mood.

The most difficult times I can recall with the nude scene were with the matinee performances. I hate to generalize but many of the matinee audiences contained mostly the elderly generation. It's kind of hard to be serious about a scene when as you gaze out into the audience, all you see is an ocean of spyglasses. Although I often found this humorous, it got to where I usually opted out of the nude scene during matinees.

It may have been cold in Milwaukee but the audience was not. We had excellent turnouts with warm receptions and great reviews. I was surprised one morning to get a call from the front desk saying some girls were in the lobby and they were requesting to meet me. Robin was always a good sport about this sort of thing and encouraged me to go down and talk to them. I was very flattered and surprised at this visit. I had experienced much admiration from young girls in Seattle but really did not expect it to continue into other areas of the country. There were about four girls in the group and they were all students at Marquette University. They were very disappointed to find out I was married and had a child, but thanked me for my time and presented me with a Marquette University t-shirt as a gift. I always greatly treasured any admiration from fans and felt honored to be a part of their "Hair" experience.

By the time we'd reached our third stop in Kansas City Missouri, Robin was beginning to get road weary. It was the first week in February and cold as hell. The first hotel we were booked into was really bad. It was dark, dingy and very dirty. The next day we found better accommodations at the Downtown Motor Inn that made Robin much happier. She was getting a little home sick and Melissa was getting crankier due to teething. I was not a happy camper either. Melissa would be crying and waking up several times during the night and I wasn't getting much sleep. The weather was also a factor in that as the winter went on it seemed to get colder and colder, with more and more snow.

The show was playing at the Capri Theatre in the heart of town and our hotel was in walking distance, which was nice. Although our reviews were good in Kansas City, this was the first stop we started receiving threats on. We also had our first encounter with direct violence lashed at us. Robert Boehm was our wardrobe manager. A gang of thugs followed him from the theatre after the show one night. They beat him severely enough to be hospitalized, all because he was gay. It sort of scared us all and made us realize we needed to stay closer to one another for general protection.

While in Kansas City we also got first hand experience on how dangerous the show could be. At the end of the show, Berger is dancing around the stage where Claude is lying on his back, as if in a coffin. The lights are slowly dimming and by the time the theatre goes black, Berger is supposed to be kneeling behind Claude, holding two sticks in the shape of a cross over Claude's lifeless body. The sticks are painted with florescent paint so they glow in the dark, which creates a magnificent effect.

The theatre in Kansas City had a giant orchestra pit in front which we did not use. Our band was located off to the side of the stage on an old flatbed truck. Greg Karliss was playing Berger and while doing his magical little dance around Claude one night, twirled around and fell into the pit. The audience and most of the cast didn't have a clue as to what was going on.

I happened to be watching as it happened and quickly looked into the pit to see my friend, lying sprawled out, face down, at the bottom of the pit. Truly at first glance I thought Greg might be dead. As it was he suffered a back injury which still haunts him to this day. Several weeks went by before Greg was able to resume his role in the show.

A Frizzy Hair Story

Hair could be a dangerous show which I can personally attest to. When playing Claude in the "Flesh Failures" scene at the end of the show, they would have a small microphone placed around my neck and under my shirt. It was a wireless microphone that was connected to a small receiving device. The receiving device was then neatly positioned in my tight nylon underwear. One night after the dressers attached the device a wire came loose without their knowledge and was pressed against my most intimate parts. Totally unaware of this, I started to sing the song. At that very moment the soundman turned the mike on for the first time and I immediately started getting a continuous shock.

Now to me this song was the climax of the show. Everything Claude said or did was working up to this moment. There was no way I could let anything interfere with the show at this point. Here I was, standing at attention, in full army uniform, wreathing in such terrible pain and I couldn't move! I wanted so bad to even touch my crotch area to try and move whatever was shocking me, even a little bit so it would shock another spot even for a second, but I couldn't!

Finally towards the end of the song, Claude lays down as if in a coffin and stops singing. At that very moment the lights dimmed and I was able to move my hand over the affected area. Just as I did the soundman turned the mike off and the pain stopped. It's very funny now but wasn't so funny then. My privates were shocked and burnt for quite sometime. . ~ Story relayed by Los Angeles cast member, Bob Corff

---

A very nice couple came to see "Hair" in Kansas City and invited the cast over to their house for a party after the show. Unfortunately I can't remember their names. I do remember they were very hospitable and generally made us fell welcome and at home. They also took us on a tour of Kansas City the following day, which included a trip to Swope Park and the Starlight Theatre. Two years later I met up with them again when I was a member of The New Christy Minstrels playing at the Starlight with Henry Mancini. They were at the show, remembered me and came up to me after the show. This time around they invited The New Christy Minstrels over as guests. I got the feeling these folks knew just about everyone who ever played in Kansas City.

On a personal aside one of our greatest family moments occurred in Kansas City. Melissa took her first steps and was off like a rocket, getting into everything. It was great fun to watch her start to make the change from infant to toddler. I was daily falling deeper and deeper in love with both of the girls. Robin wasn't feeling very good though as she was a little depressed. When I would ask her why, she explained she wished she could be working or doing something more productive with her life besides being a mom and wife. She said although she loved being a mom and was deeply in love with me, there was something missing.

She could see how happy my work made me and wanted something for her too. I understood totally, so we spoke at great lengths about what she might want to do. Without going back to school it was difficult to come up with anything though. She didn't want to act (although I thought she'd be good) and she couldn't dance or sing. Even though Robin wasn't petite, or extremely beautiful, I felt she had a special quality that might translate to some sort of photo modeling. So with that in mind, I took a roll of pictures of her and was hoping to shop them around to some agencies.

One afternoon, Robin and I had a fight over some ridiculous thing. She left and went for a walk leaving me with the baby. Because of this and her depression, I started thinking I was being very selfish by dragging them along on the road with me. It really didn't seem to be quite fair to either of them. When she returned, we made up and I asked her if she would like to go back home for a visit. She thought it would be great but she didn't want to be away from me for a long time. We both agreed a couple of weeks at home would be a fun thing for her and Melissa to do.

The plan was to have them leave from Kansas City, skip the St. Paul run and meet me back in Cleveland. The St. Paul stay was only going to last for two weeks so skipping St. Paul made sense. The best fare available at the time was on United Airlines so we made all the arrangements with them.

When I took the girls to the airport in Kansas City I began to realize being away from them was not going to be easy. After having been apart for so long the previous year, I was not anxious to let them go for even a short time.

The plane was sitting out on the tarmac and the passengers had to walk outside of the terminal to board. So I decided to walk out to the plane with them to say our final goodbyes. As we got to the plane I noticed the greeting stewardess at the top of the stairs was my dear friend Sheila. What a small world! Up to now, Robin and Sheila had never met so the two of them spent the entire flight getting acquainted. This made me feel a whole lot better about them flying off alone.

When Robin and Melissa got back to Seattle they tried to spend time with family on both sides. They spent a few days with her mom, a few with my mom, but spent most of the time at my dad's house. It was great because all of my family really got a chance to know both her and Melissa.

A Hair Tease Story

One night after the show in New York, Gerry Ragni asked Robin McNamara to give him a ride down to the Chelsea since Robin had a car and always drove home to Jersey after the show. Gerry then asked Robin to come up to his room and stay awhile before going home. While they talked and laughed for awhile, Gerry proceeded to ask Robin if he could come home with him and watch Robin and his now ex-wife have sex. Robin jokingly said sure, thinking in the back of his mind that Gerry wasn't at all serious. But Gerry did go back with him.

After arriving at Robin's, the three of them visited awhile and then Robin's Armenian wife asked Gerry if he was hungry. He said yes, but first he wanted to watch them make love. Robin's wife, knowing Gerry and his personality said "sure," but first he had to have a shot of whiskey and eat some Armenian "grape leaves," which they proceeded to do 3 times. After the third grape leaf and shot, Gerry began to nod and eventually fell asleep after a wonderful night of hard laughter.

Robin told Gerry on the ride into the city the next morning, that he had missed out on the show of a lifetime. ~ Story relayed by Broadway cast member, Robin McNamara

Our next stop was St. Paul and it was very strange traveling without Robin and Melissa. Flights with the cast were really becoming more like a three-ring circus. The show itself was very stressful and coupled with the publicity we created tended to encourage us to party hard between shows. We were sort of isolated from the rest of the world and therefore becoming more like a large family. The news that greeted us on our arrival in St. Paul was some concerned citizens had tried unsuccessfully to stop our arrival by launching an obscenity campaign against "Hair."

THE MERCURY TOUR CAST,
ST PAUL, February 23 through March 7, 1971

Richard Almack	Linda Gaines
Rose Marie Barbee	Susan Gaynes
Ferne Borke	Jo Ann Harris
Dell Cunningham	Ula Hedwig
John Dickson	Jonathon Johnson
Arthur L. Dillingham	Danny Kantner
Debi Dye	Johnnie Keys
Cecelia Eaves	Betty Lloyd
Leo Elmore	Reggie Mack
Marla Marlo	David (Kalani) Molina
	John David Yarbrough

There was quite a bit of snow the first day when we arrived. Several of us walked around the town and I took a lot of pictures in St. Paul, as I found the city to be architecturally very interesting. The area around the theatre was quite nice and felt safe to walk around. I was very lonely without Robin and Melissa to tend to so I spent much time outdoors with my camera.

The strange thing that happened in St. Paul was the great mice scare. There was an elder minister who was trying very hard to get people to stop seeing "Hair" and hopefully send the show out of town. His plan involved letting more than a dozen mice loose in the theatre on opening night. I guess he thought the mice would scare everyone out of the theatre. He actually did go through with his plan and let the mice loose in the theatre on opening night. He was however doomed to disappointment as no one even noticed. As in other cities where the show was protested, the majority of people in St. Paul enjoyed "Hair" much to his chagrin and others like him.

The Boston production of "Hair" had recently closed so we gained a few cast members from that production while in St. Paul. I quickly become friends with Dell Cunningham, Marsha Faye and Ben Lautman. Dell and Ben had been in the Boston production and Marsha was from the San Franciso show.

I had a very funny occurrence in St. Paul while doing the show. There was some blocking we referred to as the "Stoned Indians." Three or four guys would roll down to the foot of the stage and sit facing the audience as if we were stone statues.

During one particular performance I misjudged my blocking and overshot the stage by about two feet. This error sent me flying right into the lap of a very large lady who was sitting in the front row! The audience belted out with laughter while the lady was particularly excited. It appeared she (along with the rest of the audience) thought it all was part of the show. After the short uproar, I gracefully removed myself from her lap and rejoined the tribe on stage. Throughout the rest of the performance the lady deemed it appropriate to pinch my ass each time I roamed past her through the isles.

In March of 1971 another company of "Hair" opened in Washington DC. In DC, the excitement about "Hair" had started to build up weeks before it opened. Everyone in town was talking about it. The first four performances set aside for benefits.

The opening was a huge gala affair. Senators, Ambassadors and the social elite attended. There were also picketers for and against the production at the theater entrance. One woman circled in the wrong group for 10 minutes before she realized her mistake. Some of the groups picketing were the Smite Smut League and the Gay Liberation Front.

There had been a few gasps at the political satire in the show. Some in the audience roared loudly after seeing the picket sign "Nixon is Rosemary's baby." It was mentioned that even Henry Kissinger seemed to enjoy the show. There weren't many vocal protests however, only a group of Catholics and Fundamentalists who took out an ad in The Washington Star to protest that "Hair" pollutes the air.

A spokesman for the group who admitted he hadn't seen the play said, "You don't have to see it to know what's going on. You don't have to drown to know about drowning."

Just before the show in St Paul closed, I talked to Robin and she indicated she was having a great time but missed me and wanted to return early. So we made arrangements for her to meet me in St. Paul and the three of us would fly to Cleveland together. The girls soon returned and I was very happy to be reunited with both of them. Now that we were back together, I couldn't imagine ever being without them again.

11

Eyes Look Your Last, Arms Take Your Last Embrace

After our arrival in Cleveland, Robin, Melissa and I took a cab to the Pick Carter Hotel. As we were driving down the expressway we passed a cemetery and I got a very eerie feeling I couldn't explain. I'd never felt anything quite like it before and I kept it to myself. Hell, it was only a cemetery filled with dead, discarded bodies and that was probably why I got the creepy feeling. The Pick Carter Hotel (which was on Prospect Avenue) was only a couple of blocks away from the Hanna Theatre. Both the hotel and theatre were in a part of town that was not particularly appealing. It seemed more like a slum than a downtown area and we did not feel safe. Once we were settled into our room we checked around town for other accommodations. Unfortunately there weren't any close enough to the theatre. We were stuck at the Pick Carter.

There were ten floors in the Pick Carter and our room was a suite. It was on the 9th floor, room 937. Our view was of the center courtyard of the building which was not very appealing. We tried to get a suite facing the outside of the building but none were available. Making the best of the situation, we made ourselves at home. It was a large suite that had a small section with a love seat and a chair. That's where we also put Melissa's crib.

THE MERCURY TOUR CAST,
CLEVELAND, Opening Night March 9, 1971

Richard Almack
Rose Marie Barbee
Dell Cunningham
John Dickson
Arthur L. Dillingham
Susan Gaynes
Jo Ann Harris
Ula Hedwig
John Herzog
Jonathon Johnson
Danny Kantner
Johnnie Keys
Ben Lautman

Debi Dye
Cecelia Eaves
Leo Elmore
Marsha Faye
Linda Gaines
Betty Lloyd
Reggie Mack
David (Kalani) Molina
Zora Rasmussen
Alaina Reed
Doug Rowell
John David Yarbrough

Down the street from the hotel and on the way towards the theatre we found a little deli that served great rotisserie chicken. This became one of our favorite places to eat during our stay in Cleveland. As we were walking down to the deli one afternoon, Melissa stopped in her tracks and stooped to pick something up off the ground. I happened to be taking a picture of her at the exact moment she reached down. Quickly realizing she was about to pick up a piece of colored glass, I rushed to extract it from her hands. Both Robin and I were relieved Melissa hadn't cut herself.

This event segued into a deep conversation between Robin and me, discussing the effects touring may be having on Melissa. We both wanted so much to be together but we were also both starting to get real concerned about what was best for Melissa. In our hearts we knew it would be best to leave the tour but we also needed the money. It was a hard choice to make and so we decided we needed to think more about it.

Meanwhile, the eerie feeling I was getting when we first came into town was starting to also effect me at night. I was having very vivid dreams and was getting stronger impulses to leave the tour. The dreams kept reoccurring and would even turn to the point of nightmares. I didn't mention them to Robin because I attributed them to not getting enough sleep. I was up most every night due to Melissa's teething and also to our long conversations about getting off the road. It got so bad I thought I was hearing voices telling us to leave. I wasn't on drugs, so I was beginning to think I was going bonkers.

Things concerning the show couldn't have been worse. The people who attended the show loved us but there were other elements in Cleveland who just didn't want us in town. During our stay we were greeted by many bomb scares. We took all of them seriously and on a couple occasions, both the cast and the audience were forced to evacuate the theatre so the bomb squad could check the building. It was very odd to have a show interrupted and to be standing out in the cold alley along with the audience. There were also several death threats against the cast in general. Someone or some group in Cleveland hated "Hair" and all it stood for, enough to make our lives miserable.

Robin had some relatives who lived outside of Cleveland in Strongsville Ohio who invited us out to stay with them one weekend. It was a pleasure to get out of Cleveland and see a nice neighborhood for a change. They had a very nice house and I remember being impressed by seeing cardinals at the bird feeders in their back yard.

Melissa had a great time walking around their big house and just being a kid. During our stay our thoughts once again turned to Melissa. It was here we made our final decision to leave the tour. Our plan was that Robin and Melissa would fly back to Seattle and stay with my parents. We would wait until after Melissa's first birthday so we could celebrate it as a family. I would then stay on with the tour for another month or so to save up some money and then try to get into the New York Company of "Hair." As soon as I could get an apartment in New York, Robin and Melissa would join me. If I couldn't get into the New York production, it was agreed I would go back to Seattle and look for work there.

Easter came and the three of us spent time walking around the city together. We asked Ula Hedwig to take some family pictures of us with my camera. Although there was still snow on the ground, it was a very sunny day which even made downtown Cleveland sparkle. We were happier than ever before in our lives. We felt good about our decision to leave the tour but we were also sad we were going to have to part. Robin had been shopping the day before and gave me two gifts. One was a crystal and silver crucifix and the other was a leather pinky ring that had the word "Smile," printed on it in violet. I wasn't expecting a gift from her so I asked, "What's this for?"

Robin looked at me as tears welled up in her eyes,

"To remember me by," she said.

The three of us embraced and I comfortingly told her the time would go by fast and we would be back together again in no time at all.

At a rehearsal the next day, Rusty Carlson (the production stage manger) was having a difficult time keeping everyone focused. Marsha Faye had brought her little dog along with her and was continually leaving the stage to tend to it. Rusty also had words with Johnnie Keyes about his adlibbing in the show and had firmly directed him to no longer wear his leopard skin loincloth when performing Hud. After several disturbances with Marsha and her dog, Rusty finally blurted out, "Look, either you pay attention and rehearse or leave to be with your dog. What's it going to be?" Marsha picked up her dog and left the theatre.

Later in the day while at the corner deli, Rusty told me he fired both Johnnie and Marsha. I think he felt things were getting out of control and he wanted to bring more order and professionalism to the show. I'm not sure if those results actually occurred though. When Marsha left, Dell (being in love with her) handed in his walking papers as well. That seemed to be the way with "Hair" though. Folks were always coming and going, returning and leaving. It was a very stressful show for all involved, especially on the road. Many simply could not handle it without a break here and there.

One night later in the week, Robin said she and Melissa were going to come to the theatre for the evening performance as they often did. But Melissa was still teething a lot and I was not getting much sleep because of it. With that in mind I was adamant they both stay at the hotel. I didn't feel keeping a baby up late was a good thing and she might sleep better if she went down earlier. In addition I was concerned about the bomb threats. Robin disagreed and insisted they come to the show. She said it was boring, lonely and creepy staying at the hotel alone. After a heated discussion on the matter, my point of view won out and the two of them stayed home.

The evening performance went on as usual until about the middle of the first act when Rusty Carlson pulled me off the stage shouting closely in my face,

"FIRE! THERE'S A FIRE! COME NOW!!"

His demeanor was bordering on hysteria, the music from the show was blaring away and what he was saying just wasn't registering with me. I had no idea what he was talking about. Quite frankly I thought he must have been kidding at first. Then he repeated himself,

"JONATHON! THERE'S A FIRE AT THE HOTEL! COME WITH ME NOW!!"

I started to stammer, pointed back to the stage and said, "But the show," and he abruptly interrupted me while grabbing my arm and said,

"FUCK THE SHOW! THIS IS FOR REAL!"

To say I was in shock would be an understatement. My mind was whirling with many strange thoughts and fears rushing through my mind as the two of us ran out of the theatre towards the hotel. Rusty also had a wife, Carroll and a daughter. His little girl Corrina was about the same age as Melissa. With both families on the road with babies, we had much in common and had just started to become good friends. Once we got to the hotel we frantically tried to get into the building from all points but the fireman and other authorities would not allow us in. We then tried to explain where our families might be and they just said they could only pass on the information. Meanwhile they told us be calm and wait.

Jerry Arrow, who was managing the tour, soon joined Rusty and me in trying to find our families. Jerry volunteered to check with all the hospitals and emergency services to see if we could find out where the girls were. By this time Rusty and I were both a mess and Jerry encouraged us both to wait at a nearby bar while he searched for our families.

In times of crisis the mind tends to play very funny tricks on you. As the two of us sat there we began to rationalize and second-guess everything that was going on. We had by this time heard that several people were taken to different local hospitals and treated for minor smoke inhalation. Hearing this news we were very hopeful the girls had also been taken to a hospital and we would hear from them soon. While I was waiting at the bar some guy said he overheard the commotion and expressed his concern. He then began to talk with me the rest of the time we were there. He failed to mention he was with the press. His intentions were far less than admirable.

In the very early hours of the morning, Jerry walked in and approached Rusty and me. With tears in his eyes he said,

"I'm so sorry. They're gone, all of them, gone."

The three of us embraced, sobbing with tremendous pain. From that moment on I felt as though I was in a living hell. I just couldn't believe it was so. How could it be? Why them? And the worst of the guilt began to roll over and over again in my mind. Why didn't I just let them come to the theatre? If I hadn't been such an asshole! If I hadn't of made an issue of them coming to the show they would both still be alive!

It was then I was told an arsonist had most likely started the fire. The cause of the fire was of a suspicious nature. I was also told Robin and Melissa didn't stand a chance. That Robin had done the right thing by taking the baby from our 9th floor room, directly up the fire escape past the 10th floor and onto the roof. Sadly, the door had been wired shut from the outside, a direct violation of all fire safety rules! They were found lying together at the door to the roof, trapped and locked inside.

Besides both Rusty and me each losing a wife and daughter, three other people unrelated to "Hair" perished in the fire as well. All seven died of smoke inhalation. My pain was now turning to anger and rage against the hateful people making bomb threats, the murderers who had started the fire, but mostly at myself.

At this point I'm not sure where I was. Jerry and others were taking great care in making sure that Rusty and I were both taken care of as well as sheltering us from the press. News of the fire had now reached the National News. Although I had just found out myself, it was now incumbent upon me to call all our loved ones. I needed to reach them before they turned on their TV's or read the morning papers. It was painful enough to call my parents but even more so to call Robin's. There is no way to cushion such terrible awful news. I felt so guilty, as though I had betrayed them all. Here I was supposed to be Robin and Melissa's protector and I had failed in those duties.

After the calls were made, a doctor came in and gave me some sleeping pills to calm me down. The pills didn't work. I spent most of the night tossing, turning and wondering how God could allow such a thing. I thought about the events leading up to this night again and again. I thought about the eerie feelings and bad dreams I had been having. In my heart I now knew they had been warnings.

At a little before dawn I finally fell to sleep while in prayer. Once I fell asleep the reoccurring dream I had many times earlier in my life came back to haunt me. Over and over, I kept seeing Robin and me being pulled apart by some strange force. It had indeed been a premonition. My faith was completely shattered and torn.

In the morning when I awoke I was hoping it had all been a bad dream. But even more so I was devastated and felt tremendous pain and guilt. In the paper was an article by the guy who befriended me in the bar the night before. The title of his article was "He Took Pictures, She Died." Underneath the title was supposed to be a picture of me, instead it was a picture of my dear friend, Ben Lautman. This boob of a journalist couldn't even get the picture right, let alone get facts straight in an article. I thought it was all in very poor taste.

Luckily I found myself surrounded by a loving tribe, comforting me and also protecting me from the media. Several of us went back to the hotel to retrieve my things later in the day. The hotel was reeking with the smell of smoke. As we walked through the hotel I began to imagine the hell Robin and Melissa went through. When we reached the room I was disgusted to find someone had already stolen several items from the room. We quickly gathered the belongings and headed back down to the lobby. I couldn't get out quick enough.

Just as the group was about to leave the hotel, several people from the media were gathered downstairs and tried to block our passage. One of them made the uncouth mistake of asking me if I was Jonathon Johnson. Someone from our group responded saying I was not. Then the media person quickly fired back that they knew I was Jonathon and they would just like to ask me a few questions. Upon hearing his statement I was furious that they wouldn't even allow me this moment of grief. I was quick to respond with my middle finger thrust into the air and an angry explicative at their cameras. Just as quickly, they turned their cameras and recorders off. Now they weren't going to be able to use their footage on the six o'clock news.

The rest of this day was spent on the phone making funeral arrangements, transportation arrangements and so on. The management for "Hair" was very helpful and supportive to me through the entire process. It's surprising how quickly all these things can happen. Arrangements were made for me to fly back home to Seattle and "Hair" had offered to pay for another cast member to go with me. I asked Ben Lautman to go with me.

As all the cast and crew were gathered around I said my good-byes. It was an emotional moment I will never forget. As I was standing and looking around the room at my friends, time seemed to stand still. It was not easy for me to leave this wonderful support group—they were my tribe.

Having Ben with me on the trip home was really a Godsend. Ben is a very spiritual person and had a calming effect over me during the trip. I was very sad to see him return the next day though. I was hoping he could visit for longer and be a shoulder to lean on. As soon as Ben left the walls of reality came crushing in and around from all sides. As you can imagine, everyone in my family and Robin's family was an emotional mess!

The first issue was that I didn't even have any idea of where I was going to bury them. What young person plans ahead for a funeral? I ended up buying a plot my parents had once purchased for themselves, thinking they would go first. I so badly needed time to grieve, yet I was expected to take care of all the arrangements as well as comforting others. I could barely cope with the whole process.

The newspapers in both Cleveland and Seattle carried pretty much the same stories about the fire. Mention was made of the fact that a fastened door prevented Robin and Melissa from escaping the explosive fire that ripped through the Pick Carter Hotel in Cleveland, taking a total of seven lives.

The papers stated that Cleveland's Fire Chief said the fire had started in the basement of the hotel at about 10:00 p.m. and had spread very rapidly. It was just a matter of minutes before it had engulfed the basement and was into the first floor. It spread more rapidly than the average fire. They also wrote that authorities were looking for a young man who tipped off a maintenance man in the hotel lobby about the fire.

They indicated that both Robin and Carroll Carlson were found dead with their babies in stairwells. Robin was found on the 10th floor and Carroll on the 7th floor. Robin was trying to escape onto the roof, as she was found in the stairwell by the door to the roof. Somebody said the door was tied shut. If she could have gotten to the roof she probably would have been safe.

By the time the day of the funeral came I was a complete wreck. Even though friends and family tried to convince me otherwise, I opted to stay in the back throughout the service. Not only could I not bear to be present during the service but I also couldn't drag myself to view my beloved wife and child. I just couldn't do it.

Hundreds of people came to the services including many cast members from different tribes I had worked in. Tyrone Miles also came and volunteered to be a pallbearer. It was all so unreal. To make matters even stranger, Robin and Melissa were laid to rest together, easily within 20 feet of Jimi Hendrix's grave. Here Robin had just been to his funeral less than a year earlier. I had no idea this was where they would be.

Meanwhile on April 25th back in Cleveland, not quite two weeks after the fire, a bomb was finally thrown at the Hanna Theatre. It bounced off the marquee and exploded at the curb. The bomb was strong enough to blow out more than 40 windows in the Hanna building. It also caused minor damage to other storefronts. I guess the fact that seven innocent people had already lost their lives was not enough for these hate mongers.

The one thing I still question to this day is why there was never any criminal investigation into this tremendous tragedy. By all accounts from the Cleveland Fire Marshals and other witnesses, the fire was of a suspicious origin. That information, the many bomb threats and the final bombing of the theatre should have been more than enough to prompt an investigation. This should have been investigated as a multiple homicide. My feeling is it would have been investigated had it not been associated with "Hair." In my opinion the authorities in Cleveland had more than enough information to open up a case. It is a shameful mark on the city of Cleveland that they did nothing. That alone was criminal in itself.

In essence, Glen died in the fire in Cleveland too. Along with Robin and Melissa I buried much of my old existence. It was from this point on I insisted that even my family call me Jonathon. A few years later I even changed my name legally. I left no trace of Glen.

The evenings were the only time I could find solitude. I slept little, lost myself in prayer, self-doubt and depression. I knew I had to find the strength some-where to keep going. My faith in God reinforced my belief that life does go on, that our little planet is just the beginning of a long journey, that God loves each and every one of us, lives inside us and that one day I would again see Robin and Melissa. I had to raise myself up out of this darkness and move on. There was hope.

LOVE WILL FIND ITS WAY

Sometimes words are hard to find,
to fill the spaces within your mind.
All the good things friends can say,
yet still your tears won't fade away.

Listen to me, love will find its way.
Open up your heart in every way.

There is nothing we can do,
you may win or you may lose.
Guilty sorrows swallow pride,
there is nothing you can hide.

Listen to me, love will find its way.
Open up your heart in every way, today.

By Jonathon Johnson   © 1971 and © 2004

12

Good Morning Starshine

In early May, The New York cast of "Hair" celebrated its third successful year on Broadway by holding a special concert at the Cathedral Church of St John the Divine. "Hair's" 3rd birthday celebration became Galt MacDermot's Mass in F concert. It was a beautiful musical piece to which a live LP was made from. While this event was a spectacular moment in "Hair's" history, it did not escape some controversy.

While Michael Butler and "Hair" were both targets for extreme leftist groups such as The Weathermen, they were also vehemently opposed to by groups on the far right. At this particular juncture in time members of the John Birch Society had called for the assassination of Michael Butler. Bizarre as it may sound, this was a genuine threat.

Michael had received word the hit was going to happen at the birthday celebration at St. Johns Cathedral. Although the both the police and his entourage tried to encourage Michael to stay away from the event there was no way he was going to bow down to these threats.

This time the police were present in and around the church itself. While the show was going on, Michael's bodyguard (who was sitting directly behind him) gently tapped Michael on the shoulder. Directing Michael to look up at the scaffolding to the rear of the room, a person was seen climbing up the structure. The bodyguard then tried to convince Michael it was time for him to depart. Although a little fearful of the potential danger, Michael decided to remain in the theatre to continue watching the performance. As it turns out the police apprehended the person on the scaffolding; only to be pleasantly surprised it was just a young fan of the show, trying to obtain a better view.

While still in Seattle, I decided I would go back to work as soon as possible to get my mind off of things. Before the fire in Cleveland, I had met with Abe Jacob, the sound designer for "Hair," and we had talked about recording some of my music. So I called Abe to see if we could arrange something. Abe was living bi-coastal and was due to be back in San Francisco later in the month. He said he could set up some time at Wally Heider studios for me. He offered his engineering services for free so all I would have to pay for was the studio time. Because I had been out of work for a while and was running out of funds, I turned to Jim Rado to see if he could help with the recording. Jim was very quick to help out.

At the beginning of May I arranged to fly down to San Francisco to record a demo with Abe. Dell Cunningham and Marsha Faye had just moved to Berkeley so I stayed with them at their place.

After the sessions, Brenda flew down from Seattle to visit me. At the same time John David Yarbrough and Richard Almack came to visit with Dell and Marsha. It was like a mini "Hair" reunion for the next few days. I felt a little more than awkward with Brenda there. It was probably awkward for the both of us, especially since she had become Robin's very best friend. I knew she wanted to comfort me but she didn't know how to approach me. Seeing her was wonderful and I desperately wanted to be with her, but how? It was very confusing to me and it was far too soon for me to be thinking about being with anyone other than Robin. Besides, Brenda and I had already established we were only to be good friends, or had we? I was not sure at all but I knew I loved her, wanted the best for her and was happy to have her near.

The first day we all took a drive out to Mount Tamalpais State Park to go for a hike. Both John and Ritchie were quickly making plays on Brenda and she didn't seem to mind at all. Loneliness started creeping in again and I became anxious to leave San Francisco and go back to work. As soon as Brenda left to go back to Seattle, I hopped on a plane to rejoin "Hair" in Baltimore.

More Personal Reflections on "HAIR," Act II

The second act of "Hair" begins with "Electric Blues" and ends with "Flesh Failures and Let the Sunshine In." It moves at a fast and furious pace and is more surreal than act one. Claude has returned from the induction center and spends a great deal of time trying to convince both himself and the tribe that he is not going into the Army.

It's in act two that Claude gives his poster of Mick Jagger as a present to Woof. Woof then goes wild over the poster and proceeds to lie on top of it. Squirming on top of the poster, he tells the audience he is not gay, but he does love Mick Jagger and would go to bed with him anytime.

Act two is also where the great Supremes gag is found. High up on scaffolding, three young black girls (or so you think) are dressed as the Supremes in wild red sequence dresses. They are singing the song "White Boys" with much power and zest. As the song builds, the three break out in dance and you realize it is only one dress they are occupying! Also, in most cases a young black man would be playing one of the Supremes. It was a very entertaining and fun scene in the show.

We then move into Claude's party. All the doors are locked and the joints begin to go around from tribe member to tribe member. "Were the joints real?" Many people have asked me this throughout the years. The answer I give is no and yes.

No, they were not real. We had specific props, fake tobacco joints laced with smelly stuff that were to be used in the scene. They were actually pretty disgusting and it was sometimes difficult to inhale them. We couldn't have real pot because pot was and still is illegal. After all, we wouldn't want to get the entire show and theatre busted over a joint, would we?

For the most part we were all faithful to this rule. However on occasion, a real joint would somehow mysteriously make its way into the scene. When that did happen, most of us would quickly smoke it up and make it surreptitiously disappear. It can never be said "Hair" isn't a fun show to do. It may be hard and strenuous work to perform in a production of "Hair," but it can also be an extremely fun, exciting, as well as rewarding experience.

The next several scenes become Claude's bad trip. When I was in the show the hardest part for the actors during this segment was the smoke drifting on and off the stage. It was created by dry ice and was heavy on your lungs to breathe. The scenes change fast and end with the Shakespearean rendition of "What a Piece of Work is Man." The song ends with a chorus of,

"Our eyes are open, are eyes are open, wide, wide, wide."

As the song finishes, Berger shakes Claude awake from his nightmare and the party moves on. Soon in the song called "The Bed," you are led to believe that maybe Sheila will finally relent and go to bed with Claude. You never really know though. Claude is soon to be left alone, gunshots are heard and he disappears from the stage while backing up.

You are suddenly taken back to the park, it is snowing and all the tribe members are calling out for Claude. This brings me to the snow. Little flakes of plastic created the snow effects we used. I would much rather breathe in dry ice all day than get one of these nasty little flakes caught in my wind pipe! The effect was great, but it was very unpleasant to achieve it.

While the cast is getting frantic looking for Claude, he is busy backstage. Claude is standing in a large bucket, while two or three people wet his hair down completely. He is then dried off and steps into a full army dress uniform that is actually a one-piece suit. As he is jumping into the suit, his hair is being tied and pinned back as close to his head as possible. Soon after, it is stuffed under an army dress cap and disappears completely. This transformation begins as soon as he has left the stage and is completed within 5 minutes or less.

Claude then jumps back out on the stage while the rest of the cast freezes. The audience is shocked and the reality of his death is apparent. Claude, just another number, has joined the ranks of a very large number of young boys who are sent off to die in a foreign land. Claude then reminds us of society's failures in the song, "Flesh Failures," which leads into the brilliant and thought provoking, "Let the Sunshine In." You are left with a grand feeling of love and hope.

Once again for the disbeliever's out there, "Hair" does have a plot. Like a parable, you just have to work a little harder to ascertain the message.

THE NATIONAL TOUR CAST, BALTIMORE, Opening Night June 15, 1971

Jeannie Arthur	David Lasley
Rose Marie Barbee	Betty Lloyd
Linda Compton	Reggie Mack
Arthur L. Dillingham	George Mansour
Bill Dobbins	Arnold McCuller
Cecelia Eaves	Tyrone Miles

Linda Gaines
Susan Gaynes
Jo Ann Harris
Valentino Harris
John Herzog
David Hunt
Jonathon Johnson
Lyle Kang
Randy Keys

David (Kalani) Molina
Lynn Pitney
Zora Rasmussen
Gayle Riffle
Alaina Reed
Doug Rowell
David Stidwell
Naomi Wexler
John David Yarbrough

Returning to the show wasn't as easy as I thought it might be. Not so much the show itself, but day-to-day existence. When I was on stage it was easier and a relief to throw myself into a character rather than to come to grips with my own reality. The good thing was I was surrounded by loving friends who had in every sense become my extended family. Knowing I was extremely fragile, a few of the girls in the cast kept an almost constant vigil around me. There were some who thought I was having a harem of sorts going on but it wasn't anything like that at all. It was very innocent and sweet. The girls were just concerned about my well being and therefore spent a lot of time with me in my room before and after performances. It was like being back at home with my sisters.

After our stay in Baltimore the show moved on to Buffalo NY. It was in Buffalo that I started to indulge more in drugs and alcohol to hide my pain. I needed to talk to someone about what happened in Cleveland. But I was also becoming acutely aware that any discussions with others along this line were met with avoidance, as it was depressing for others to hear. Hell, I was used to being a very cheerful person and fun to be around! I wanted that back and partying seemed to loosen me up in that way.

I met a few nice girls in Buffalo who had each seen the show and wanted to meet me afterwards, so I decided to start dating. Not dating in a serious sense. I wasn't interested in sex with another woman just as yet, I still felt married. I primarily wanted companionship which unfortunately was hard to find with groupies as my primary source for meeting women. Also, I was more than aware I would probably never see any of these girls again after leaving town.

One of the girls I met in Buffalo was Nan. She was a nice girl who had a good job and was living with her mother. She was about my age and seemed to want to be "just friends," which was appealing to me. Nan may have felt differently, I don't really know. All I knew was she was friendly and seemed to care for me more as a person than an entertainer. Our relationship was strictly friends as we never even exchanged a kiss. She drove me around the city and showed me the sights. She also introduced me to a friend of hers who had seen the show, Andie.

Andie was into fortune telling, the mystical and metaphysics in general. She was a single mom and an interesting person to talk to. Andie was much older than me and had an apartment across town. Nan took me over to visit her once or twice while I was in Buffalo. I remained in touch with both Nan and Andie for a couple of years.

Another girl I met in Buffalo was Maryanne. She was very pretty and I was extremely attracted to her. We spent an afternoon or two together and I retreated from the potential relationship because it scared me. I did not want or need to be in a serious relationship with anyone at this time in my life.

Flipping His Wig

My brother lives in Brooklyn and has always been very conservative. He's a college professor, has a PHD in mathematics and is a Rabbi. His friends and associates are equally as conservative. I seriously doubt if any of them ever knew his brother was an actor, let alone an actor in the musical "Hair." In order to save my brother from the least amount of embarrassment (and because I love my brother dearly), I went out and bought a short hair wig. So every time I visited my brother I would put on this wig. It looked as though my hair was a little bit long but not terribly long. Not like it really was anyway.
~ Story relayed by cast member, Ben Lautman

On one of these afternoon dates I had arranged for my date to meet me at my room. I invited her in for a few minutes and then we headed out the door. Just as I was locking the door, two other girls I had been seeing came walking down the hall. What an uncomfortable feeling. Here I was, awkwardly standing with three girls, trying to be polite yet trying to shoo off the other two. They probably all thought I was some sort of cad, yet I wasn't intimate with any of them, nor had I invited them all over. In any case I never saw or kept in touch with any of them after that day.

While in Buffalo I received a cash gift collected from various "Hair" tribes around the world. They had pooled together as a gesture of kindness for both Rusty and me. It was very thoughtful and touched me immensely. I knew I could use a companion so I decided I would get a puppy. I always wanted an Old English Sheep Dog so I began to look for one. I checked all the pet stores in Buffalo but couldn't find one. That was okay because the search was half the fun—it kept me busy. I'd look more at our next stop in Toronto.

Upon arriving in Toronto we had a dinner party of sorts at a restaurant on Young's Street. Some of the members of the original Toronto Company of "Hair" came by to meet and visit with some of us from the touring production. It was at this dinner I became friends with Tabby Johnson. Tabby was very beautiful, sweet and kind, yet quiet and reserved. We got along well and spent a good deal of time together while I was in Toronto.

Instead of renting hotel rooms, a group of us got together and rented a dormitory at a local college that was out for the summer. There were about six rooms with a common living area and kitchen. It was much cheaper for all of us and made for more of a home environment.

I was still determined to get a Sheep Dog, so I went out to a pet store to see if I could find one. The only sheepdog available was in a pet store I found in a mall. I can't remember exactly but I think I paid about $600 for a little male pup. I named him Noah.

Noah was absolutely the cutest puppy I had ever seen. I had no idea how beautiful these dogs were as puppies and I immediately became attached to him. Unfortunately within the first two days of getting him home, he got severely ill and wouldn't eat. I called the pet store and they paid to have me take Noah to a vet. After his examination I was told he had coccidiosis, a disease that usually only chickens get. The vet said it was a common problem in this breed due to mass breeding in England, in what he termed as, "pet factories." It would probably never go away and could only be treated with medicine which would be costly. The store offered to take him back and return my money.

After everything I had gone through I just couldn't take Noah back. After all, he wasn't a just a thing to be returned or discarded. He was a wonderful living creature. Fearing he would inevitably die if I returned him, I decided to deal with it and keep him. What a chore to take on, but if busy work was what I needed Noah provided just that.

Soon I started to come down with what I thought was a bad cold. I remember walking to the Royal Alexandra Theatre just before show time, sneezing all the way. Just before turning to go into the stage door, I sneezed very loudly and scared two girls in front of me so bad they screamed. When they turned to look at me, I apologized and they just gave me a very funny look. I'm sure they had no idea I was in the show, but probably got a good laugh when they saw me later on stage.

A Much Needed Respite

Sometime later in the tour I was still sick and decided to take a break and return to Seattle. Upon arriving I checked into a clinic only to find I did not have a cold. What I had come down with was mononucleosis. I was told I had become susceptible due to all the stress I had been through. Hearing that I decided stay at my dad's for a couple of weeks to get well.

While staying at my dad's in Seattle a different touring company of "Hair" came into town. I called the theatre to see if I could get tickets and was invited to the show. I was happy to see many of my friends were in this cast, including my old friend Kenny Ortega. Kenny was playing Berger and Les Carlsen was playing Claude.

While "Hair" was in town, Kenny and I went out to lunch one day at the Space Needle. We hadn't seen one another since San Francisco so we had a lot to talk about. During our conversation I asked him about arranging to get back all the things Robin and I had stored with him. Kenny then informed me our stuff was destroyed in a fire at his parent's house in Redwood City. This coincidence was very ironic and was a real shocker to me. Sadly, all the many pictures Robin and I had taken of each other over the years, along with other irreplaceable family mementos were gone.

Tommy was playing at the Moore Theatre and Kenny wanted to stop by, so I drove the two of us over. It brought back a flood of good memories to see the theatre where "Hair" played in Seattle the first time around. There was a day rehearsal going on and Kenny introduced me to a friend of his who was playing the Acid Queen in Tommy, Bette Midler.

Although I was missing "Hair," after a few weeks of recuperating, I decided I should start working on my music and possibly put a band together. I didn't want to stay in Seattle though, so I decided to buy a car and drive down the coast to San Francisco. My brother-in-law sold me his station wagon and I put curtains in it so I could sleep in it if necessary. I thought I would make a vacation of it, take my time and drive the coastal route, camping out along the way. Before leaving I called Abe in San Francisco to let him know my plans. The next day I packed up the car, Noah hopped in and away we went.

Along the way I stopped in Astoria to visit Robin's mom, who had recently moved there. I only stayed for a day or so as it was a real difficult situation. As always, she was very sweet to me and said something very touching before I left. While holding my hand in hers she said,

"You know, I just didn't lose a daughter and a grand daughter, I also lost a son."

The thought had never occurred to me but she was right. She knew I was young and had to move on from this very sad situation. I felt so bad for her. I knew her pain had to be much greater than mine. This was the last time I ever saw Robin's mom.

Riding down the coastal route with a little dog that could barely stand up straight on level ground was quite an experience. As we went down those twisty curvy roads, Noah would be sliding from side to side in the car. I gave him free rein of the car so he'd be jumping all around from window to window.

As soon as I arrived I got in touch with Abe and stayed with him for a few days in the city. Abe told me that David, who had played on my previous recording, was interested in putting something musical together with me.

So we arranged to go out to David's up in Marin County. David had a great little house in downtown Fairfax on Bolinas Road. It had a very tiny living room, two small bedrooms, one bath, a small kitchen and an enclosed back porch. It sat behind the main business section in the town of Fairfax, right across from a little baseball field. The road out the front door would take you up to Bolinas Ridge and on to the top of Mt. Tamalpais.

David and I hit it off well and within a short time we formed an acoustic trio along with David's long time friend, Robbie. I sang lead vocals and played rhythm guitar, while David played lead guitar and Robbie played electric bass. Both David and Robbie sang backup vocals which made for some nice harmonies. We concentrated on mostly my original material and this became a fruitful time for me writing songs. My guitar playing also improved as David took the time to teach me some finger picking techniques I had never known.

The three of us got along good and because David and Robbie were both north county natives, I was introduced to a large number of their friends. The stress of touring and eight shows a week was gone. Still missing my fellow tribe members in "Hair" though, I continued to keep a pulse on the show. Between practicing and rehearsals I was introduced to and fell in love with northern California, specifically Marin County.

One of our favorite things to do was to drive up the mountain to Bolinas Ridge. Most of the area high on the ridge was either undeveloped or State Park. The views were spectacular and it was the perfect place for me to just let Noah run free. One time when we were up on the ridge, it was decided by the others that we would hike down the cliffs to Stinson Beach. I wasn't up for it because I was not dressed for the occasion, but was outvoted so down we went. It was a rough hike and so steep it was hard not to run or fall. In the end though I was glad I participated.

Many times on the weekends there would be an impromptu softball game across the street. Usually anybody could play, so often I would join in to play a game or two. On a few of these occasions members of the Grateful Dead would come to play softball as well. Fairfax was a unique little community that had a quiet village feeling to it. It was not strange to see famous folks just hanging out and being real. It was a safe place to hang out.

Somehow cocaine use started to become a more frequent event for me. We would rehearse pretty regularly and many people knew it. Folks would drop by to listen and ultimately brings gifts of pleasure for us to indulge in. Although I enjoyed it immensely at the time, I believe it was also leading me into a deep depression. So deep, that on one occasion I even considered taking my own life. I drove up to the ridge by myself, indulging in self pity and raced my car back down the winding roads, all the while toying with the idea of flying off one of the many cliffs. Luckily I didn't have the courage to do so. Poor Noah was with me, flying all about the back of the car.

Around this time I woke up one morning with severe chest pains that would come and go. During a phone conversation with Abe I mentioned the chest pains and he immediately arranged for me to see his doctor. Knowing I was short on cash he also paid for it. This is the kind of friend Abe was and I will forever be indebted to him for helping me so much through those tough times. After many tests, the only thing the doctor could come up with was stress.

Taking care of me was hard enough and I found I was really losing it with Noah. He was getting very large and was extremely unruly. I called my mom in Seattle and asked her if she would take him for a while. She consented and so I flew him back to stay with her for the time being. It was a relief to me and probably for him as well.

Robbie had gone to visit his sister in Flagstaff for a while and came back with a brown paper bag loaded with peyote. Although we were all interested in trying some of it, both David and I were extremely nervous about having it in the house. We were worried and rightfully so, about the illegal aspects of having so much of this. Robbie agreed to get rid of it the next day and in the meantime, David promptly hid it in the attic.

That same night at about 8 o'clock we sat down to rehearse in the living room. We had our makeshift wine bottle water pipe out on the table along with some other paraphernalia to help us get into the mood. About 45 minutes into playing, there was a loud knock at the door. Robbie was expecting some friends to drop by, so assuming that's who was at the door he said,

"If you're a friend come on in. If you're a cop, fuck you!"

As we all start to chuckle, the door knocks once again. Robbie quickly repeats himself much louder this time, "I said—if you're a friend come in! If you're a fucking pig, then fuck you!"

The door knocked very firmly once again. David and I look at one another thinking the worse. While he and Robbie quickly whisked away everything on the table, I went to the door to play the straight man. As soon as I could see they had removed all the illegal stuff, I opened the door.

There in front of me stood one of Marin County's finest, a sheriff. By this time David and Robbie were both behind me, peaking over my shoulders. We must have looked like the Fabulous Furry Freak Brothers. The air in the house was thick with pot smoke. A cloud of it must have nearly knocked this guy over as we opened the door.

Before I could finish saying "Can I help you officer," he interrupted me saying, "Don't worry, I'm not here to get you. I was just wondering if you might know who owns this car out here."

As I stared at the Sheriff standing on the porch, visions of jail rushed through my mind, only this time I was of legal age and definitely holding contraband.

Scared stiff and suddenly straight as an arrow, the three of us walked outside with him to look at a car that had been parked in front of our house for a few days. We said we didn't know anything about it. He thanked us and went on his way. As soon as he was gone, David gave orders to Robbie to remove the bag from the house.

Abe had some business in L.A. and asked me if I would like to tag along. He was doing the sound for James Taylor at the Hollywood Bowl and Tommy at the Aquarius. It was a fun getaway for me. Because Abe was doing the sound we were able to get back stage passes and had free rein of the Bowl. I was also pleasantly surprised to see my friend Tabby Johnson from the Toronto Company of "Hair" was in Tommy. We had a good visit with each other at a cast party before I returned to the bay.

The band soon broke up and as my unemployment benefits were about to end, I decided it was high time I got back to work. Christmas was coming around the corner, so I thought I'd go visit my family in Seattle. I would then go back to New York to see if I could get in the Broadway Company of "Hair."

13

Let The Sunshine In

When I arrived in New York I was happy to find Dell and Marsha were living there as well. Marsha was in the cast of Jesus Christ Superstar and Dell was in "Hair." Auditions for "Hair" were only held one day per week and the day had already passed. Ben Lautman was also in the Broadway production during this time and it was equally good to see him. He was living in a very tiny room in a hotel around the corner from the Biltmore Theatre. I was shocked when I saw how small it was and was worried I may end up in similar digs.

Within a week I found an apartment and auditioned for "Hair." I was hired as a tribe member with understudies to Claude and Woof. My apartment was located a half a block away from Central Park on West 83rd Street. It was in an old brownstone and it had just been refurbished into an apartment complex. It was up three flights with no elevator. It was a great place, in a safe neighborhood and had close access to the park for Noah. Also, I could easily take the bus to the Biltmore. I arranged as soon as possible to have Noah flown to New York.

Scumbag For President

Dell and Marsha had told me stories about a street person that everyone referred to as Scumbag. The man looked like an anorexic version of Santa Claus who had traded in his red suit for a beige trench coat. His clothes, long gray hair and beard were completely unkempt and covered in dirt and grime.

As if it were his job, he would sit everyday on Broadway at 50th Street, directly facing a coffee house called Chock Full of Nuts. As people would walk by him, he would gruffly mutter obscenities. His favorites being,

"Scumbag," "Shit," "Diarrhea," followed by "In your mouth."

Unlike many other New York street people, he would never ask for money.

Knowing of Scumbag, I had already thought about what I would do if I was to see him. As a joke I would say something nasty to him before he could say anything to me. It just so happens that on the way to the Biltmore one night, I got off the bus on 51st street and there was Scumbag sitting in his spot across the street. As I approached the other side of the street where he was sitting, I went directly up to him and said with a gruff cartoon-like voice, "Shit, in your mouth, scumbag." Then, I turned and walked away.

Scumbag was absolutely taken back at this. As I was walking away he called back in his trademark raspy voice saying,

"Hey wait a minute! Come back here! You can't say that to me!"

I went back to him and I said with a laugh, "Why not?"

"Because, it's my thing. Besides, my name isn't Scumbag. It's LaRee. Not Larry, LaRee."

And then he proceeded to spell it out,

"Capital L, small a, Capitol R, small double e."

I then asked him, "How come you're always saying nasty things to people?"

He replied, "Because people think they're too good. They think they're better than me and they're not."

He asked who I was, so I introduced myself to him. He also asked how I knew of him and I said I was in "Hair" and fellow cast members had told me about him. LaRee then said, "Oh, I like that show. Lot's of dirty words."

I heard later that Alan Braunstein and some other cast members had gotten him in to see the show before. Alan had also taken LaRee to see Jesus Christ Superstar and had taken him out to dinner a few times as well. In the New York production of "Hair" we even had a sign in the protest scene, which said "Scumbag for President."

LaRee told me about his life, that he was once a musician and he basically felt the whole system had let him down. From this time on I would visit with him whenever I saw him. He was always quite friendly and appreciated the company. I always got a kick out of him. He was really a kind person, just a bit misguided.

I soon came down with bronchitis but continued to work and in doing so I developed laryngitis. Fred Reinglas (production stage manager) was very understanding. He basically just used me as a body on the stage for a couple of weeks while I tried to shake it. I couldn't sing and could hardly speak. In fact, I sounded like a frog. I ended up spending hundreds of dollars at a voice specialist, Dr. Wilbur Gould. He was famous for treating both entertainers and politicians. He said my vocal chords were close to hemorrhaging so he put me on cortisone shots. That seemed to work.

After my voice came back Margaret Harris (musical conductor) took me under her wing and started giving me some voice lessons. She was very patient and diligent with me. She told me her objective was to have me be the primary understudy for Claude. At the time there were about three or four different folks who were understudying the part. Anyway, I would come in early before every performance to work with her.

Soon after joining the Broadway production I was one of the many tribe members who occasionally played the role of Woof. During this period it almost seemed like there was no permanent Woof. Although there were credits given in the Playbills, I'm not really sure if anyone was actually signed to the role. Woof was a role I was very comfortable with and I always enjoyed playing the part.

Shorter, Rock Star type shag haircuts were also starting to be fashionable at this time and several of the guys in the show starting getting them. Fred Reinglas, becoming increasingly concerned the show might stray away from the hippy look, put up a sign on our bulletin board. The sign said something to the effect of, "No more haircuts. If you want to cut your hair then go to work for No No Nanette."

Although it made sense, this also cracked me up. The irony was for so many years I had been told to cut my hair, now I was being told NOT to cut my hair!

After the shows many of us would gather around the corner at the Hay Market pub for burgers and beer. Performing in "Hair" consumes a great deal of energy and we would consequently need to unwind. It was also a good social outlet and allowed for everyone to get to know each other better.

I hesitate to write this, but one night as my girlfriend and I were on our way over to the Hay Market, Bert Sommer was outside the stage door waiting for us all to come out. I hadn't seen him since my first visit to New York and now he was no longer in the show. From what others had said and we could now see for ourselves, Bert was pretty well strung out on drugs. On this night he was trying to sell a microphone. It was a very sad sight as well as frightening.

Here was an incredibly talented young person who had somehow taken a wrong turn in life. We were witnessing first hand the worst of what drugs can do. I had previously heard of Bert's problem from other cast members. This evening it was known throughout the theatre that Bert was around trying to get money for drugs. The message was basically, "So if you really love Bert, please do not give him any money and do not buy anything from him."

Before I ever joined the New York cast I had heard rumors of heavy drug use at the Biltmore. There were stories about the use of heroin and also vitamin shots laced with speed which were administered by the company doctor. Perhaps this was all true, but by the time I joined the Broadway production, I never saw any of this. For the most part all I ever saw was a joint here and there and maybe a little coke. Only one time did I ever see any real hard drugs around the theatre. That was when I walked into one of the dressing rooms and saw some white powder on some tin foil on the dressing table. I looked at it and someone said, "Help yourself." Thinking it was coke; I decided to snort a line. After taking the one snort I immediately realized it wasn't coke. When I asked what it was, I was told it was heroin.

My girlfriend was in the theatre that night and I told her right away what had just occurred. She began to freak out, especially after recently seeing Bert. She was now worried I was going to be a heroin addict. I calmed her down and explained that for one, I didn't like it at all and secondly, it takes more than once to get addicted.

Shelley Plimpton was back in the show and as always played the most remarkable Crissy ever. I used to love to hear Shelley sing Frank Mills. Her voice was very angelic and always seemed to melt the audience. Many times Shelley would bring her daughter Martha (whose nickname was Bunky) to the theatre with her. It was not unusual to find Bunky crawling around backstage or in the dressing rooms. It was okay with everybody though. Having a baby around just made us feel more like family.

A "Sweet" Snip of Hair

Nina Machlin-Dayton worked at the concession room at the back of the Biltmore for the last couple of years of the Broadway run. The concession room was a tiny little room, more like a walk-in closet. The walls were covered with shelves of the candy that was sold and stacks of programs.

One night as Nina and the other concession workers were putting stuff away after intermission; there was a knock on the door. It was Gerry Ragni with two of his friends. Gerry convinced Nina and the others it would be a good idea to take one chocolate covered almond out of each box in the storeroom. No one would miss them he said, and it would be their own little feast.

So very carefully they opened every box and took one almond out of every one, resulting in an enormous pile. After which they spent about twenty minutes gorging themselves on chocolate covered almonds. Now whenever Nina sees chocolate covered almonds, she happily thinks of Gerry. ~ Story relayed by Nina Machlin-Dayton.

After working with Margaret for a while it was finally my turn to play Claude. Up to this point in my career I can't ever remember having stage fright. I must have been saving it all for this night because I was absolutely petrified. I haven't the slightest idea why I was so scared either. I only know I could barely sing at all. I couldn't catch my breath which made it nearly impossible to reach any note. I was okay with the group songs, singing "Hair" with Berger and the dialog. It was when singing the solos that I froze up.

The tribe was very supportive during this time. They were whispering positive things in my ear and giving me reassuring touches throughout the show which helped a lot. It took a few performances for me to finally get over it and feel one with the role.

Galen McKinley, who was the stage manager for Jesus Christ Superstar, saw me playing Claude a couple of times and he introduced himself to me after one of our shows. He asked me if I would like to be in Superstar. I was flattered and really considered making the move over to the Mark Hellinger Theatre. It was a chorus part he could offer with understudy to Jesus. He invited me over to see the show a couple of times and gave me a grand tour. Because of my personal religious beliefs however, I declined to investigate the move to Superstar any further. Although I liked the show and thought the music was awesome, I also thought Christ was portrayed as a weakling and I couldn't have portrayed him in that manner.

The same thing came up later when going in for my audition for the Jesus Christ Superstar movie. About 15 minutes before my scheduled audition, I decided not to even try and left. Instead I stopped at the Sherwin-Williams store, bought some paint and went home to paint my apartment. Looking back I think I probably should have put my own religious beliefs aside. After all, it was only one interpretation of Jesus' life and it was only another show. Both the play and the movie would have been good moves for my career.

In May the cast of "Hair" on Broadway celebrated the shows fourth anniversary to a crowd of approximately 15,000 people. Like the second birthday bash, this free 90-minute concert was held in the Central Park Mall. It was slightly tardy because April 29th was the official day marking the shows four year run at the Biltmore Theatre. Members from "Hair" tribes from London, Mexico, Tokyo, Israel and Broadway sang songs from the show as well as some specialty numbers. There were hundreds of yellow and red balloons, along with dozens of orange Frisbees flying through the air at the close of the program. The grand finale was of course, "Let the Sunshine In."

Backstage at the Biltmore the Alessi twins and Peppy Castro (formerly of the Blues Magoos) would often be jamming in their dressing room. Peppy would usually be playing a very funky old acoustic guitar with the three of them singing. I used to like to drop in to hear their incredible harmonies. After "Hair" closed in New York, the three of them formed a band together called Barnaby Bye. They released a couple of albums on Atlantic Records before breaking up.

Meanwhile ticket sales were in a slump so management decided to start selling tickets, two for the price of one. It seemed to help fill the seats at first, but rumors of the end were starting to go around quickly. On Broadway, selling tickets two for the price of one is usually a sign the end times are near.

On May 17th the New York Times prematurely reported that the Broadway production of "Hair" might close at the end of the week. They were wrong with their predictions but were not too far off. The show did not close as predicted as it continued its run until July.

Sometime in late May or early June Willie Windsor (who was playing Claude) hurt his back during a scene. The injury was serious enough to land him in the hospital and out of the show. After Willie's back injury, I stepped in to play Claude throughout the remainder of the Broadway run.

Playing Claude was much different for me than playing Woof. Personally, I could relate to Claude on many levels much easier than I had Woof. I saw Claude as being somewhat aloof, confused and scared of being drafted. All these were feelings I could personally relate to and so I drew upon those feelings.

When I first started understudying the part of Claude in New York I was extremely nervous, which really affected my performance. By the time I took over the role from Willie, it began to fit me like a glove. I loved playing Claude and wished I had played it much earlier. Unlike playing Woof, I was able to immerse myself into the character and in many ways was able to transform myself into Claude.

I remember one performance in particular I really got into. Just before "Flesh Failures" the tribe is frantically searching for Claude. It's snowing, everyone is cold and they can't find him. They are yelling out,

"Claude, where are you?"

As they go through these motions, suddenly Claude appears amongst them shouting,

"I'm here!"

Just as he makes this entrance, the entire tribe freezes in position. Claude is now dressed in full military dress. His hair is all gone and while standing at attention he is saluting towards the audience. After a pause, where the audience has a chance to catch their breath, he begins to sing "Flesh Failures." The audience now realizes Claude has gone to Vietnam and has died.

It is normal for the audience to be shocked at this juncture and it is not unusual to hear sighs and groans expressing shock and sadness. On this night though, I heard a woman laugh very loudly at that moment, which in turn caused a short hail of laughter throughout the theatre. With the seriousness of the scene, I took the laughter personally and delivered probably the most cutting rendition of Flesh Failures I had ever performed. I took my anger and threw it into each and every word so the audience would have no doubt in the tragedy of Claude's death.

After the show was over I quickly retired to the dressing room instead of staying to greet the audience as I usually did. I was still feeling the effects of the laugh and had assumed this audience just didn't get it. I had been in the dressing room for about five minutes or so when Greg Karliss came in to find me. Greg said,

"What are you doing up here man? The audience is going nuts. There are people down there asking for you, wanting to meet you."

I said to Greg, "Didn't you hear the laughing?"

Greg then said, "Man, the lady felt so badly. She was just so shocked and saddened that it just accidentally came out as a laugh. You were dynamite man! Get your ass down there!"

With that, I followed Greg back down to the stage and mingled with the crowd.

After the experience I always sought to find that same place when I performed Flesh Failures, since it obviously had a great effect the first time on accident.

Soon it was June 25th (my birthday) and I was still filling in as Claude for Willie. That night before show time as Greg and I were backstage dressing up, he asked me how old I was now. After I told him I was just 21, he asked me a very poignant question.

"Man, do you realize how cool it is to be only 21 and star in a Broadway show? You're gonna look back on this moment forever."

The thought never really occurred to me. Up to that moment, I hadn't thought about anyone in "Hair" being a star. This was sort of a no-no in all the casts of "Hair" I had been in. Oh sure, we had a prima donna here and there, but star's, never. But in a way Greg was right. To the audiences we were stars and I have always looked back proudly on those special moments. It was a privilege indeed to be a part of it all. What's interesting is that 30 years later, I hear the same sentiments from the kids who are now playing in companies of "Hair" around the world.

When the news came the show was really going to shut down, I don't think any of us truly believed it. Up until about a half an hour before show time we didn't even know who was going to play what role. It was Gerry and Jim's show, so it was sort of assumed they would play Berger and Claude one last time. It would have been fitting and well deserved. But Greg and I were also hoping we would get a shot at playing Claude and Berger for the last night on Broadway.

As it turned out, both authors decided to let Greg and me play the leads. The house was packed and everyone in the cast put on a very powerful performance. I had never seen the Biltmore so crowded. Like Seattle's closing night, this one was way beyond standing room only. The audience was filled with many of the people who had made the show happen, tribe members from all over the world, along with years of die-hard fans. It was both a happy and a sad occasion. After one of the longest and most successful runs in the history of Broadway, "Hair" finally closed after 1,742 performances.

THE BROADWAY CAST LIST,
Closing Night July 1, 1972,
as listed in the June 1972 Playbill

Billy Alessi	Stephanie Parker
Marjorie Barnes	Shelley Plimpton
Beverly Bremers	Carl Scott
Patrick Carlock	Kenny Seymour
Zenobia Conkerite	Mary Seymour
Stephen Fenning	Dale Soules
Robert Golden	Bryan Spencer
Gloria Goldman	Oatis Stephens
Ula Hedwig	George Turner
Jonathon Johnson	Valerie Williams
Gregory V. Karliss	Willie Windsor
Debbie Offner	Kathrynann Wright

Hair employs over 300 members of Actor's Equity Association.
~ From the July 1970 "Hair" press kit.

14

Ain't Got No

The evening after the last show I had my girlfriend cut all my hair off into a shorter shag style cut. I hadn't had my hair this short in years. I decided to move back to Seattle the next morning, so I called up Bobby Alessi to see if he could give us a ride to JFK.

Bobby arrived at our apartment with a van at about 6 in the morning. We didn't have a whole lot of stuff, just a large travel trunk, a large rug, my guitar, Noah and a few carry items. We didn't have airline reservations and were planning to fly standby, so we made arrangements to ship almost everything back to Seattle via cargo. That way we wouldn't have to worry about it getting there and my parents could pick it all up, including Noah.

After arriving in Seattle my girlfriend and I made our spilt official as it just wasn't working out. I found myself really relieved to be single again and spent the next few months visiting with my family. I began to work diligently on my solo act and song writing. I was making plans to go back to New York in the near future.

I soon returned to New York and stayed with some friends from Seattle, Tom and Sheila. They were always such great friends and were also fun to be around. It was an odd feeling though, being back in New York with no "Hair" to go back to.

A week or so after arriving in New York I went down to Times Square and was just walking around. As I was walking down 42nd Street someone came up from behind me and grabbed me. With their arms hugging me tight around my chest, this person picked me up off the ground and began to turn me in circles! I'm thinking and probably saying out loud, "What the hell?"

Within seconds the person puts me down and then turns me around. Now I can see it is none other than my good friend Ben Lautman! What a marvelous surprise! What are the odds in a city as large as New York? We spent an hour or so talking and walking through the streets of New York together. I hadn't seen Ben in at least a year so it was such a pleasant surprise to run into him again.

Learning I was looking for a place of my own, Ben offered that I room with him at his place in the West Village for a while. I took him up on his offer and moved in. It was a small apartment, up five flights of stairs on 11th street, just around the corner from the White Horse Tavern. The White Horse is a famous pub that has been designated a historical site. It was often the place where Ben and I would hangout and visit over a brew or two.

Ben and I had many good times together living in the village. It was like living with a brother I had never had before. Besides writing a lot of songs, I wrote a children's story called the Sun and The New Forest while living with Ben. The complete story came to me in a dream and its moral was about not taking people you love for granted.

As soon as I got settled in I started making the rounds and playing many clubs throughout the Village as a solo act. I suppose the place I played the most was Gerties Folk City on 4th Street. It was a pass the hat club and besides being an avenue to showcase new material, it was also a great place to meet other talented acts. There were also great stories to hear about the many famous folks who got their start at Folk City.

In the early Spring I was talking to Nan in Buffalo and she suggested I take a bus upstate to visit her. I needed a break from the city and decided to go. On the way up I started to get strange feelings, like those I had when I first came into Cleveland, only now I was a bit more aware of them. I tried to put them aside and enjoy the ride but it was difficult. What did they mean this time?

Once I arrived in Buffalo Nan took me over to meet her brother and his family. They had nice little home in the suburbs of Buffalo and five beautiful children. Her sister-in-law was very friendly and was interested in talking to me about spiritual things, so my interest in the Urantia Book came up. We had some nice discussions and later returned to the apartment where Nan and her mom lived. They were both very hospitable and I spent the night on the couch.

The following day, Nan let me use her car while she was at work so I could go over to visit Andie. After visiting for some time with Andie, I headed back to Nan's. While I was at their apartment the phone rang. It was Nan's sister-in-law. She said she was hoping I was around and wondered if I could stop over by their house. She said there were some more things she wanted to talk to me about. I said I would be happy to come by and made plans to go over in the afternoon. Before I left I called Nan at work to let her know where I was going and why.

When I arrived, Nan's sister-in-law thanked me for coming and said she felt a strong leading to speak with me. She then went on to ask me many spiritual questions and was especially interested in what I knew about life after death. We visited for about two hours, after which she thanked me and also asked me to keep the details of our visit in strict confidence. She said,

"Please, do not tell a soul what we talked about."

I assured her I would respect her wishes and would keep the contents of our discussions private.

When I got back to the apartment, Nan of course wanted to know how things went and I just said something to the extent of "Just fine, we had a nice visit."

Late in the evening after we were all asleep, the phone rang. It was around 1:00 a.m. and since I had been sleeping on the couch in the living room, I answered the phone. It was Nan's brother and he was very upset. They had been out to dinner that evening and his wife had choked on a piece of steak and died. She couldn't have even been 30 years old and she was gone!

So the feelings I had on the way up to Buffalo had to of been premonitions of some sort. In truth, although it was a very sad weekend I was glad I had gone and was able to consult with Nan's sister-in-law. I also recognized this whole event would have happened whether I was there or not. Because of the nature of our meeting and that it was requested by her, I believe it was all predestined.

I stayed through the weekend in order to pay my respects at the funeral. But for the rest of my stay, Nan continued to press me for details about what her sister-in-law and I had talked about. I tried to explain that I had given her my word, but Nan didn't or couldn't understand why I wouldn't share it with her. Her feelings were, her sister-in-law was now dead so what did it matter?

To me though, I had made a promise to her sister and I would not break it under any circumstances. All I could say to Nan was that nothing bad was said. Our discussions were all of a personal and spiritual nature. By the time I left home for the city, Nan was very angry and stopped talking to me altogether. I tried several times to contact her afterwards, all to no avail. It appeared our friendship was lost.

It is my conviction that trusts between people should be considered unbreakable bonds. When honored as such, they show the true integrity and spiritual growth of those who honor the sanctity of that trust.

If you believe life continues on after leaving this planet, then the mere fact of death does not null or void the trust. Death is only a transformation from one plane to another. It is my belief when you leave this planet you take up on the other side exactly where you left off here. The experience of death does not add anything to your knowledge or spiritual growth other than the resurrection experience itself. Although I am deeply saddened that Nan chose no longer to be my friend, I am also confident and secure that my choice not to give in to her desires was the right and therefore only decision I could make.

When I returned to the city I resumed my club hopping activities. If I wasn't playing I was networking with and listening to other acts in town. Feeling I might be out staying my welcome at Ben's place, I moved back to the upper west side with Tom and Sheila for a short time. Shortly thereafter I subleased a loft in the east village from Reggie Maack and Shezwae Powell. They had both been in the San Francisco company of "Hair" and Reggie had been one of the few black Woof's. They were both going out on the road at the time.

The loft on the lower east side was kind of a scary place. There were several bars on the doors due to previous break-in's and the neighborhood was a little on the rough side. One time a fairly nice car broke down on the street in front of this place. I don't know where the owners were, but within a few days there was nothing left but the frame. The first day the tires disappeared, the next day the seats and electronics, followed by the doors, engine, you get the picture. It actually gave me a chuckle or two.

At this time there wasn't much happening in the way of theatre that I would have felt comfortable doing. There was Grease, National Lampoon's Lemmings and Godspell. I went to see Lemmings and I loved the show. John Belushi, Chevy Chase and Christopher Guest were unknowns at the time and all three of them were in the show. They were hysterical! I believe it was in Lemmings that John Belushi first did his Joe Cocker impression. The entire show was made up of impressions of various rock stars. Abe told me they were going to open up another company of Lemmings in Toronto. I auditioned for the show and did well as they said they were interested, but it never came to fruition.

Soon my sublease was up and I moved back in with Tom and Sheila once again. Sheila was off flying quite often, so Tom and I spent a lot of time together when I wasn't playing.

One time Tom and I were hanging out in Central Park enjoying the Puerto Rician Day festivities. Tom had some acid so we both decided to take it and go to see "2001 A Space Odyssey." Neither of us had seen it in a long time and we thought it would be fun to see it on acid. It was playing at a theatre on the upper east side so we had to walk across the park to get to it.

By the time we got to the other side of the park the parade down 5th Avenue was just about over. There were thousands of people in the park and on the street that day. There also appeared to be tons of trash strewn everywhere. By then we were really flying high and we're curious as to what would happen to all the trash.

As we continued walking on towards Madison Avenue we noticed a hot-dog vendor pushing his cart up the street. Just as we were both looking, a large jar full of mustard and onions fell from his cart and onto the hot, dirty street. The vendor then stooped down, checked to see if anyone was looking and scraped back into the jar much of what had fallen onto the street. We were both hysterical with laughter and sick to our stomachs! No way were we ever going to eat from a local street vendor again!

We found the movie to be fun, but acid really didn't make much of a difference. Still high, we started making our way back to the west side. As we got to 5th Avenue our curiosity was answered as concerned the trash. It seemed all of it had been pushed knee deep onto the road, where these little space age looking sweepers were moving down the street and sucking it up. We stood and watched them for quite some time before making our way back across the park.

While looking through the trades, I saw an add that The New Christy Minstrels were holding open call auditions. I always liked the group and although they were a little straight laced I went ahead and auditioned. There were literally thousands lining up to audition over a few days. If I remember correctly, I was one of the first to audition. I would later find out over 5,000 people were auditioned that week for only one position.

The New Christy Minstrels

"The New Christy Minstrels," a folk group started by front man Randy Sparks, made their debut on the Andy Williams Show in the fall of 1962. The group became very popular and had several hits, such as: Green Green, This Land Is Your Land, Saturday Night, Chim Chim Cher-ee, Chitty Chitty Bang Bang and Today.

In 1964 Randy Sparks sold his interest in The New Christy Minstrels for two and a half million dollars to George Greif and Sid Garris of Greif-Garris Management in Beverly Hills. Not long after in 1965, Barry McGuire left the group for a solo career and soon had a number one hit with his song "Eve of Destruction". By the end of 1965 all the remaining original Christy's had left the group.

For the next 15 years "The New Christy Minstrels" continued as a concert draw, while countless young performers passed through the group. Some of these performers went on to far greater successes. Some notable Christy's were; Kenny Rogers and the First Edition, Kim Carnes, Gene Clark of the Byrds and John Denver to name a few. Although there are some who doubt as to whether or not John Denver was actually a member, the official group advertisements made such a claim and Sid Garris stated so to me as well.

Sidney Garris was who I auditioned for with the Christy's. The audition was with just me and my guitar. Sid must have had me play bits and pieces of over 12 of my original songs. I would start to play one and he'd interrupt me asking for another. Because I never got to finish one complete song I figured he wasn't interested in me.

A few days later at around noon I received a call at Tom and Sheila's from Sid asking me to join the group. I said I would love to and he then asked me if I could be at the airport for a 4:00 p.m. flight to Harrah's in Lake Tahoe! I said yes and had barely enough time to shower and pack a bag. I was only able to say goodbye to just a few of my friends. Both Tom and Sheila were out so I had to leave them a note explaining where I had gone.

So I joined and toured with the New Christy Minstrels for the summer of 1973. The New Christy Minstrels lineup at the time was: John (Lamont) Pulsipher, Drew Daniels, Valorie Haggins, Vivian Wesson, Christopher Parks, Minako Kobayashi and Myself.

Even though I only stayed with the Christy's for a summer, I have many stories of what went on which I won't go into here. I don't want to stray too far away from my "Hair" experiences. The best time I had with them was playing with Henry Mancini at the Starlight Theatre in Kansas City. It was an amazing experience to play and sing being backed by one of the best orchestra's in the world. Besides being an incredible talent, Henry was a very nice and congenial person. He was also very easy to talk to.

Growing Back My Hair

Back as a solo act again I was happy to get a call telling me there was going to be a revival of "Hair" in Paramus NJ. I was invited to a meeting with several past cast members at Wesley Fata's apartment. The meeting turned out to be sort of a reunion and I can't recall any auditions whatsoever. Wesley had worked with the New York production and was familiar with all our work. The cast wasn't going to be as large as the New York cast, but most were alumni and some of the best.

A HAIR REVIVAL
PARAMUS NJ, Opening Night March 1, 1974

Michael David Arian	Soni Moreno
Robalee Barnes	Nathaniel Morris
Roberta Baum	Allan Nicholls
Alan Braunstein	Angie Ortega
Bobbie Ferguson	Janet Powell
Sheila Gibbs	Mary Seymour
Jonathon Johnson	Dale Soules
Larry Marshall	Bryan Spencer
Victoria Medlin	

Since almost all of us lived in the city, several of us pooled together and rented a station wagon for the duration of the show. Of course none of us wanted the responsibility or pressure of either driving it or finding a place to park. Somehow we all worked it out though and it made for an interesting experience.

I remember a horrible accident happened one day while we were driving on the west side of Manhattan during one of the trips back into the city. It involved a car, which was literally driving right along side of ours. We were all a little shook up but Alan Braunstein broke the ice by saying,

"That's it. Tomorrow I'm buying a lunch pail and I'm going to get a real job."

Not long after the Paramus Company of "Hair" folded, many of us received calls from Wesley Fata saying there was going to be a summer stock version of "Hair." Once again I joined up and if I recall correctly our first stop was in Philadelphia. Steve Curry was also in the cast this time and I had a great time working with him as well as hanging out after the shows and listening to his old "Hair" tales.

While in Philly I became pretty close friends with Danny Beard, who was our Hud. Danny was a great guy with a lot of class and even more talent. A couple of years after leaving "Hair," Danny ended up joining the Fifth Dimension and then broke off into a solo career. We kept in touch for quite awhile but then he sort of disappeared. Sadly, I found out he hadn't disappeared at all. He lost his life in a fire in the mid-eighties.

Grease was playing around the corner from us. Danny had a friend named John who was in Grease, so the cast members from both shows used to hang out quite often with each other. Seems I do remember us partying quite a bit.

The stage set up in Philly was very tight and they did have an old truck as a stage platform for the band. The passageway to the stage near this platform was only about two feet wide. This was not nearly enough room when running on and off stage. During one of our last performances in Philly, I accidentally jammed my foot into a rusty bar that was sticking out from the truck as I was leaving the stage. I was barefoot so there was a hole about half the size of a dime in the center of the top of my foot. I have a high tolerance for pain but rightfully so management thought I should go to a hospital and get a tetanus shot.

After getting the shot I returned to finish our last evening performance. During the show I started feeling faint and developed a fever. It turned out I had an allergic reaction to the shot. It lasted a whole day and I can remember Steve Curry kidding me on the train ride back to New York,

"Don't die on me now."

Unlike the official tours of "Hair," with this one there were a few unpaid breaks in the tour between stops. During those breaks I would return to New York. Since I no longer had my own place I would stay with a musician friend of mine at his apartment on the Upper East Side. Victor lived six floors up with no elevator. The great thing was he had a piano and you could also easily get up on the roof. I used to love to go up on the roof. It was as if you had your own yard with a view of the city.

There was a club around the corner from Victor's called JP's. I used to play there a lot and developed a nice little following. I also made good use of Victor's piano and within a short period of time I started to write as much if not more on the piano than I did the guitar.

I was playing at JP's on my birthday and had invited a lot of friends to see me. My set was a little later in the evening so I just had fun with everyone. Needless to say I got more than a little high. About half way through the evening the owner asked me if I would give up my time slot for a special guest in the house. Not knowing who this person was, I of course said no problem.

It turned out the special guest was the now late and great Steve Goodman. Steve of course put on a fantastic performance, which made me very nervous because now I had to follow him. There were also rumors of record company execs in the house so that didn't help matters. As it was I put on a very good show, splitting my act between the guitar and piano. After the show the owner of the club came up to me and asked what I was drinking. I said beer and he bought me one, which was in itself unusual. Putting his arms around me, he then let me know Nat Weiss was in the audience and wanted to meet with me. The owner was real excited and led me over to Nat's table.

Nat proceeded to give me his background, saying he had once even managed the Beatles for a short time. He said I had great potential to be a big star, blah, blah, blah. I was very happy to hear all this but as the conversation grew, it appeared to me he was interested in me for something other than my music. He noticed I was uncomfortable with the situation and asked if everything was okay. I said yes, but really wanted to say no. He then asked if I had any tapes so I arranged to send him some. I must have been right about the vibes I was getting because I never heard from him again. The good thing was that beers were always on the house for me from that point on at the club. I must have at least impressed the owner.

Another stop on the "Hair" tour was Detroit. In Detroit the "Hair" band got a whole lot better by adding a local Detroit guitarist named Kevin Russell. Kevin was a fantastic guitar player. Kevin and I had much in common and became good friends. Later on in the late 70's Kevin would form a band in Los Angeles called 707. They were a very successful touring group and had a few great albums. To this day he is still a highly respected guitarist, producer and recording artist.

I think it was in Detroit that I also finally started feeling better about myself enough to out with a lot of different girls. Not being married or having a steady girl, I clearly took advantage of all the groupies who seemed to hang out around "Hair."

We moved on to Baltimore next and played at the Morris Mechanic Theatre where I had played with "Hair" on the first tour. While in Baltimore, Danny Beard, Willie Windsor, me and some other folks rented a condo together. It made our stay in the city a comfortable one. Danny, Kevin and I hung out more with each other and explored the city together. We went to the beach one day and I was surprised at the response we received from the people on the beach. Danny thought it might have been because it was a beach where blacks were usually not present. That could very well have been so, but in any case it was weird.

After Baltimore the show moved into the typical summer stock territory of Connecticut. The first stop I can remember was in the little town of Ivy. Kevin, Mike (The drummer for the "Hair" band) and I rented a small cabin outside of town for the duration of the show.

Soon after we got settled in we met up with the rest of the cast at the theatre. I could hardly believe my eyes as it was so small. I've seen grade school auditoriums much larger than this theatre. It had a lot of history though. The locals said it was the first theatre that Katherine Hepburn had ever worked in.

We partied an awful lot right from the start on this tour and this continued when getting into Ivy. After our first night the three of us were in for a rude awakening staying in the cabin. We didn't realize there was a farm adjacent to us, so at around four o'clock in the morning we were abruptly awakened to the sound of several roosters crowing. We were all hung over and although we found humor in it later, it was not so funny the first time around.

I started drinking way too much while in Ivy and almost got my ass kicked for it. We were all out drinking at a local bar and I was with this cute young lady who I later found out was only 15 years old. Lucky I didn't end up in jail. Anyway, while we were sitting at this table a local guy across from us was making rude comments to the girl I was with, along with disparaging comments about the show. I guess he knew her and had worked with her before. When I asked him to stop he then made some sort of remark to the effect of, "Well what do you know, you're just an understudy."

Hearing him speak and not even taking the time to size him up (I'm only 5" 7"), I took a full bottle of Lowenbrau and poured it over his head saying,

"Well, you are a nothing."

After which, the girl and I walked out to the sound of sighs, moans and a little laughter from the rest of the folks at the table.

The girl was staying with a friend at a nearby hotel so we went up to her room. By the time we got there, I had enough time to reflect on my behavior and was not pleased with myself. I felt bad and within about ten minutes I made the decision to go back and apologize, regardless of the consequences.

Just as I opened the door of the room to leave, the guy was standing right before me. Before I could say a word, he threw a glass of scotch at me which completely soaked the front of my shirt. I looked at him, smiled and said,

"Thanks, I deserved that. I was just on my way out to apologize to you for what I did and said."

He seemed shocked at my response and also a little amused.

"Well," he said, "It's a good thing you did because for revenge I was going to turn your mike off during your next performance as Claude." I had no idea he was the soundman for the show.

He also apologized for his remarks and the three of us stayed up pretty late just talking. It was a real wake up call for me and I slowed down on my partying from that point on. Still feeling bad, the next day I went out and bought the guy a bottle of his favorite scotch as a gift.

Shelley Plimpton was in this production with us and with the help of her boyfriend, she brought her daughter Bunky along on the tour. Working with Shelly, Larry Marshall and Vicky Medlin brought back lots of good "Hair" memories for me. It was just like time had stood still.

After Ivy we moved on to Danbury and it was pretty uneventful. We did the show there for a short while and moved on to New London.

I really enjoyed New London. It was a picturesque little town on the water with a quaint little marina. The theatre was actually in some sort of school auditorium. Dorm arrangements were available which some of us stayed in. I went to visit Old Saybrook with someone while I was there and they showed me Katherine Hepburn's house on the beach. I walked a great deal around the area and was enjoying being a part of the "Hair" experience once again.

In Westport we were playing in a real theatre again. Kevin had flown home to see his girlfriend Sue and had driven his van back with him from Detroit. Having the van made for a bit more freedom for us. Towards the end of our run in Westport, I received notice of a small settlement offer from the Pick Carter Hotel in Cleveland. I had to quickly decide whether to settle or fight. Because I wanted to put it behind me as much as possible, I decided to settle.

Although close to nothing considering settlements these days, it was enough to put me in a position to quit for a short time. I knew Willie was leaving the show and they would probably ask me to play Claude. I decided I would stay if they gave me a small raise. I asked and they said no, that they wouldn't pay me any more for the role than what was currently offered. So I quit "Hair" when its run in Westport was finished.

Kevin also decided to leave the show after Westport and the two of us drove to New York to pick up my things. From there we drove his van all the way to Detroit. I stayed with Kevin and his family for a few days after which I flew to Cleveland and then back to Seattle.

15

Although My Hair Is Gray

Time moves on and as they say—time heals all wounds. As for me, I married again in the spring of 1975. Although the marriage was both short lived and tumultuous, those four years did produce two wonderful sons. Also during that time I recorded one solo record album and continued to write music and perform.

By the middle of the summer of 1979 I was living on my own again. In February 1980 I met and fell in love with Betsy. Ever since then Betsy has been my partner and best friend. In 1983 we got married in a wonderful outdoor setting in Topanga Canyon State Park, California. Our greatest accomplishment together has been our lovely daughter, who came to us exactly eight years after we first met.

Even though "Hair" is no longer the focus of media attention it was in the sixties and seventies, it still enjoys a strong following. Each and every year over the past 30 plus years, casts of "Hair" have popped up all over the world. Even with the demise of the dreaded war in Vietnam, people are still attracted to spirit and music of "Hair." After all, the real message of "Hair" will continue to be viable, at least until world peace ceases to be a movement and evolves into the institution that mankind has always prayed for.

As I write this there are many newsgroups and webpage's on the Internet where you can find up-to-date information on current and past tribes of the show. More seem to jump on board every week and the cast members themselves are just as excited, if not more so than the original members were in the beginning.

The messages in "Hair" may seem old but they all still hold true. There can never be enough love in the world and peace—well it hasn't come to this planet as yet.

When the "Hair" movie premiered in Hollywood in 1979 Michael Butler invited a bunch of us old "Hair" alumni to the premier. We were all so excited the show had finally come to the big screen! We had no idea what was coming though. I can still hear Greg Karliss' shock at the end of the film when Berger dies.

"No, Berger can't die! Over one thousand performances and I never died!"

Greg's reaction caused much laughter from the large group of us who were sitting together. The rest of the audience probably didn't find our laughter as amusing though.

Although the movie had good moments I don't think any of us who had performed in the stage productions ever thought it was how "Hair" should have been filmed. The entire plot and feel of the show had been changed and it just didn't seem right to us. I'm one of those who believe the real film of "Hair" is yet to be made.

The Movie Reunion Party

When the movie premiered in LA at the Film Festival in 1979 I called Michael (Butler) and asked what about those of us who had been in the show? He said nothing could be done for the festival, so I suggested a party at the Cinerama Dome when the movie opened for the general public the next night.

Well, understand that this was about a week before the event. Michael agreed to foot the bill, so Sally Kirkland and I started getting on the phones and networking, even calling AEA for names and phone numbers and they were actually very helpful! Sally found an artist's studio, which was like a NYC loft, we got someone to bring in tables and food, and VOILA, the first reunion party happened.

It was wonderful. Everyone looked so great dressed up like real adults (it was 1979 you know) and we had about 450 former cast members from all over the world, plus wardrobe, stagehands, musicians, everyone we could find that "Hair" had touched over 10-12 years. Funny, we had not aged a day. We sang along, ran up and down the aisles during "Starshine," yelled "sing the song girl" during "Easy to be Hard" (wasn't she wonderful?) and cried like babies when Berger died at the end. We were traumatized, screaming "No! NO!"

At the party Milos Forman came up to me and asked "Why didn't I see you people when I was casting?" Actually, we had been told that we were "too old!" (How ridiculous, we are still not too old!) Gerry and Jim came up to me and said, accusingly, "YOU! You are responsible for this. No one else would have cared that much." That made me feel very, very good. I just loved those guys. Michael looked wonderful; I had not seen him for about 10 years! Gerry and Jim looked great, even Ted Rado looked good. LOL Ted.

It was such a great night, full of love and friendship. The Reporter or Variety wrote that although the film had premiered at the Festival, the real event was the following night at the Cinerama Dome (Which I think is gone now, just like the mural on the Aquarius Theatre a block away and the old Brown Derby where we would have dinner between shows). Sally and I had done a good job and I was very proud.

Thank you Michael for throwing that wonderful party for us. ~ Corinne Broskette (Corn Mother)

If you were to ask me if I still believe in everything "Hair" stood for, with a few exceptions I would have to say yes. Nowadays however, I have some great concerns and reservations about drug use and free sex. I'll attempt to discuss my opinions on some of the issues "Hair" brought into the limelight and I'll start by addressing drugs.

First of all I want to make a clear distinction concerning drugs. I do not believe marijuana should have ever been considered a dangerous drug. In my opinion it should be controlled in a similar manner as alcohol and tobacco are. If you really want to get down to brass tacks, between alcohol, marijuana, and tobacco, pot is the least harmful of all three. If marijuana is ever legalized I think there should be limitations on it as there are on alcohol. For instance; you shouldn't be able to use it until the age of 21; not while driving; etc.

In all my years of living, I have never seen anyone who was addicted to pot. I have also never seen anyone die or be hurt in anyway by pot. Marijuana is considerably less intoxicating than alcohol and I don't care what the textbooks say, it is not addicting, nor does it lead to stronger drugs. People lead people to stronger drugs, not marijuana. By making it illegal you turn its control over to the black market, which is run by thieves and gangsters. Those are the people who need addicts to support their business. Pot won't do it for them so they talk people into using other drugs, the real ones.

On the other hand I have indeed known many folks who have killed themselves and others by abusing alcohol, including my own mother. Each and everyday countless people are killed due to the abuse of alcohol. Pot should be legalized without question. The laws concerning its use are outdated and maintained by those few narrow minded individuals who refuse to even have it tested, let alone ever try it.

I have not personally indulged in any real drugs (all except marijuana) since 1973. I also never did drugs of any sort around my children, including pot. After my last LSD trip in 1973, I made a conscience decision to quit doing drugs altogether because I felt they were bad for me and could only do harm. I had seen enough of my friends, peers and idols fall victim to drug abuse by this time. I saw when you allow drugs to take over your life, you not only hurt yourself you also hurt your family, friends, loved ones, and the fragment of God within you. You cloud the natural highs that are all around you and destroy the essence of love.

Again making a clear distinction between drugs and marijuana, I did continue to smoke pot on occasion until completely quitting in the mid eighties, just before the birth of my youngest child. I quit smoking pot for two reasons, the first being it is illegal. Secondly it is my belief both pot and alcohol can be inhibitors to spiritual growth. I did not quit smoking pot because I thought it was bad. Quitting was my own personal decision and I do not put down others if they choose to do otherwise. I will say this; if pot were legal I might choose to smoke it socially on occasion just as I now have an occasional drink. I believe moderation is very important when indulging in either pot or alcohol.

I personally see no purpose at all in tobacco. It has absolutely no redeeming values in my opinion. Although it has long been proven to cause great bodily harm and death, it continues to be sold and marketed freely. As soon as heavier restrictions were levied upon tobacco within the United States, the large tobacco companies took their marketing strategies abroad to become an exporter of death. Yes I used to be a smoker, but I got smart and quit many years ago.

Having said all that I strongly believe drugs are not really necessary for anyone unless used for medicinal purposes. I especially do not think young people should use drugs of any kind. In this thought I include alcohol, pot and tobacco.

Am I being hypocritical?

Perhaps I am, but times were really much different back in the sixties and seventies than they are now. Our generation experimented with everything and anything in order to find new meanings and values. We were so perversely lied to about so many things that it was very difficult to know right from wrong. Consequently we distrusted all the dogma that was spoon fed to us. This included the notion that drugs are not good for you. The world is now a much different place in which to live. Accurate information and knowledge is readily available through many sources other than the approved textbooks of the authorities. Remember, we were the generation subjected to the so-called educational films such as "Reefer Madness."

I believe ALL drug use should be decriminalized. I think the current methods of regulating the use of drugs has failed. It is far more a crime that we have filled our prisons to the brim with non-violent drug offenders. Especially since it is a known fact that it's very easy to get drugs in jail. If what I'm saying is true, then where is the rehabilitation the politicians speak of?

In California and many other states, referendums have been passed by the voters to make marijuana legal for medical use. This is a great step in the right direction. Pot has been proven to be extremely helpful to those patients suffering from cancer as well as AIDS. What is unfortunate is the Federal Government does not recognize the states individual rights to pass such laws and has been prosecuting individuals for medical marijuana use, even though the states say it is legal. So we go one step forward and two steps back.

I think we would be better off scrapping the current system and approaching it from an entirely new direction. Marijuana should be controlled in a similar manner to which alcohol is controlled with all other drugs falling under the supervision of the physicians. If someone is addicted to heroin then let him or her get their drugs through a doctor with supervised care. Only then will there be any real chance for rehabilitation. In most cases it certainly won't happen in a prison.

What are my thoughts about free sex?

Well, although it was accepted and enjoyed by many of my generation in the sixties and seventies it also killed many of my dear friends in the early nineties. As I said earlier concerning the drugs, "We were so perversely lied to about so many things that it was very difficult to know right from wrong." We threw out the baby with the bath water. But we did so because we were told sex was dirty, perverse and it was something not to talk about—end of story. Sex was a mystery that could only be understood after marriage. Sex education was unheard of in the sixties and seventies, frowned upon in the eighties and finally accepted by the general populace in the nineties. Although there are still many communities to this very day who continue to find issue with it.

If you look back on our generation you will also see that teen pregnancy was at an all time high. Fortunately the only diseases we had to worry about were gonorrhea or syphilis. Not that they were good ones, but they certainly weren't as deadly as what the kids today have to be concerned with. I truly believe if AIDS had been a factor during the sixties and seventies, millions upon millions would have died—quite possibly me included.

What I learned through the sexual attitudes of those times is that sex in and of itself, although stimulating, is void of any real value without love. And love, true love, is of much more substantial value and is independent from sex. Together, love and sex create a symphony of human expression and emotion. Apart, one is cosmic and eternal; the other is sweat and flesh. When you're young and the hormones are bursting out through every pour of your being, it's very difficult to listen to someone telling you to hold back the floodgates. That you must wait to experience such a mystical and magical part of life itself.

The real catch is though, the direct correlation between sex and family. Many young people in my day as well as those today, have no real idea how hard it is to raise a child. They also haven't a clue on how to really get along and communicate with the opposite sex. How could they? They haven't been taught anything about marriage and family. To drive a car, you must take a test in order to get a license. But anyone can have a baby and all you need is a blood test to get married. How bizarre is that!

What are really needed now for youth are marriage and family classes that begin as an integral part of early education, before puberty. They should cover all aspects of family life, from balancing a checkbook to changing a diaper. I'll share an idea I had after attending a marriage and family class many years ago.

The class would be an integrated part of both middle schools and high schools. It would also be a working daycare center which would help fund the classes. The teachers would be rotating husband and wife teams. The teacher's aides could be single moms or college students earning credits. Instead of having the students working with textbooks only and plastic dolls, the curriculum would be real life situations as they occur. Because real people are involved, emotional ties, concern and love would develop, creating a real understanding for families that some children may not get from their own home environment.

Are these radical thoughts?

Maybe, but remember so was the birth of a new nation back in the 1700's. What is our society so scared of when it comes to change? Why is it we so readily admit our successes and ignore our failures? We need to be brave and step outside of the box. I'm not saying my ideas are the right ones to use. I'm simply stating what we are doing is not working and we need to be courageous and try something different and new.

Let's talk about peace. Take a look around the globe. Do you think we are any closer to world peace now than we were two thousand years ago? Sometimes I get very sad because in the big picture I don't think we've really changed much over even the last century. Oh yeah, we've accomplished great technological milestones, but there's always a war, people are starving and children continue to be neglected and abused.

"Hair" did so much as far as getting the message of peace out to the masses. It woke up many to the evils of one particular war in time. It did so without the pomp of one particular religion, without the zeal of a particular party, yet "Hair" was in a sense religious and political. It was as if the children had spoken. It was simple, it was truth and it touched the world.

To me it now seems as though the peoples of this planet have fallen back to sleep. The time is more than ripe to awaken them once again to the message of "Hair." Different voices, different wars, singing sweetly in the name of love, freedom, equality and peace.

Sometime around 1995 (thanks to the Internet) I began to get back in touch with many people who were involved with "Hair" back in the old days. On May 2, 1998 Michael Butler held a 30th Birthday reunion party at John Phillip Law's house above the Sunset Strip in Hollywood. It was an incredible night I will always remember. After 30 years it was as if time had stood still for all of us. Of course much of the hair in the crowd was now gray and for some gone altogether. But even with our aging and physical changes we were still one big tribe.

Following are the names from the signed guest book at the party. There were also many attendees who for some reason didn't sign the guest book. Of those I also included a few names of some folks I personally recall seeing at the reunion party.

"30 years of "Hair" in one night!"
30th anniversary party May 2, 1998

Guest Book

Leata Galloway	Cara Robin
Bruce & Janin Paine	Alan Martin
Karen Back	Misty Reams &
Rolan Bolan	Christian Kiley
Susan Morse	Barbara Lauren
Dan Kern	Gregg Smith
Nancy Boykin	Deborah Offner
Griffin Drew	Katherine Iacofano
Omer Ganin	Toad (Toni) Attell
David McCormick	Lee Mallory
Rick Kurek	Trey Selvage
Debra Ortega	Erroll Booker
Ethlie Ann Vare	Nathan Sanford
Doug Rowell	Laura Hart
Tisk Diskin (& son, Paddy)	Tom Propofsky
Joan & Gary Quasar	James Finnerty
Beverly Bremers &	Chris Comer
David Lipton	Bill Dobbins
Danielle Bisutti	Kathy & Ron Pittman
Efren Bojorquez	Les Carlsen &
Jim Carrozo	Joyce (Macek) Carlsen
Jonathon Johnson	Melodie Wilson
Tera & Stu Yahm	Lelan Berner

Randal Hoey   Valentino Harris
Ellen Crawford   Bob Corff & Claire
Christine Adams   Sacha Vaughn
Tadg Galleran   Ben Lautman
Charles Valentino   She
Ted Lange   Christine Mackenzie
Cliff Lipson   Steven Menkin
Chip Matthews, Esq.   She She aka Martha
Charlotte Crossley   Yvonne Tramel
Gene Krischner   Charles O'Lynch
Marsha Faye   Paul Leight
Sharmagne Leland-St. John   Kevin ("Pigpen")
Richard Almack   Flaherty
Sharon Simon   Barbara Leighton
Merria Ross   Mary Lorrie Davis
David ("Pappy") Hunt   Michael Butler
Lee King   John Philip Law
Lydia Phillips   Linda Rees
Moreno Kline   Robert Rubinsky
                                     Kenny Ortega

Towards the end of the evening, someone grabbed a guitar and we all gathered in the living room for one more encore. Truly we must have sung every
song in the show and with the windows wide open for all to hear on the Sunset Strip below us. The rush of emotions and feelings were overwhelming and
made the hair on the back of my neck rise.

Later on in the summer of 1998 my then 21-year-old son and I attended a
matinee of a revival of "Hair" at the Candlefish Theatre in Hollywood. Greg
Karliss joined the two of us, along with Robert Rubinsky from the original
cast. Both Greg and Robert decided it was too hot to wear shirts, so in typical
"Hair" fashion they went into the theatre topless. It was a super feeling to see
my son fall in love with the same show I had some 28 years before! What was

really fun was when Berger decided to crawl over the seats and into my lap to ask for spare change.

The torch has now been passed to future generations of young people, expressing both their frustrations with society and their delights with life. "Hair" undoubtedly will continue to grow (pun intended). No matter how many times you cut it, it will always grow back. "Hair" was and always will be the journal of one generation of youth, passed on to all future generations.

16

Voices of the Tribe ~ A Tribal Pow Wow with Chats, Interviews, Anecdotes and Love Will Steer The Stars

Michael Butler
Worldwide Producer of HAIR

MICHAEL BUTLER (Producer) has wide and diversified business interests in real estate, paper, aviation, recreation and sports, banking, electronics, ranching, utilities, and other fields. Among his myriad activities are posts as Director of International Sports Core, the Chicago Regional Port District and the famed New York discotheque Ondine, and Chancellor of the Lincoln Academy of Illinois. ~ *From the First HAIR Playbill at The Cheetah, December 1967.*

MICHAEL BUTLER (Producer) has seen his now-classic musical in 25 countries in 14 languages. A *Medici of the Counter Culture*, Mr. Butler is thought of by those around him as a bridge between new talent and those able to give that talent exposure. In addition to his continuing activity in theatre (he is a producer of *Lenny*), Mr. Butler is an international promoter of polo. Butler's Great Harmony, an organic restaurant and boutique on East 60th Street, is evidence of the versatility of this "21st Century Renaissance Man" who has been cited by *Who's Who*, *The U.N.* (for making possible the *U.N. World Youth Assembly*), *The New England Theatre Special Conference Award* and *The National Educational Theatre Conference Special Award*. Mr. Butler's papers and clippings were recently requested by and presented to *Boston University's Contemporary Documents Library*. Besides his newly founded project, Revelation Records (which will continue to utilize the energies brought together on stage in *Hair*), Mr. Butler is planning a musical adaptation of Frankenstein. ~ *From the Last HAIR Playbill on Broadway, June 1972.*

Some thoughts from Michael ~

Before I got involved with "*Hair*," I was very active in politics and I was getting ready to run for the U.S. Senate from the State of Illinois. I had made a major change from being a very military, establishment guy, to being very much against the Vietnam War. I was totally unprepared for what I saw in New York.

I went to New York with the Governor of Illinois, Otto Kerner, to meet with Mayor Lindsey. The two of them were co-chairs of what was known as the Kerner Commission for Civil Disorder, about civil rights in this country. While in New York I discovered this ad for "*Hair*," the tribal love-rock musical. It had a picture of Indian braves and I thought, "Oh my God the Indians put a show together." Indian rights had been a major concern of mine at that time and they still are. So I went down to see a preview of "*Hair*" at the Public Theatre, Joe Papp's place.

After seeing the show I thought, "My God, this would be fantastic to have my constituents in Illinois see this show," because it was the strongest anti-war statement I'd ever seen. So, I didn't know Papp, but I did know Roger Stevens who was the head of the Kennedy Center. From Roger, I got an introduction to Papp and went to talk with him. I said I'd like to take the show to Chicago and he said, "No we don't do that. Like most Rep companies we run a show for a month, six weeks, then we close it, shut it down and that's it."

I went back to Illinois disappointed and a few days later a call came through. It was Joe Papp saying, "Listen, we'd like very much to do a co-production of the show. What would you think of that?"

I immediately said yes. I decided I would do that instead of running for political office. So I came to New York, made a call to the Mayor and the Governor (Mayor Daly and Governor Kerner) and told them I was not going to run.

We moved the show to the Cheetah. The Cheetah was a big discothèque that had been built by a partner of mine in other discothèque's, Olivier Coquelin. Olivier was one of my best friends, a guy I stayed with whenever I came to New York. We had built the Hippopotamus, the Ondine, the Talisman, the Ski Club Tannin, a whole bunch of them. I also was involved; we were heavy investors in Westside Story (which I found), a play called Ondine and another one called the Golden Apple—three musicals. I love straight theatre, but I've always sort of been more interested in musicals.

So anyway, we went into the Cheetah discothèque and the show didn't really work. It was sort of limping along and in the process of trying to figure out what was wrong with the show, we found a few things. Number one, the authors wanted to make some changes. Number two, the director, who was a fabulous director, but he'd never smoked grass. He was more into beatniks than he was into hippies. He didn't really understand where it was coming from. Another problem we had was we would have the show early, about seven or seven-thirty and then we would have to close down after that for the dancing. It just didn't work. We had to move the sets, but it was not so much that as it was just a non-theatrical venue.

The real problem was the show needed some changes and the show had a very tough ending; there was nothing pleasant about it. The ending was very negative, there was no hope and there was no "Let the Sunshine In." That was fine for a very esoteric audience that is used to 200 seats or 99 seats, people who are deeply into theatre and all that. But for getting a message across to the general public, you've got to feed them a little hope. Otherwise, it becomes a pretty dark scene. The other factor I felt stronger about all the time, is that I felt that this show, that the book, was very autobiographical. I thought Jim really represented Claude and therefore he should play Claude.

Olivier Coquelin brought two incredible people into the mix. One of them was Michael Gifford, who previous to "Hair" had sold a Batman poster very successfully. Olivier said, "This lady has a terrific ability in sales and promotion." So I took her on for that purpose. The other person Olivier introduced me to was Bertrand Castelli. Bertrand came in, ultimately as the Executive Producer. Bertrand was the mad Corsican who had incredible ideas and a very high degree of intelligence and taste. He was a very interesting counterpoint to the hippie, anti-intelligence attitudes.

Finally, I went to work out a deal with Papp, seeing if we could work together and he changed the terms a couple of times. So in going for the first class rights, I found Joe Papp had not optioned the first class rights. He didn't take advantage of his option to do that. So I went on and took on the first class rights and did it alone. Joe Papp's focus was with getting the Public Theatre off the ground. We wound up giving royalties to the Shakespeare Festival that kept them alive for many years. Papp and I became very close friends. In fact, he stayed at my home with his family one year for Christmas. And I really miss him, he was a fantastic man.

Tom O'Horgan really came into the picture, mainly as far as I was concerned, at the recommendation and insistence of Bertrand Castelli. But I think Bertrand probably was plugged into Tom by Jim and Gerry. I had never been to La Mama, I knew about it, but had never gone. So I had never seen Tom's work before. But I took their combined advice and he was a good man to work with. I certainly was happy about the decision. I found his sensitivity exercises fascinated me. I think they had a tremendous influence on bringing things together.

One of the major things I think about "*Hair's*" opening and it's become very important in my thinking about producing further companies, is the need for the cast to become a tribe. When we first opened on Broadway, that tribe had been together about six months. So you had a very cohesive group of people who really were a tribe, a serious tribe. Beyond that, they were an extended family. And I think that had a very big influence on the success of "*Hair.*"

That in my opinion, is the reason the 1977 show, the second time it went to Broadway, did not work. I think that was the main reason. I don't think it was that the timing was off or anything like that. I think it was the fact that the tribe was totally professional and they had no real love for the piece. They weren't really anchored in to it. Tom was directing it, but we didn't have all that time of being together. You really need that time. That's why in the new tour; we are going to have five weeks of rehearsal and a month to six weeks of running before we go into a main market. I also want to get everyone out of their hometown and into an atmosphere where we are living together. We are looking at some places in both Santa Fe New Mexico and Ojai California.

When I got involved with "*Hair,*" I had no idea it would be the success it was. When I first met Jim, Gerry and Galt, I of course thought they were very interesting people. I was fascinated with Gerry. He was a very strong and unusual personality. Galt was totally in a different sphere. A nice guy that I got along with and liked, but he wasn't into the philosophy of the show or anything. All Galt really cared about was his beautiful music. And Jim, his whole attitude is a story. He was totally different than Gerry.

The interesting thing is that I almost immediately began to equate the story with Huckleberry Finn. I began to think, well now here you've got Huckleberry Finn, you've got Tom Sawyer and you've got Becky Thatcher, but moved into a hippie philosophy. That is the story and you've got a terrific black man who was a very important factor in Mark Twain's story and "*Hair*." By doing that, I was able to have a certain feeling of the underpinnings of the book.

I personally do not buy this business that the book is unimportant. I think the book is the important thing about "*Hair*." I think it existed before the music did. I think it's very critical that one understands it is what "*Hair*" is all about. And I personally feel my interest in "*Hair*" came from the book. It came from the story and I feel it is a very real story, and as far as I'm concerned it's a play about Claude. Claude is somebody you have to love. He's like your younger brother, going off to war.

Once "*Hair*" took off on Broadway, I came up with the idea of taking it out to the world, outside of confines of Broadway. This was an unusual approach and the master plan was to go after the main targets of influence. You have to remember I was very politically stimulated and involved as far as this whole show was concerned. As was Michael Gifford and Bertrand Castelli. Everybody involving the show, one way or the other, had the same basic interest. Which was, the show was a very political statement, entertaining at the same time.

Michael Gifford figured we could do it. We broke all the rules by going into Philadelphia, Boston and Washington. Which everybody said would hurt us in the New York market, which it did. "*Hair*" probably would have run twice the length of time in New York if we had done the standard scene and just kept in New York. What we did with Boston, Philadelphia and Washington is we penetrated the New York market. But we also got a lot of people who wouldn't have made the trip to New York. So I figured we wound up doing much better. It was so current, as it is today. If you do a good job with the productions, you'll find an immediate audience for it.

Looking back, the only regrets I have are that I left "*Hair*" for a while. Right after the film, I was really burnt out and very tired. So I went back home and just spent my time playing polo. I figured I just wanted to rest up. So after about a year and a half I was ready to come back and get back into it because I knew certain things needed to be done. Not so much artistically, but from a marketing point of view. But just at that time, my father was killed in an auto accident. He was hit by a drunken driver.

So I had to take over the Butler Company. My sister couldn't do it because she had her own businesses to run and my brother wasn't capable of running the company. It was a very big company, paper, aviation, some electronics, and real estate was its heaviest interest in those days. But it turned out to be ten years of absolute hell. I stuck it out as long as I could, but working for my family was just unbelievable. Most of them lived back with Louis the Fourteenth, not even the sixteenth. So I regret doing that because it would have made life a lot easier now, with what we're trying to do, had I not left.

From the time "*Hair*" closed on Broadway, it has gone on continuously since then. I haven't actually broken it down, but I think it's more popular now than it was ten years ago. In stock, amateur, high schools, colleges and community theatres. I went up to Salem Oregon in October to see a version of "*Hair*" and it was incredible. Especially with what they had to work with. It's amazing how involved they all get. "*Hair*" is different from any other show. It becomes a part of you, you are tribe.

I missed the final performance on Broadway in 1972. I'm pretty sure I was in England at the time. I was concentrating very heavily on the film then. We were with Paramount then, which of course fell apart. Then there was a big internal fight at Paramount. Hal Ashby, was to direct. Hal had done Harold and Maude, Landlord, and others. Collin Higgins was writing the screenplay. It was an incredible team we put together. We started and then Hal Ashby blew up. He got very heavily into drugs and it ultimately killed him. When we lost Hal Ashby, everything else became unraveled. After Hal left, I wanted Higgins to do it but we couldn't get Paramount to agree. After the deal with Paramount was finished, it took about two more years to get the deal with United Artists, where Milos Forman was the director.

In the movie, I really don't like how they changed the story. I didn't like the screenplay. I mean, who do you care about in that film? I want to be able to be concerned about Claude. Well, in the screenplay version, that just didn't happen. You didn't feel any empathy. Also, maybe that's why they sent Berger off to be killed. Berger's job wasn't to add that. It's sort of like Berger, to be a funny, outrageous teddy bear. It was also unrealistic that a switch like that could happen, Berger going off in the place of Claude. The movie wasn't believable; where as the original story was very believable.

My years of involvement with "*Hair*" have been filled with so many unique and good experiences that looking back; I couldn't possibly pick out any as being my favorite. The whole experience has been incredible and as far as "*Hair*" is concerned, I have no regrets. There are though, many great experiences I could share if there were only enough time. I will share one with you that comes to mind.

At one time we had so many tribes going we couldn't keep track of them. With *"Hair,"* you had to keep a constant eye on the productions to see they didn't stray too far off track. So we drew straws. We divided the tribes up and each one of us took the responsibility for one of them. I drew San Francisco as my particular responsibility.

The principle thing was to keep the show going, working with the stage managers to be sure the show was not getting too long, or that bits and pieces were not being destroyed. The usual for *"Hair,"* too much improvising, taking over the script, etc. Also, watching the business aspects of the show. So, I spent a fair amount of time out there. Enough so that I got involved with a couple who were in the show. I was living with them. So I was really quite into what was happening.

So, while back in New York, the phone rang and there was going to be a big peace moratorium in San Francisco. The tribe wanted to go to the moratorium and they wanted to cancel the show. Well, there wasn't time enough to advise the public. I think we were talking about three or four days. Tickets were already sold far in advance. You'd have a couple thousand angry people; also the show must go on. And I said no, we couldn't do it. The cast in turn said they were going to go ahead and do it.

I then put together a team of people from companies all over the country and flew them into San Francisco. And I flew in myself with Paul Jabara. The deal to get Paul Jabara is I had to offer him Teru. Teru Kawaoka was my close friend and bodyguard at that time. I told Teru, I said, "Teru, I'm not going to force you to do it, but this is a situation." It was very funny and is still good for a laugh. Teru was a terrific guy. Anyway, Paul and I flew out together from New York. And Teru had decided he wasn't particularly that fond of Paul. I had to laugh and said, "Well Teru, it's up to you. If the show goes down…. no I'm just kidding."

When we got to San Francisco, I told them what we were going to do. That we were going to replace the tribe entirely. And everybody started to freak out, cry and everything else. To make a long story short, after exhausting negotiations it was decided everyone would go on, except the two ringleaders—they were out. So, they agreed to do so under the condition that I would appear in the nude scene. And they gave me a peace pipe, which I have to this day. I went in the nude scene three times. It's an extraordinary feeling, being in the nude scene.

So many people were moved by the *"Hair"* experience that it's hard to put a finger on any particular event at this moment. I do remember one incident where at intermission; I was walking down the isle towards the stage of the Aquarius Theatre in Los Angeles. And I heard coming up from behind me, a voice I knew immediately. It was Diana Vreeland, who was a great fashion dragon of the world. She was the head of Vogue and Harper's magazines. Now they even have a whole exhibit at the Metropolitan Museum in her honor. Just an incredible lady and a great fashion editor. Anyway, she said "Michael, this is the ninth time I've seen *Hair*." I can't off-hand remember the instances, but I know there were several times where people were totally changed by *"Hair"* that I knew of.

The show changed my life. It made me a much kinder, compassionate and understanding person. Before *"Hair,"* I would describe myself as ruthless, at least in business. I truly still subscribe to the hippie philosophy of life. Peace, love and freedom. The best thing that comes out of *"Hair"* is friendship, family. It's the password to Nirvana. You can meet someone who's a complete stranger who is involved with the show and almost instantly they're like family. It's not just another show.

The most important ideal and condition of all our lives is freedom. The destroyer of freedom is war. It allows the forces of evil to exercise control over us to preserve our sense of security. Benjamin Franklin said, "Those who seek after both freedom and security shall have neither". Intolerance, fundamentalism are all methods of control. Lack of compassion for different thoughts and attitudes breed contempt for other human beings. Religious beliefs, sexual preferences, rights of choice are just the beginnings of a list of prejudices.

Love is the only antidote and *"Hair"* is a messenger of love. Our concern for Claude comes from our love of Claude and what he is going through. *"Hair"* is a message specific to all times and all eras. It addresses the age-old conflict of ideals vs. humanity. I hope I always have the courage to stand on the side of humanity.

We are the messengers of a spiritual quest for Peace. We are fortunate to be involved with *"Hair."* It has changed all our lives to a greater or lesser extent, but change is there. Our minds have been expanded. Gerry and Jim wrote an incredible story, which was surrounded with Galt's beautiful music. Tom directed with great feeling. So many others assisted in the production of *"Hair."* Many continue to carry this message. Nothing in the theatre compares to the effect *"Hair"* has had on everyone who has become involved. Certainly it has had an effect on all who have seen it. That is our joy and our task, to let the sunshine in.

What does the future hold for "*Hair*?" I think "*Hair*" is about to become more popular and a more important political statement than it was in the sixties and seventies. The time is once again ripe for the message of "*Hair*." Look at the political climate in the world, or just in the United States for that matter. Once again we have the religious political right, working hard to usurp their power. In the process, everything is at stake and up for grabs, including the environment, peace and freedom itself. There is already a growing interest in "*Hair*" among the youth. Just as in the sixties, they are steadily becoming disillusioned with what is happening in the world today. Also, from a marketing standpoint, you have the baby boomers who loved the show when it came around the first time, who will now want to see it again. They in turn will want to share it with their families.

Freedom, Peace and Love,   *Michael Butler*

Michael David Arian

Michael David Arian was a member of the German and Spanish productions of "Hair" as well as several touring companies in the USA.

MICHAEL DAVID ARIAN (Father, Young Recruit, General Grant, Tribe) originally performed in "Hair" in Germany. Back in the states, he now works with John Vacarro's "Playhouse of the Ridiculous" and has played the Father in "Rainbow." He is looking forward to doing the show in English here at the Playhouse. ~ *From the March 1974 HAIR program at the Playhouse on the Mall in Paramus, New Jersey.*

Michael recalls ~

Where do I begin? I saw the show on Broadway dozens of times and auditioned 13 times between 1967 and 1969 alone. I could say something about how it affected people globally, about being in Spain when Franco died, or seeing one of only two performances in Rome. I also met people who'd done the show all over Europe, who just could not get into "real life" after being in the show.

Well, here goes.......

Before getting involved with "Hair" I was in Memphis, Tennessee clamoring to get out of high school. I was being influenced by the Beatles, my hormones and the ferment of the 60's. As a teen I had stayed apart from politics choosing to concentrate not on school but the theater. As the world went from one crisis to another in the 60's, I started to realize a world outside of my hometown. So when I came to NYC to study at the American Academy of Dramatic Arts in 1967, the first show I saw was "Hair." I was 19 and was taken by Cass Morgan to see the show, inspiring both of us to audition later on. She made it to Broadway and I went to Europe and did the show in Germany. I knew when I first stepped into the Biltmore Theatre, this was for me.

For my first NY audition in 1967 I brought a friend to play guitar for me. I did a terrible version of "Take Another Little Piece Of My Heart." They asked my accompanist to sing. Oddly enough, neither of us got a part. On a subsequent audition the same thing happened to another pair. The difference was that before the eyes of all assembled, including the girl singing; the casting director dragged the accompanist out to sign a contract, leaving her song unsung.

My first contact with "Hair" in Germany came about by my having been sent with a letter from Bertrand Castelli to the casting director in Vienna. She was out of town so I didn't see her at that time. I went on to stay in Amsterdam and do theater workshops until one day I got a telegram from Fred Reinglas to come be in the show. I got on a train to Germany and got to the theater just before curtain. It happened to be my 21st birthday and the stage manager told me to just sit out in the house and enjoy myself. I said I'd rather join in and did.

The cast didn't know me from Adam but the spirit was overwhelming. They led me by the hand through the Aquarius circle and after the singer sang the first verse, not in German but in French, she handed me the mike and I sang it in English. The audience loved it and it was one of my best moments on a stage ever.

In Germany I played the Pill Lady and was to do several other small parts that needed coaching in the language. Peter Kern, who was playing these parts and was slated to leave the show, was my teacher. We would get together to rehearse, and before I could learn my part he'd pull out his hash pipe and all thoughts of studying would soon be forgotten. Consequently, I would go on and do the role in a mix of English and Pigeon German. Peter went on to be a star throughout Austria and Germany.

At the time I joined up in Germany, there were three different productions going through the German speaking countries. Our group had a band that had defected from Czechoslovakia. When we were about to open in Hamburg, I found out that the producer (Werner Schmidt, who later brought Uri Geller to the world) had not paid the band what they were promised. I decided to right this wrong with a well-timed strike. We waited until intermission on a sold out opening night and I told the office we would not continue until they were paid. They were paid faster than any band in history.

When I joined the cast in Spain in the summer of 1975 we were warned to be on the alert as Franco's death was rumored to be days away. It was still a running joke on Saturday Night Live. The show opened in Madrid at a state run theater. Under Franco strikes were illegal. Our producer was an Italian pornographer. To just mix it up and get under his skin, I spread a rumor that we were to strike on opening night, with no intent to do so.

Well the producers spy pipeline was working and he got the word because at the 15-minute call, soldiers came rushing into the backstage area, machine-guns drawn and proceeded to herd us toward the door. After vacating in my pants and being the one looked to as the origin of this conflict, I was able to talk the soldiers out of busting up the place.

In Spain I played and sang many small parts including a Mom, General Washington and "What A Piece of Work is Man," until finally taking over as the Tourist Lady for 10 months, 10 shows a week. Which brings me to another story about the producer in Spain. He had wanted to go on with me as Mr. Tourist Lady, so I finally let him do so. But, first I loaded my purse with a heavy weight. All thru the scene I smashed his head repeatedly with my weighty handbag. When we exited, while rubbing his head in agony, he said he'd had a good time but it was too much work being on stage. He couldn't imagine that I had sabotaged him.

Later on, I was in the "Hair" production at the Paramus Mall in New Jersey where I played the Young Recruit. I had already done the show in Germany so when I auditioned I asked to sing "Oh Great God of Power" in German. When the pianist said he could only play the song in French, I knew I had the part.

I met Jim Rado and Gerry Ragni as fans of The Playhouse of the Ridiculous when I did my first show with them at La Mama. They said they had loved me and wanted to talk about the show, but I was too in awe of them to speak. I worked with them on YMCA and later auditioned for Dude, but got into Rainbow as a last minute replacement before the show opened to the controversy it created.

I did a theatrical happening that Tom O'Horgan put together at St Clements Church called "Fun-House of the Lord" in the early 70's. At this point I was friendly with Tom too and it couldn't have been more fun.

I was present for the final performance of "Hair" on Broadway. I signed a bunch of papers freeing the production from liability before they would let me on stage, but I could only watch totally transfixed by the moment. I was moved to tears throughout.

Being in "Hair" was the most fun I ever had on a stage ever. Being paid to do this show and travel through Europe was a great and high point of my life. Even with the low pay and cruddy producers nothing has ever been able to touch these moments.

After "Hair," I returned to New York and continued being an actor. Today I work in the administrative offices at La Mama, which Tom O'Horgan refers to as the spiritual home of "Hair."

"Hair" gave me a new awareness of the world and the theater in particular. It was more an education than just a show. Not a day goes by when I don't think on some level about some aspect of the show. There are days I spend in quiet reverie seeing the choreography in my mind and stretching my arms and legs out like I was 20 years old again. If only acid would take me back there.

XOXOX M

Beverly Bremers

Beverly Bremers was a two-time member of Broadway production of *"Hair"* in *both 1969 and 1972*. She played the roles of Sheila and Crissy. Beverly was also the last Sheila on Broadway.

BEVERLY BREMERS (Sheila) made her Broadway debut in *HAIR* in 1969 and now returns, after a successful run in the original cast of the hit musical *The Me Nobody Knows*. She has also appeared in productions of *Babes In Toyland, Skin of Our Teeth, South Pacific, The Sound of Music, J.B., The Ghost Sonata* and *The Miser,* and has appeared often on TV talk and variety shows, as well as the film-TV *Good Morning, Freedom,* and numerous commercials. Beverly records for Scepter Records and her follow-up to her hit recording of *"Don't Say You Don't Remember"* is called *"We're Free." ~ From the last HAIR Playbill on Broadway, June 1972.*

A few story's from Beverly ~

When the Shakespeare Festival production of "Hair" first held auditions in 1967, I had an appointment for an audition. A few days before hand though, I cancelled it. I was thinking "Hair" was a strange name for a show and it probably wouldn't go anywhere. Who knows what might have been.

I soon forgot all about "Hair" until the following year when I ran into Lamont Washington, a good friend of mine and fellow actor. Lamont was going on about this great Broadway show he was in called "Hair." He was telling me I would be great in the show and should go to see it. Lamont convinced me to go but sadly, he died in a tragic fire shortly after our conversation.

Lamont was the reason I was going to see the show, but after he died, I just couldn't. I mean the papers had a photo of him literally on fire. He had fallen asleep while smoking and jumped out of a third story window. It was just a horrible thing, so I lost all interest in "Hair."

Months later, while on my way into the city, I ran into some people I knew at the train station. They were coming back from a matinee of "Hair." They said, "Beverly, we just saw this show that you are so perfect for. You have the voice, the hair, everything. You've got to get down and see it." So I finally went to a matinee and can still remember sitting there going, "Oh my God, they are absolutely right."

I had already heard about the major cattle calls to audition for the show and wanted to avoid them. So, I called an agent I had met once briefly who had offered to help me and said I would like him to arrange an audition. He said, "I have a client, Lynn Kellogg, who used to be in the show and she's the only one. I've arranged for many of my clients to audition, but none have ever gotten in." I said, "trust me I know I'm perfect for the show." He said "fine," and arranged an audition for me.

When I showed up for my appointment, I remember singing "Somebody to Love" by the Jefferson Airplane. I got about one line out and that was all I needed. They said, "We must have you for this show. You have two choices, we are opening up a show in L.A. and you'd be perfect for the role of Sheila. Or, we could really use you here because we've lost a bunch of cast members. We don't know what part you'd be playing in New York though."

I didn't have to think about it very long. It was Broadway and I wanted to be on Broadway. So that was the choice I made and I think for me personally, it was the better choice. They said I could start immediately. Most of the original cast was still in the show at that time. I was hired along with a beautiful black woman named Carolyn Blakey. They brought the two of us in after eight people had quit and they literally said, "You two have to replace all eight people." It was really baptism by fire because they only taught me one number, "Black Boys." They said, "You can come in tonight and you're going to do the show." I told them I only knew one number and they said, "Oh don't worry about it. We'll start paying you and you'll do that number."

After about a week of working with Julie Arenal on the choreography and the stage manager on blocking, I finally started having rehearsals with the cast. This was very interesting because they taught some of the Tom O'Horgan sensitivity exercises. The scariest one was where everyone's in a circle; they blindfold you and make you run. No one allowed me to get hurt and they didn't even know me! I realized this exercise was to develop trust, because when Berger takes the leap off the platform, he's gotta know people are going to catch him. I remember once when there were only about four people there to catch him and I'm shouting, "Don't do it, I can't catch you. Don't do it!" Gerry did it anyway and we caught him, but it was a bit much.

Shortly after getting into the show, Shelley Plimpton left and they asked me to do "Frank Mills." I thought the key was a little high, but they said they didn't care. They needed someone fast and they would change the key. They said, "You're the smallest person in the cast and you look the youngest too." So I ended up playing Crissy pretty much the whole time. They forgot all about

Sheila. They had Heather McRae who was pretty consistent and they didn't have to worry about her. This was a great disappointment; since that was the role I knew I was really suited for.

I was known as Beverly Ann at this time. I had made some records and had dropped my last name because it was difficult for some people to remember. Robin McNamara, Allen Nicholls and Keith Carradine had also come in about the same time. Bert Sommer was playing Woof and then Keith played it later. Keith was kind of goofy, sort of like a country hick. It was really funny to me because he was from L.A., from this big, famous, show business family. And he's just like, "Hey how are you?" Like a big puppy dog, very sweet, but no one took him very seriously. He would hang around backstage in between shows, play around on his guitar and write songs. Ironically, he said a couple of years later that the Oscar-winning song, "I'm Easy" from the movie "Nashville," in which he starred, was one of the songs he had written backstage at "Hair."

I made a lot of good friends during that time. Paul Jabara was a hoot and a very talented songwriter as well. I did another show with him later in L.A., "The Rocky Horror Show" at the Roxy. Tragically, Paul is gone now as well as a lot of talented, wonderful people. Susan Morse joined the show from the L.A. cast and I'm still friends with her today. Also a girl named Barbara Lauren, who is now a casting director in L.A., Carolyn Blakey, who came in the show with me, lasted about two weeks. She was very prim and proper, and I still remember crawling on the ground next to her in the second act, with the dry ice surrounding us, both of us coughing. She said, "This is way too much. This is stupid. I'm out of here!" She quit soon after.

I shared a dressing room with Denise, Melba and Sally Eaton, who was the freakiest of all. Melba and Denise had sort of taken me under their wings, telling me things like, "Don't go to Fire Island." Because the first week I was hired people were saying, "Let's go to Fire Island, we're having a party." I didn't know any better and was ready to say yes and go. But Melba and Denise are saying, "Do not go. This is way beyond any experience you want." I was a baby. I mean I basically had no experience with anything whatever. The Fire Island parties were notoriously wild. Not going probably saved me from something I was not prepared to handle.

I joined the cast at a really awkward time. One of the reasons why they had lost so many cast members was because there was extreme racial tension. There were a lot of bad feelings: number one over Lamont, the way they treated Lamont's death. Melba and Denise had told me all about it. Melba was always very sweet; she wasn't into a lot of what was going on. She basically told me that when Lamont died, the producers wouldn't cancel the show for the funeral. Well, the black members of the cast in particular found that to be extremely insulting and disrespectful. Most of them went to the funeral anyway and skipped the show. Hostile feelings started erupting and it sort of carried over into everything. It was kind of a shock to me because I'm going into a show about peace, love and flowers. I get in there and it's quite different. There was quite a bit of tension there, certainly against management.

There were all kinds of people who came and went during that time. One guy who was playing Claude had a nervous breakdown. I was there for the show when he freaked out. He ran up to the upstairs bathroom, locked himself in and wouldn't come out. It had something to do with either the director or the stage manager, giving him mixed messages of some sort. Anyway, he left and I never saw him again. He was probably high, because there was a lot of that going on. There was a lot of politics going on as well and it became increasingly difficult to do the show.

I still remember Gerry Ragni going on with this whole rant, explaining some of the songs in "Hair," such as "Air," and "Flesh Failures." He was explaining that we put all this artificial stuff like deodorant, perfume, etc. on and that's not the real thing—that we should all be natural. A lot of people took it to heart, so about half the cast didn't use any deodorants. Now when you do as much sweating as you did in this show, that could cause some conflict! I must say this was one of those shows where you had to let a lot of that "natural" philosophy go because you were right in there with them.

The only time I ever smoked dope and did the show was with two other cast members. We used to see everybody do this but had never done it ourselves. So one night we thought, "Hey let's try it". I'll never forget because we were like three klutz's. We kept bumping into each other and falling down. We were a mess and I thought, "Never, ever will I do anything like that again". So although there was real stuff being passed around on stage (it was supposed to be tea) I just didn't do it.

In the six months or so that I did the show, I think I did every number that was conceivable for me to do. On stage and off, "Hair" taught me the good, the bad and the ugly of life. The best thing it taught me was spontaneity and to just go with whatever happens. I tell my singing/acting students now that you CAN fool all the people all the time. I learned that in the show. There were things that happened in the show that you just went with. When I think of it, it was absolutely incredible.

First of all, you're sitting in the dressing room a half hour before show time, talking, putting on your clothes, your makeup, and over the loud speaker the stage manager is saying; "Okay, so-and-so is playing this, you're singing the solo, you're playing this, you'll do the solo in "My Body," etc., etc. Rattling off about fifteen minutes worth of stuff that you would do in the show that night. And you'd just sort of be half listening and you'd go out on stage and do it.

On top of that, the person who was supposed to be standing next to you, who has the solo, doesn't show up for whatever reason and you learned to just do it. And then they would pay you for it! I got paid more money when I was in the tribe than later when I was the lead because there would be so many times when people just didn't show up. They were backstage, getting high or whatever. It was all great though because it really did train you to be on your toes and be ready for anything. You could just never settle in and be on autopilot.

There was sort of a strike while I was there. All the people who were doing the nude scene thought it was unfair that they would do it all the time and other people never did it, yet they all got paid the same amount of money. So they demanded to get paid extra for it. I remember one night, only one person stood up because everyone else was on strike. And that was when management said, "Okay, we'll give you an extra fifteen dollars a week to do it."

The other thing was that there were so many accidents. People were getting hurt all the time. One night during the shirt scene in "Easy to Be Hard," Berger (Greg Karliss) was just doing his thing, ripping the shirt and I was standing in the same place I always stood. While he's ripping the shirt and we're doing the dialog, he accidentally pops me in the eye with his elbow. I mean this is full strength. His elbow went just below my eye and nobody knew what happened but him and me.

Well, the show must go on and my next line happened to be, "Why did you do that?" And his next line was, "I don't know." So we're doing the dialog and as we're talking, my face is swelling, big time. Still, other than Greg, no one was aware of what was happening. With my back to the band, Charlie Brown, the guitarist, started to play the song, so I just started singing. Of course, I'm crying through most of the song. It was probably the most realistic rendition of the song ever done. About midway, I composed myself and actually finished the song. After the song, I walked off stage and said, "I need ice and an insurance form" on my way up to the dressing room. That's how used to accidents we were. I was prepared to finish the show but they talked me out of it and had Gloria Goldman finish the show as Sheila. I still wonder if anyone in the audience noticed that Sheila looked completely different. For the next two weeks, I was so battered and bruised that I must have looked like a battered wife or something. But you know that was the one thing about the show, they just did not care. The show had to go on.

The most horrendous accident I ever saw was with Red Sheppard. He came from the L.A. show and was just filling in for a couple of weeks as Berger. He was at the side of the house getting ready to swing on the rope, over the audience. Someone on the crew had set the two knots on the rope in the wrong location. When he swung out on the rope, he went flying into the third row and hit the back of a chair. Both his legs were broken and it was amazing he didn't hurt anyone in the audience.

This was at the top of the show, during "Donna." I never saw anyone move as quickly as I saw Allan Nicholls and Robin McNamara that night. Allan, who was playing Claude, had been sitting cross-legged in the middle of the stage with his Indian blanket draped over him. While a few tribe members and stagehands were carrying Red off, Allan had taken off his blanket, grabbed the mike and finished singing "Donna" without missing a beat. While he took over as Berger, Robin, who had been playing Woof, just as quickly donned the blanket to play Claude. The show went on without another hitch. I don't think the audience had a clue! That was the worst accident I saw but there were many others. The dry ice, snowflakes, water and mud on an inclined stage too small for the size of the cast made it a slippery and danger-ous place.

When I went into the show the second time in 1972, it was much different. Everyone was a professional and it was much more professionally run. Jim and Gerry would come in still, but they weren't speaking at the time, so it was really hard. Consequently, they played at different times, but I played with both of them. A lot of good things happened then. Ted Lange and I became good friends; we stayed in touch and ended up writing a musical together.

Many other people came and went. What really struck me the most were things like you'd be in the middle of a number, you'd look over and there would be somebody new sitting next to you who you'd never seen before in your life. Sometimes they'd be there for about a week and then they'd be gone. And then of course, Michael Butler would make appearances. You'd look over, see this guy with Indian garb and it would be Michael Butler sitting on stage. Galt MacDermot would do the same thing in the band. He would show up for "Easy to Be Hard" a lot. I always knew when he was there, because all of a sudden I would hear all these beautiful jazzy chords coming from the piano. I'd think "Oh, Galt's here!"

On the audience: The first time I was in the show, was right before "Aquarius" and "Let the Sunshine In" were hits. So when I'd tell people I was in "Hair," they'd think I was a beautician. Those who had heard about it would say, "Oh you mean that show with all those freaks, the nude scene, whatever". So when we would go out in the house, crawling over the audience and whatnot, the people were horrified. It became a challenge during every show you worked to win the audience over. But then of course, the songs became hits and almost overnight, everybody knew what "Hair" was. Then all my friends wanted tickets. It took months to get house tickets. It was a big switch.

When I came back the second time, what an easy gig! The audience knew all the songs, because by that time there were seven or eight hits. Plus, in that year and a half period of time, all their kids, grandkids, or someone they knew, had long hair. So the shock value was gone. The good news was instead of a hostile audience that you needed to win over; you had an accepting crowd from the beginning. So in the end, it was an easier show to do.

There were lots of groupies at this time too. There's one kid who was a groupie that I'm still friends with now. He's a director, Dennis Erdman. Dennis was this cute little blond kid who came every Saturday. He sat in the front row, was always there and was absolutely enamored with the show. There was another kid we called Tie-Dye Eddy. He was a curly headed skinny kid who would hang out back stage and would tie-dye shirts for people. He was really good at it, hence, his nickname. Both of them used to hang out back stage with us. To this day, whenever I see Dennis, the "Hair" days are all he wants to talk about. It made him decide he wanted to be in show business. He was absolutely the most adoring, loveable fan you could ever want.

Beverly Bremers

Corinne Broskette

Corinne Broskette played the roles of Sheila and Jeanie in the Los Angeles, Mexico, Las Vegas and National touring companies of *HAIR*.

On October 6, 1971, Las Vegas "Hair" (Pakalolo Tribe) closed at the International Hotel (now the Hilton, the show room is now Benihana's restaurant). Some of the Tribe returned to Hawaii and a good group went on the road with the FIRST road tour, the Rainbow Company. We opened in Indianapolis at the Circle Theater, with Sherman Warner, Director (now head of Dodger Productions in NYC) and Chris Comer (SM). Sheila was Patti Keene, Susie Allanson was Jeanie, Alan Martin was Claude and Greg Karliss was Berger. Ted Lange, Doug Rowell, Frankie Karl and Gregg Smith were also in the show. Leland Berner (costumer) was along to sew our jeans.

When we arrived in Indianapolis, we definitely were not wanted in that town. There were protests, etc., and the theatre that had been rented (an old vaudeville house) had been used as a movie theatre for years. Because of that, all of the rigging needed to be replaced.

But, the story I am here to tell is about finding places to live. We were doing a 4-week run in each city, to go on to the Shubert Circuit. But in "India-no-place," there were no theatre hotels. So we started looking for apartments. There was a bunch of us, all piled into a VW van, roaming the streets looking for rooms, anything to rent, armed with a newspaper.

Along came a truck and these red necks started throwing stale bread rolls at us. Well, never one to miss an opportunity for good improv, we began to scramble for the rolls, saying "Hey, thanks man! We are so hungry." Well, they were not impressed.

Some of us finally settled into a rooming house run by this gay couple who did interior decorating. Some of us had rooms, Chris and I (we were a couple back then) and our cat Uronamus Baste ("Ronnie Mouse") occupied a furnished apartment on the top floor. Ronnie would go out the window and chase squirrels all day. At night he would come to the theatre and chase the mice. Sometimes, Sherman's wife Elaine would baby-sit him and he would then chase Sherm's socks around their apartment. Ronnie was cool, would walk on a leash and sit on your shoulder if his feet got too cold.

The Union rules required we hire 4 musicians, so they hired a string quartet to play classical music in the lobby before the show and during intermission.

One night, Greg, Alan and others dressed up in tutus and did an impromptu ballet through the lobby. You had to be there. It was really very funny.

The Rainbow Company was eventually split apart in Cincinnati, November of 1971, with 1/4 of the cast fired and the rest split between Chicago (Venus I think), NY and Mercury (formerly Rainbow). It was pretty sad, because we were quite a family.

Corinne

In 1970 and 1971 over 2/3 of the actors working in the USA were working in HAIR.

Robert Camuto

Robert Camuto played the role of Woof and Claude in several touring productions of "Hair."

ROBERT CAMUTO (Woof) A resident of New York City, Peter Roberts is a double Libra with moon in Aquarius. He has acted in two previous productions of *HAIR*. Since making his stage debut at the age of 14 as Oliver Twist in *Oliver*, he has been seen in several shows including a college tour of *Jesus Christ Superstar* as the Apostle Paul, *In White America* as The Narrator, and in numerous roles for regional and children's theatre. ~ *From the Rock Talent Production HAIR program.*

Robert remembers ~

Some of my memories of the sixties are terrific and some are an absolute horror. Michael Butler was correct when he said our country was headed for a civil war. Not only was the whole country in an upheaval, but so were people's homes. I had trouble expressing my opinions of what was going on in the world in my own home. Having grown up in the era of "Duck and Cover" air raid drills and "Cold War" horror films about the possibilities of a nuclear disaster, I was convinced I wouldn't live past my 20's. The fact that my draft lottery number was 7 on the last drawing our country made didn't help much either. Both of my very conservative parents thought we belonged in Viet Nam and that it was my duty to go if called. "Didn't I want to preserve the wonderful lifestyle I had, by fighting off the communist scourge?"

My point about not having any life much longer didn't seem to faze them. It made me not want to be in my home, or my country. That doesn't mean I wanted to leave the country. It just meant I wanted to do something to change it. And I felt it would be changed for the better. I attended rallies and moratoriums and found contemporaries with the same beliefs as myself. I became an outcast in my home and looked forward to the day I would leave it.

Before "Hair" I was a student and did some winter stock productions of The Sound of Music, Oliver and Camelot. I also did several unsuccessful Off Broadway shows. I had unfortunately reached the age where I was too old to play Oliver or one of those fucking Von Trapp kids, but too young for the other roles in traditional musicals. I also found them fairly inane considering the world in the state it was in. I changed from listening to show tunes to listening to folk and protest rock. I loved Janis Ian and Country Joe and The Fish.

My cousin had seen "Hair" at the Cheetah and recommended it to me. I went to see it and decided I wanted to get involved by about the third musical number. Although I thought the production was really lame, I loved the pop rock score and almost everything it had to say. I felt some of the characters were written to be bad as opposed to rebellious though. I could personally relate to what "Hair" was about. Oh God yes, I really, really, really could! I can laugh when I look back on it now that I've lived significantly longer than the 20's I had expected. And lo and behold, here was a show that I was not too old, or too young for. If I did this show I could continue to consider theater as a possible way to support myself.

When the show later moved to Broadway and became really controversial, I realized it was a different show then the one I had seen at the Cheetah. It wasn't until October of 1968 that I saw the Broadway production. Barry McGuire was Berger, Joseph Campbell Butler was Claude and Diane Keaton was Sheila. I WAS HOOKED!!! I saw it again soon after with Heather Mac-Rae as Sheila and was totally smitten.

I later auditioned for the Broadway production in the winter of 1969. I believe it was February. I had to get permission from an adult to come to the callbacks because I was a minor, not yet 16. I arranged for a sympathetic aunt (my mother's sister) to do this for me. It was a very amusing experience. I brought music to "Sixteen going on Seventeen" from the "Sound of Music" and a book of Beatles songs. I ended up singing "If I Fell in Love With You" and a rock version of "The Star Spangled Banner." It was a very informal audition, and Fred Reinglas, Julie Taylor and Mary Davis were there. Actually, there were several cast members lurking about. I had 3 auditions, including one for Tom O'Horgan; before they decided they wanted an actual parent there to make sure it was a really possible for me to do the show. My mother decided she should see this show before she signed anything giving me permission. It turned out the nude scene was the least offensive part of the show for her. She said she was not giving me permission to be in a lewd, communist show. She told me to forget about "Hair," and study real acting if that's what I wanted to do. Shit!!!

During my auditioning period I became friends with Sally Eaton. She is still one of my oldest and dearest friends. She introduced me to Jim and Gerry after my parents told me that doing Hair was impossible. I found Jim to be very handsome and charming. Gerry was slightly intimidating, wild and scary to me. I was short and very thin (5' 6" and 119 lb.) and Gerry would some-times pick me up and spin me around. They both seemed to be very sincere and pleasant without being overly friendly.

When I finally got into Hair, I had to change my name because my parents didn't want anyone to know I was in the show. I decided to go by the name "Peter Roberts." I was originally hired to play tribe and understudy Woof in a tour that was already out on the road. We (8 actors) rehearsed in NYC for 3 weeks with an assistant musical director, the director and a dance captain who was in the show but back in NY to train us. I rehearsed the role of Woof the whole 3 weeks and wondered what I was going to do when I actually got to the first town and had to be part of the tribe.

We got to South Bend, Indiana, secretly watched a performance and were not introduced to anyone in the tribe. We stayed at a different hotel than the rest of the cast. The next day we rehearsed with the tribe and found out that 8 actors had been fired after the evening performance we had watched. The actor playing Woof was nowhere to be found, so I was rehearsing Woof once again. He showed up when we got to the movie scene and staggered on stage. He told me to go back to the tribe where I belonged and since the stage man-ager and the director didn't say anything I went back to the tribe and just sort of tried to fit in somewhere. The rest of the tribe was great and very helpful with all of us who were there as new members. Three days later after several unpleasant situations and 2 1/2 performances in the role of Woof (I had to take over in the second act) I was issued a new contract and given the role of Woof.

My understudy was the man who played the Tourist Lady and would occa-sionally ask if he could play Woof. If the director allowed it, I would sit out and take notes. One time the stage manager and company manager made me go on as the Tourist Lady. I was terrified. After that I made sure I knew every-one's lines and blocking as well as I could. I was asked to play roles with a few minutes notice on many occasions because the managers were confident I knew the lines and blocking. At one performance during a second act I ran off stage from being a paratrooper, ran back on as the drummer boy, ran off and was handed General Grant's costume and ran back on again. Then I was a monk in the strobe light sequence and I also had to sing "What a Piece" that evening without any rehearsal. It kept me on my toes. I also played Claude twice with only a brief run through some of his songs as the audience was fil-ing in. I wasn't terrified by that point, but I always felt more comfortable play-ing Woof.

I grew up in NYC, which despite the "Hair" controversy was a very hip place. I was very unaffected by controversy until going on the road. Then the "shit hit the fan" and I was thoroughly shocked by it. We had a bomb threat and were escorted out of town in Augusta Georgia, by a squad of police cars in the middle of the night. Someone tried to bring a rifle into a performance in Atlanta. Georgia, as lovely as it is, is not some place I care to visit again.

Our tour was famous for being denied a permit to perform in Nashville. My mother tracked me down after reading about it in the NY papers and suggested I might want to leave the show. She would look for any excuse. I went to festivals and peace rallies with the NY cast because Sally and I were such close friends. They were great learning experiences. I once got a $3.00 fine for smoking a joint on the street in Ann Arbor, Michigan.

One of my favorite stories happened in Oakland, California at the Paramount Theater. The Paramount Theatre was a beautiful old movie palace that was refurbished into a playhouse. Our Crissy, Suki Vasquez, was pissed at the management and claimed to have laryngitis right before the show. When none of the women knew the whole song, "Frank Mills," they asked me to absorb her songs and lines into the role of Woof.

We had a huge gay audience being so close to San Francisco. No one in the cast knew what was going on—since being a last minute change, no announcement had been made. The audience not knowing the show very well didn't realize I was doing her lines or her harmony in the song "Air." When I got the words "I met a boy called Frank Mills" out of my mouth, the audience went wild and started clapping. At the end of the number I got a standing ovation. It was great playing Woof in a place where there was such a huge gay turn out. I was getting encouragement from the audience for the whole performance and had a terrific night all around. Bo Golden (Robert Golden) had tried to upstage me during my opening monologue, but the audience was with me. It turned it right around on him and we came up with great ad-libs.

Gosh, there are just so many memories both good and bad, but I suppose the fondest is actually getting to preach the "Hair" message of peace and love and equality in which I firmly believed—and getting to do that preaching in every state but Alaska.

Besides making me believe I could get the peace and love point across to the whole world, the experience of "Hair" made me a better person all around. I went from a skinny, frightened teenager to a more confident adult. I learned I was attractive, had some talent and I learned to love and to not be afraid of having my personal space invaded. I also learned how to let people know when

I didn't want my personal space invaded in a kinder and gentler manner. I also learned how to role a terrific joint. (Auntie Mame says, "Knowledge is power").

There were hundreds of special moments being in "Hair." Like getting told I had the job. Being told by Sally Eaton and Ron Dyson that I was a wonderful Woof. Memories of the great audience responses and of young people telling us how seeing our production of "Hair" had changed their lives. Doing awful local morning talk shows with Ruta Lee, who was touring in "Everyone Loves Opal." Doing a cerebral palsy telethon in Kansas City, Missouri and being thanked by Paul James on national TV. The whole cast band and crew taking over a fun house on a pier in Wildwood, NJ between shows. We also got to meet Bruce Springsteen in Wildwood.

When "Hair" closed on Broadway on July 1, 1972, I was there. I was sitting in the Balcony in front of Jim Rado, wondering how I got a better seat than he did. Wow! Considering it contained the largest tribe to grace any stage ever it was amazing. People showed up, were given costumes and sent out to do "Hair" from memory with a tribe that had been working together for quite awhile. The stage barely contained them all. The Aquarius circle had no way to open up when the cue came. It was a boisterous performance that went from high to low with the beginning and ending of each musical number. I remember the gong sounding at the end of Aquarius and bursting into tears, thinking I would never see that ritual ever again except in my head. Each number went the same way—a glorious high as it started and tears when it ended.

After "Hair," I fell in love and moved to L.A. I did a television commercial for Two Guys (a crappy store) and some movie extra work in "Looking for Mr. Goodbar" and "Rollercoaster." I fell out of love and moved back to NY and auditioned for lots of stuff before going into box office management, which I had learned in school. I fell in love again and am still in love 24 years later. I currently live in Connecticut with my partner and I'm a support counselor for people who are mentally challenged. I love my work and have taken some of my consumers to see productions of "Hair." I have recreated Tom's staging for a national tour of "Hair" produced by Pink Lace Productions and was a consultant on another production in Pennsylvania. I still have all of my own hair and actually now have some on my back and in my ears (gross)! Most of it is still brown too!

Love & Peace & Best Wishes to you and your loved ones ~ Robert P. Camuto (Formally Peter Roberts because my parents didn't want anyone to know I was in "Hair")

Bob Corff

Bob Corff played the role of Claude in the Los Angeles cast of *"Hair."* Bob went on to star in many other Broadway shows and appeared in the film *Gas-s-s.* Bob is a well-known vocal coach in Hollywood and his clients include a long list of Hollywood stars.

ROBERT CORFF Scorpio, From Redding PA.; a charter member of the Shakespeare Society of America. Believes we don't need drugs—"A natural high can be found." *~ From the Los Angeles HAIR program.*

A chat session with Bob ~

On my first day in January of 1969, I had seen a little rehearsal but I really wasn't even ready to go into one number. I came to the theatre that night and while I was backstage, Gerry Ragni grabbed me and said, "Let's do the nude scene."

I stammered and said, "But, but, I don't know what to do."

Gerry said, "What do you have to know? You take off your clothes."

So the first thing I ever did in Equity and got paid for was I just walked straight out there and stood naked. Nothing else—that was my first Equity experience. I went on and then I went off.

When I first got into the show, before I took over as Claude, I was tribe. And so when my mother came to see the show—I had a few little parts and I wanted to do the nude scene. So I did the nude scene and when the show was over I said, "Mom, what did you think?"

She said with disgust on her face, "You were the first out there."

I thought it was a funny thing to say. I was aching to get to her. I was thinking, "Does this upset you? Good!"

Talking about the sexuality that was going on in those days, if you talk about it through the filter of today, you sound like a sick, crazed, demented person—someone who has no taste, a low class person. I mean, how could you do it with so many people? What's wrong with you? Don't you care about relationships? It was a totally different time with a different vision. I think those of us who grew up in that time, had the greatest opportunity for sex in the history of the world. Unless you were a king, you could probably get more sex then, than any other time in history—at least with that many different partners.

"Hair," gave people an opportunity. This is really an area that I usually don't talk about, as it's not politically correct or good for business, but I tried everything. And I'm glad I did because now I know what I like and there's no mystery for me. There's no thinking that maybe I am really attracted to men. No, I know I'm not. But it was all okay then, it was not like you're bad. I think it was a wonderful opportunity to be able to not feel guilty about experimenting, to find what you like.

Today, it's really scary. Back then sexuality was just a delicious experience. There was no down side to it. Today, you look at some beautiful girl and think; I could have a horrible death from this. It sort of takes away from the tastiness of it all.

The thing I want to communicate is that if you can see that it was a different time, it was really a beautiful time. It wasn't like—bad girls could have it. It was like, good girls could have it and good boys could. It was just as good and spontaneous as it could be—with none of the dark, heavy, things that can come with it. And you could still turn out to be good person and end up happily married as I am. I don't feel like I missed anything. It's good, it was good to be able to play and enjoy it. Today there are so many rules. You can't do that; women have to give you permission. It's like we were all giving each other permission. It wasn't like a big wrestling match. I don't know if it's ever going to be like that again. I hope it could be again, but I doubt it.

The sixties were an interesting time in history, as were the twenties. There have been some times that were not so interesting. But this was like a real moment of things coming together, an awakening of sorts. I look back on it now and I mean I enjoyed it but I didn't appreciate the sexual freedom. I just assumed that's the way it was and it would always be like that. Who would have ever thought there'd be AIDS? When you're young you don't think you're going to get older and you don't think anything's going to change.

I remember the Moratorium Peace March in Washington DC. It was November 15th 1969 and I had been in the show for about 11 months. They took a few people from each tribe, so Ben Vereen and I represented the Los Angeles cast. Somehow June Lockhart got to go along with us, I don't remember exactly how, but we were together then and so we thought this will be great.

We all met in Chicago and picked up all the San Francisco people, Chicago people and members from other places as well. Then we went on to Washington DC. I was lucky, because I was with June and we stayed in some really nice places. And she was able to work it so we could get around these crowds. But some of the people, Ted Rado was one of them, were tear-gassed. So some of the kids in the cast were actually in the midst of it. I was lucky to have missed the tear gas and only have beautiful memories of our time there for peace and send a message to stop the war.

What happened is at night; there were so many people in town that the kids from all over the country were sleeping in gymnasiums of colleges and high schools everywhere. And they took us from "Hair," to each one of these gymnasiums where there were thousands of people, lying on the floor. And they asked if I would introduce June to them.

That was the first time I ever did an introduction and I just said something like, "I want to introduce to you somebody who we all know and love, and somebody who's here to march for peace with us. Lassie's mother, please welcome June Lockhart."

Well people stood, they cheered, they stomped, because it was the mother who was saying, "It's okay what you're doing." Because our mothers were not saying that, right. We went to three or four different schools that night and it was the same reaction every time. It was like a thunderous five or ten minute ovation for her. And then she would give a little talk and they would just go crazy.

The next day, we sang, "Let the Sunshine In" for people as far as you could see in any direction. We were on the stage and you know the scene in the movie Forrest Gump, well that was the view.

It's nice to be around people who want to create a positive change in the world. "Hair" was all about that. Now, when I watch a news show or a documentary and I see somebody whose making a difference, it just reminds me of my original impulse. I think everybody, if you really scratch deep enough; we all really have that impulse. When I think of race relations and all that stuff, I thought it was all going to be taken care of. There was so much hope.

I'm always fascinated by people who will say, "That's a bad show, I hate that show." Then you say, "Did you see that show?" Then they say, "No and I won't." But they don't really know if they like it or not. If they saw the show and hated it, at least I could respect their opinion about that show.

One night we were doing the show and all of a sudden, we started to smell something pretty intense. Finally, the stage manager had to make an announcement, "We have to clear the theatre, there's been a stink bomb." So the show stopped and we all went out into the parking lot of the Aquarius Theatre. It was interesting because the show was already going and then all the characters got to interact with the people who were watching it. We spent about 45 minutes talking to the people and then they announced the theatre had been cleared. So we all went back in and started the show up again from that place on. It actually sort of expanded the experience of the show.

About two weeks later, I'm up doing a change with my dresser, Earl Scott. And Ben Vereen comes running by the dressing room and says, "There's a bomb, let's go."

Earl and I figured, well it's a stink bomb and we're continuing with the change. All of a sudden, we hear Ben running back up the steps and he says, "There's a BOMB, let's go!"

And we went, "You mean a bomb, bomb?"

Ben says, "Yes, a BOMB, BOMB!"

Then you should have seen three people flying down the steps!

One of the exciting things was when you'd leave at night; there'd be all these lines of people outside the door just waiting to talk, or whatever else they wanted to do. That was sort of the rock star part of it—it was nice. I don't know what it was like on the road, but in a big town like L.A. you took advantage of all the good things that were there.

There were always these little things going on. You know, Claude was in love with Sheila; Sheila was in love with Berger and Jeanie's in love with Claude. And there were always those little things going on, "in the cast too."

Jim and Gerry were in the show then. I related more to Gerry because I'm more of the Claude type. So Jim, the two of us were sort of like, too much alike. Gerry was an amazing Berger. His energy, the way he crawled over the seats and swung on the rope over the audience, was like Tarzan. Gerry, I thought was one of the greatest experiences I ever had. To me, he was the neatest guy I ever saw. He was talented, beautiful and homely. He was everything.

There was a lot of creativity then. Sometimes that was what would get Gerry in trouble. He'd say things like, "You know this scene, let's do it different tonight." He never stopped being creative. He would often change, which was very upsetting to the production. Because hey, you've got a show that works, you've got a cast, a lot of people who work here. You can't all of a sudden—not do that scene like that anymore.

I remember one time that was probably the first time I was ever hypnotized. Gerry said, "Just lie down. You don't need your voice. You don't need your hair. You don't need your talent." And he slowly took away everything. We weren't even high, but it was like I went to another plane. Because you know, you're working so hard to be something. Then he took away all things I thought I needed to be. He was an amazing person and he created an amazing peace.

And he was so strong. He had his young son there one time and they played this game for about an hour. The kid would run as fast as he could from the back of the stage, all the way out to the front and dive like Superman. Way too far for any child to do and Gerry would catch him. Then he'd run back and do it again. My arms got sore just watching. He was an amazingly strong man.

He once said to me, "The way you should do the show every night, is to give so much of yourself, that when you go home, you just fall in your bed and fall to sleep. You've worked so hard, that you just have to sleep."

And I thought, "Wow, that's how much I need to give."

I'd admired both Jim and Gerry. Jimmy Rado is a wonderful singer. He did some wonderful plays before this show. I think Jim and Gerry were at least ten years older than I was. You could ask them about anything. Ask them about the most intimate thing, but you just had the feeling you shouldn't ask them how old they were! They must have been 30 or so, but they were playing characters who were 18.

I remember one time after being in the show for close to eleven months; somebody asked me, "Do you want to go horseback riding?" I started to say sure and then I realized I had thought about doing something that Claude might not have done. I'd gotten so much into that part that I wasn't doing anything the character wouldn't do. I started thinking, "Wait a minute, I'm not Claude so maybe I can go horseback riding."

I never got high on the stage; I was too busy doing other things. One night it was my birthday and a bunch of people thought it would really be wonderful as a gift, to hold me down and blow hash into my face. So, I got up and I did the show.

What was interesting to me is I'd start to sing something and then all of a sudden my mind would go off. I'd think, "I just sang something. Wow, I never thought about that before." I'd just get lost in that line, then all of a sudden I'd wake up and go, "Oh my God we're in the next scene, how'd I get here?" Because your mind would just trip on something. So I'd try and concentrate to stay there, then I'd go, "Wow I never saw that thing before, look at that. Oh, wait, I'm talking." It was exhausting and frightening to have to concentrate so hard to stay on track.

Another time while doing the show as Claude, a good friend of mine showed up at the theatre. This man was an unbelievable talent, but also became a drug casualty. This was a guy who took too many drugs and eventually wiped himself out.

So, I'm doing Claude and he is on acid or something. He just walks in, because he'd been to so many theatres that he walked in with kind of authority and they just let him in. So he's sitting down next to the stage manager, just sitting in a chair. And the show is starting; everybody's touching and moving their arms for "Aquarius." Now he's got a hat on and he walks out on the stage. He touched somebody and they just lift their arms and he just walks right up. He sees me sitting in the center of the stage, walks up to me, whispers and waves in my face, "Hey Bob it's me."

I'm stunned and thinking, "Oh my God, what is this?"

Everybody's thinking this and somebody finally grabbed him and took him off. People are saying, "What the hell was that?" I just said, "A friend of mine, sorry." These are moments that couldn't have happened anyplace else.

I just feel so fortunate to have done "Hair," as well as Jesus Christ Superstar and Grease. They were fun shows, uplifting and about something. Well, except for Grease, but it was fun. It was a good time to be alive.

Bob

---

30 years before the Rent phenomena, people started lining up for tickets to "Hair" at 4am.

Charlotte Crossley

Charlotte Crossley was a member of the original Chicago Company of *"Hair"* and was also a member of the national touring productions of *"Hair."*

CHARLOTTE CROSSLEY (Tribe) Charlotte Crossley sees the Tribe as "real together people who vibrate on each other and life itself." She counts *Three Penny Opera* and *West Side Story* among her musical experiences, although she claims no formal dramatic training. Born under the sign of Taurus, she's a native of Chicago and a June 1969 graduate of South Shore High School. During lulls in her theatrical career she's been employed as a hospital aide and a clerk. ~ *From the October 1969 HAIR Playbill for the Shubert Theatre in Chicago.*

Charlotte raps about Hair ~

I was in the Original Chicago cast and both Tom O'Horgan and Julie Arenal were there to help open that show. It was very exciting and intense! There were a lot of barriers broken. You had kids fresh out of High School (me) and seasoned stage folk, some college theatre folk (a lot of them). It was 1969 and for many, this was their first legitimate show.

I went to a cattle call in downtown Chicago, at the suggestion of the director I was under at the South Shore Jewish Community Center. We had just finished Three Penny Opera, West Side Story and a bunch of musical reviews. I first auditioned just before Graduation and I got the call back in August. I went all the way to the end.

My father was so through with me! I had gotten accepted to Southern Illinois University in Carbondale, Illinois, I had an Illinois State Grant and another grant to go down there. The last day of call backs he basically cursed me out and said "He hoped I wouldn't get in the show and that I would take my a** down to Carbondale at the end of the Week!"

I prayed and prayed I would get the show and God blessed me and I GOT IT!!! I was able to leave home and have a life of my own. God had a plan and "Hair" was my way out. It was the Way out for a lot of us, coast to coast. It made me grow up and made me commit to a career in show biz. I did the show in Chicago and then got traded to Las Vegas. Those kids were basically from the Hawaii Company.

Everyone had a common experience and that was one of becoming free in areas of relating and experiencing life. We were all at the vortex of the hippie movement and were often criticized at being commercial and not really living the "so called-hippie life." Some of us were the Mr. Natural Types and some were that wild oat and hickory nuts type! We had it good. We had youth, and beauty and money. We had all of the pot we could smoke and all of the psyche-delics we could possibly trip off of. Talk about; My Body is Walking in Space! It is a miracle of God that we are still here!

We could do what we wanted and be whoever we wanted to be. We had strong political opinions and the War was a bad thing. Ironically, that song at the beginning of the 2nd act (the victorola playing White Cliffs of Dover) was a WWII song. That went into the Electric Blues.

I really loved Gerry Ragni. I really was sad to know he had passed and had been so sick. He never looked sick to me. He was always so pumped up and buff. He was the ultimate Berger, He WAS BERGER!

I loved working with Tom O'Horgan. I completely surrendered to the pro-cess, but some people didn't do that. It was hard for them. Tiny Reed was one of them. She took a long time and there were a lot of tears. She was very reserved and tried to play it off. I guess the only thing that mattered was she could sing her but off, was a soprano and sang all of that high stuff. I had to sing White Boys with her in that Supremes dress. Sometimes she was fun to work with and other times she was not.

That was another thing—the beads, flowers, freedom-happiness trip. Some folks could not get with that and working with them was a drag! There was also competition and that seemed weird to me. Especially in NYC, the tribe there was so hard and heartless (Easy to Be Hard). I guess they started out all flowery and sweet, and that gave way to the hardness of life there.

The West Coast and Midwest tribes were so idealistic. Tom and Julie were purposeful to see that we retained some form of idealism while doing the show. That was an essential element. Gerry and Jim were very present in our company and helped us focus. Other people were always trying to suck up to them. They liked me right off and thought I was funny. Galt was always so sweet. He is a visionary musically. He was present to see that the music was true to the rock element and all of the other intricate styles of music that the score held.

God Bless you! ~ Love, Charlo

Over 10,000,000 people have seen hair and Over 5 million cast albums have sold worldwide.
~ From the July 1971 "Hair" press kit.

Walter Michael Harris

Walter Michael Harris was a member of the original Broadway cast of *"Hair."* He played Woof and can be heard on the original Broadway cast recording singing *"What a Piece of Work is Man"* among others.

WALTER MICHAEL HARRIS ~ Born May 7, 1951. Presently living in Margaretville, New York. Hobbies?...Composing and creating new music and musical instruments...and then some. Seven first years in Bronxville, New York...six then in Clearwater, Florida; last three in NYC....traumatic experiences throughout. ~ *From the original Broadway HAIR program.*

Here Goes ~

I was 16 years old in 1968. At that age I was only beginning to develop political awareness. My older brother, George (a.k.a. *Hibiscus*) was ahead of me in that respect. He is the young hippie in the famous "flower power" photo, gently placing flowers down the gun barrels of army soldiers at the Pentagon demonstration in 1967. My association with "HAIR" brought my first real exposure to many of the issues of the day: the war in Vietnam, the civil rights movement, Black Power, women's rights, the youth culture (hippies, Yippies, Diggers, etc.) and the early environmental movement.

"HAIR" addressed current issues during a period of social chemistry that was immediate and volatile (Martin Luther King was shot just weeks before we opened). This supercharged environment made "HAIR's" message highly relevant to the moment. It's impossible these days to understand how passionate young people were about changing the world. Broadway musicals of the time like "Cabaret," "Man of La Mancha" and "Fiddler On The Roof" were all excellent shows and (like "HAIR") addressed serious social problems, albeit in a historical context. But only "HAIR" had the impact of headline news. During the Broadway run of "HAIR," history was being made all around us and was being reflected—no, *amplified*—back at the audience through the show. The authors could even change lines and references depending on what had been in the newspapers that morning (and often did!).

"HAIR's" rant against the warmongering U.S. government was easy for young people to embrace. Every night on the evening news we saw live, bloody battle footage from Vietnam covered by journalists who still had their integrity, unlike coverage of the early 1990s Gulf War, which was packaged and presented for consumption by the spinmasters in Washington, with the media's assent—or the recent Iraq war in which reporters were "embedded" (emphasis on "bedded") with the military. The assassinations of Martin Luther King and Robert Kennedy had a big impact on us coming as they did early in the run. They served to amplify "HAIR's" message and fuel our performances.

Then in my teens, on a personal level, I was very much in favor of human beings learning to live together in peace and harmony. The ideal of "free love"—being free to love anyone, anywhere, any time, any way—was seen by the youth culture as a social and political ideal. "Free love" had great appeal to me (and to youth around the world), being at the age where we were beginning to sort ourselves out, socially and sexually. I came from a family of theater artists who understood. My older brother's gay-ness was never an issue for my parents or siblings.

Before "HAIR" I was primarily involved in the off-off-Broadway theater movement in New York, which was chock full of young artists with a message about the culture. As a teen I was very drawn to rock and roll music and the social commentary of Bob Dylan. As an artist I saw myself as having a role to play in the enlightenment of society through theater and music. During and after "HAIR" I felt obligated to be more proactive against "the establishment" through changing my lifestyle. In less than I year I came to believe that staying in the show (as a performer) was hypocritical, because I needed to get out and start living the hippie life as my older brother Hibiscus was.

I knew director Tom O'Horgan years before "HAIR" because we were both working extensively in off-off-Broadway, particularly at La MaMa Experimental Theater Club in Greenwich Village. I was acting in a production of Paul Foster's "The Madonna In The Orchard" that Tom directed for La MaMa in 1965 or 1966. That production traveled to the Eugene O'Neill conference in Connecticut during its inaugural year. It was staged in classic O'Horgan style, influenced by his wild "kinetic sculpture" ideas and reflective of his infamous "happenings," where anything could happen—and did.

I first learned about "HAIR" from my friend Michael McClanathan (Arlo Guthrie's sidekick in the movie "Alice's Restaurant"), who gave me the off-Broadway "HAIR" album in late 1967. When he landed an audition for the Broadway remount, I agreed to be his accompanist. Tom O'Horgan invited me to audition as well. The rest, I guess, is history. Tom knew my work and wanted me in the show. I was happy to have an opportunity to work with

Tom again, especially on Broadway, where I knew he was eager to shake things up.

In the original Broadway company I played a tribe member named "Charlie," (later renamed "Walter"), understudied "Woof," and had the good fortune to play the role a dozen times during "HAIR's" first year. One of my favorite experiences that first year was "subbing" on drums for Idris Muhammad (then Leo Morris) when he was too ill to play. What a thrill it was playing Galt MacDermot's awesome score alongside greats like bass player Jimmy Lewis and trumpeter Don Leight! I also performed in "HAIR's" 20th anniversary concert at the United Nations and produced a 25th anniversary concert at Pilgrim Center for the Arts, Seattle, Washington.

I first met Gerry and Jim and Galt at my second (and last) audition. I believe it was at the Waldorf-Astoria. I memorized "Dead End" from the off-Broadway album and used it for my singing audition. I remember the guys being impressed that I used an actual "HAIR" song for my audition (apparently few, if any, others did). Gerry Ragni went out of his way during rehearsals to make sure that I had some special bit of business in the show. That's how I got the duet with Ronnie Dyson, "What A Piece of Work Is Man."

Another Gerry moment was during the 20th anniversary concert, "HAIR for the Next Generation" at the United Nations in May 1988. During rehearsal of the song "HAIR," Gerry and I spontaneously launched into a square dance! It was fun, goofy, typical Gerry, and we kept it in for the evening performance. I'll always remember it as the last personal moment I had with that big overgrown kid who was the heart and soul of Berger and muse of "HAIR."

"HAIR" has affected many peoples' lives. I've heard countless testimonials from people about how "HAIR" transformed their lives when it played their town. For hundreds of thousands of young Americans, touring companies of "HAIR" brought political awareness and news of the youth culture movement to small towns and college campuses all across the country. For many, it was a wake-up call. As "the groovy revolution" espoused by "HAIR" became an international phenomenon, a permanent family was created that now communicates via the Internet.

Some of the most profound "HAIR" stories I've heard are those expressed so eloquently by our "cyber-tribe," especially young people in high school and college productions. Their experiences and stories prove the dynamic power of "HAIR" as a theater and the relevance of its message today.

In the course of producing and presenting two concert versions of "HAIR" in Seattle, I discovered how relevant the message of "HAIR" is for audiences of the 1990's. Both concerts generated a lot of excitement and played to sold-out houses of every age, color and sexual orientation. Both concerts generated that "magic" spirit of "HAIR," which is love and the hopefulness of youth. The intense interest in these concerts prove that "harmony and understanding, sympathy and trust abounding" are not merely trite truisms of 33 years ago, but qualities that our hearts and souls yearn for, never more than now. Our casts were primarily performers in their late teens and twenties, who were born long after the last Human Be-In and long after the civil rights movement and Vietnam had faded from the headlines. Because these young people were able to tap the power of "HAIR," because they "got it" and were transformed by it, is reason enough to continue producing and promoting "HAIR" in every format.

Special memories from my year with "HAIR" on Broadway include—eluding the night guards in order to spend the night in the Biltmore "on vigil" with three of my castmates in order to "purify" the theater and ourselves in preparation for opening night—playing "Woof" to Steve Curry's "Berger"—singing "What A Piece of Work Is Man" with Ronnie Dyson and occasionally with Melba Moore—slipping off the stage into Salvador Dali's lap—chatting backstage with Janis Joplin and Sidney Poitier—a "lost weekend" on Fire island with the company—performing on the Ed Sullivan and Johnny Carson shows—recording the Broadway cast album—performing at Madison Square Garden—my friendship with Michael Butler—and being invited by the band to play drums at "HAIR's" first anniversary show at the Wollman Skating Rink in Central Park after I had left the show. There are sad memories as well. A tragic hotel fire in New York claimed the life of Lamont Washington (Hud), early in the run. This was an enormous tragedy because Lamont was a gifted all-around performer in his twenties. "HAIR" would have certainly launched his career.

One of my fondest memories happened 25 years later. At one of our "HAIR" concerts in Seattle, my then 16-year-old daughter, Kristin Green, took it upon herself to lead the cast in a version of the nude scene. Who was I to object? She was the same age I was when challenged by Tom O'Horgan to bare all for a Broadway audience. By challenging herself and then the cast, Kristin made me very proud.

After leaving "HAIR" I embarked on a 13-year odyssey of self-discovery across the country and through many adventures. The star of destiny that

"HAIR" encouraged me to follow eventually led me to Seattle, where I met my wife, Patricia Mansfield Harris. Life since has never been better! We are perfectly matched. We share a deep love of the American Tribal Love-Rock Musical. When she was a girl, Patty used to play the "HAIR" album incessantly and *LOUD*, driving her mother crazy.

I currently serve as artistic director of a small professional arts center in Seattle, ArtsWest Playhouse and Gallery (www.artswest.org), and play occasionally in local rock bands with my fifty-something friends. I do a lot of musical volunteer work, leading sing-alongs in senior centers, hospitals and for children.

I joined "HAIR" as an actor and left as a hippie. "HAIR" expanded my sense of mission, opened my eyes to the multi-layered universe and the political world, allowed me to challenge myself and gave me the courage to leave New York and follow my star of destiny. The central messages of "HAIR" are the joy of life, the unity of the human family and the need for people to transcend whatever keeps them apart. I will always believe that these are goals worthy of struggle and sacrifice.

WMH

(Walter Michael Harris)
Seattle, Washington

Jolie Kanat

Jolie Kanat played Crissy in the original San Francisco Company of "Hair."

JOLIE KANAT (Crissy) has performed as a member of a madrigal singing group and made solo appearances with a large choir in Berkeley. Besides being an accomplished singer, she has also performed as a primitive and modern dance soloist.

~ From the September 1969 Performing Arts magazine for the American Conservatory Theatre in San Francisco.

Jolie tells a story of how the entire San Francisco cast of HAIR got "fired! ~

As I recall, it was either late 1969 or early 1970. The Vietnam War was still raging. At the same time we were performing every night, sending the message to literally millions of people, from every "Hair" tribe in the country and the world, that the war was a hideous violation of our deepest beliefs and morals. (Actually as I think about this, the story takes on more interesting layers).

We were all screamingly young, as well as ardent in our beliefs about the message of the play. Many of us were not veteran professionals. We had been chosen for not only our talent, but our freshness and energy as well. It was different than, say, performing in Bye Bye Birdie, where the underlying message was not necessarily on the front page of the newspapers daily.

During the first year of the very successful and remarkable (sold out, standing room only, talk-of-the-town) San Francisco run, a general business "moratorium" was called by political leaders of the anti-war movement. All businesses were asked to close for a time in protest of the US bombings in Vietnam and Cambodia. It was not a small issue—especially in the San Francisco area, where the anti-war movement had a stronghold.

In our enthusiasm for this anti-war effort, the entire cast (or most of us) decided to stop working in the play for…I don't remember how long…a night? A week? We were sure the director, stage managers, writers (Mr. Rado and Mr. Ragni) and producer (Mr. Butler) would support us in our valiant effort to send the message to Washington. Can you see where the layers come in here?

Looking back I can see clearly that we had a contractual obligation to the 1,400 people who had bought tickets each night and that by performing the message that was in the play, our effort against the war could be more powerful than not performing it for the moratorium! Yet at the same time we wanted to send a message that we agreed with the anti-war movement in every way. We were willing to lose money, willing to risk our jobs. But...we didn't really think we were risking our jobs!!

I believe it was on a bus on the way to an anti-war rally with 300,000 people waiting at the Golden Gate polo field, that the entire cast was told by our stage manager that we were all fired.

I still do not know what the point of view of management was at that time, but having owned a business since then, I can imagine the feelings were very mixed.

A show or two was cancelled and our paychecks were docked appropriately. However, we were re-hired shortly thereafter. As I recall, the cast published a full-page explanation in the San Francisco Chronicle for the missed shows.

This story is a perfect example of how there are no absolutes in this life. For example—it would have been right to perform and it would have been right to join the moratorium. It was a time that is hard to describe to anyone who was not there.

I can only imagine the consternation we must have caused Michael and the people running the production. But perhaps they had their own uncertainties to grapple with, too.

Jolie Kanat

Lyle K'ang

Lyle Kekahi K'ang was a member of the Hawaii, Las Vegas and National touring productions of *"Hair."*

LYLE K'ANG (Tribe) A member of the tribe, he also understudies and plays both the lead male roles of Claude and Berger. Lyle was in the United States Air Force in the U.S.A. and Okinawa from 1962-66, where he formed his own singing group called *Emanons*. Lyle plays autoharp and sings the blues. He would like to live somewhere in the Pacific—in his own words "Hawaii has had it." ~ *From the July 1971 Scene magazine for the Royal Alexandra Theatre in Toronto.*

What Lyle remembers about Hair ~

…remember rehearsing in Hawaii?
Kicked off the island with no island theater open to us to call home? We were sad.

…remember October 1969 arriving in Las Vegas as the Pakalolo *"Hair"* tribe? The Hilton International's Theater Royale would be our home for over a year. Unlike other National tribes that had hundreds of fans that were in fact a support group—we had none, at first. Cold dead hands fed the one arm bandits, no smiles for the 'Children of the Rainbow,' just cold robotic humans in the casinos. We now lived with paranoia under the watchful eye of the Las Vegas Police who knew each of us as registered workers assigned to the theater, specifically in Las Vegas. We only had each other for a while and then we remembered to remember why we were there? We were disciples to spread the word of Peace and Love.

…"remember to acknowledge your audience. Look them in the eye, speak to them in the front row and project your voice so it will carry to the back of the theater. And oh…yea, remember all those souls that are too drunk to be in the casino will be given free passes to see the 'nude scene' in *"Hair"*…words spoken by our Stage Manager, a former University of Hawaii teacher.

…and so it was. During the shows 'Be-In,' we got to know 'Hud' and his personality. He was a muscular gigantic man, a former disk jockey in Hawaii. Out of self-defense, he socked one of those intolerant, foul-mouthed, members of a Georgia junket group that found their way into the theater via the casino courtesy tickets one performance night. 'Hud' later was crying and wanted to quit because he said he did not feel like he was practicing what he was preaching. He felt he let us all down and didn't have peace in his heart for that man that had yelled to 'get them dirty niggers away from them white girls on stage' and then proceeded to beat up on 'Hud!' We were a very diverse tribe, card carrying, brand-new actors; White, Filipino, Chinese, Hawaiian, Negro, Japanese, Korean, Portuguese, Hapa-haole and the enviable Poi dog.

The head electrician from the Nevada union, who was running the show said; "Lyle you really want to know about show business?" I said, "Of course!" "Then go on tour, you'll know all there is to know about show business!"

...Mercury and Venus Tours; a whirlwind, of meditation, Yoga and T'ai Chi. Christians protesting, a tornado of fire-bombings, deaths by fire, beer bottles smashed on heads and yes, drug famine...then there were more mountains of cocaine and numerical counts of Quaaludes and the occasional weed...and the tribe sang, 'Aquarius'.

We had a fast track life and watched tribe member after tribe member burnout not knowing the 'secrets.' Mere moments and we were ready, willing and able to search, deep down for more of the good stuff within ourselves to bring to "*Hair.*" We had to all find our longevity. Companion ship with the deserts of Nevada and the various Native Indian tribes; the Hopi, the Oneida and all our Brothers and Sisters from time were important for us. We criss-crossed America; from the Grand Canyon to the 'four corners,' City after City, State after State, down to Florida, up through Canada, back to Hawaii, then on to Alaska and back again across America during the early 70's. Our memorable trip ended in Niles, Chicago, in December, 1972.

It took about seven years to heal upon going 'back to the land.' I was 'Claude' and understudied 'Berger' on the road, but I could not shake the personality that 'Claude' had given me. It was one of the most difficult tasks to find where 'Claude' left off and Lyle began.

"*Hair*" gave an opportunity and provided a vehicle in which to glimpse into that world. A Reality that echoes our past mistakes and forgives our present ways. Ever increasing spirals of energy to use as we will to heal...because of

"*Hair*" I was able to start my journey in understanding eternal Love in passion for Nature and internal Love for being Human!

Peace, Lyle K'ang

Jessica Kluger

Jessica Kluger was a member of the Los Angeles production of "HAIR." Jessica played the role of Crissy.

Thoughts from Jess ~

In June of 1969 I was 18 and met an agent from William Morris while I was singing (illegally) in a Vegas lounge. I had already been a 12-year-old recording artist (Jessie Paul) with Capitol records and had opened for Santana, Three Dog Night, Steppenwolf, Sweetwater and The Grateful Dead. My life had been blessed and success was handed to me. The agent liked me, flew me to L.A., put me in a hotel, and my first audition was "Hair!"

While waiting for my audition, I was staying at the Bel Air Motel. I was raised in L.A. so I could have stayed in the valley with friends, but the agent was footing the bill. So anyway, I would frequent this market for snacks, because I hated to go into a restaurant alone (I survived on trail mix and carrots). One day, this hairy hippie starts to talk to me in Produce. I was pretty lonely—so we chatted. He said he was Charlie, a songwriter and wanted to know if I would come over to sing and jam with him. He said he had a ranch with a lot of friends living with him and he said he had connections.

A few hairs on the back of my neck stood up when he pierced his gaze on me. I continued to listen to him, but I never had any intention of going with him. We walked out to his car, he got his guitar out, and while leaning on his car he played for me. He said he wanted to sleep with me. I found him to be dirty and strange, so I said goodbye and Thank God did not give him my number. I remember this was before Sharon Tate's murder, when hippies were still trusted and considered peaceful beings. After Sharon's death, everything changed in L.A. and you could trust no one.

Shortly after, I got a call back and the second audition was for Teddy Neeley. I was asked to dance and he also asked if I opposed nudity. I replied, "No problem," although my heart was pounding. Later I got the call saying I was hired but it was on the same day my mom called to say that granddad had died—so it was bittersweet. A few weeks later, I was rehearsing for the show of the decade right out of high school.

The show had been in L.A. for two years, so I literally had to learn the show on the sidelines—watching from the floor at the theater. I had some blocking rehearsal with Kay Cole. I parted with the agent, as he wanted to sleep with me—not just once, he wanted to get me an apartment and be my—well you know. I was 18 and he was in his 40's and married—welcome to L.A.!

I remember Janis Joplin coming to the green room with Heather MacRae. Heather had left the show but brother Gar was still in our show. Janis was small and prettier than in photos. She was very insecure about her musical chops—she was a singer from her heart not from school. I found her to be sweet and shy.

After I was in the show a few months, the La Bianco/Tate murders happened, but I still didn't know about Charlie until they connected him 5 or6 months later. When I saw him on the news, I knew who he was right away—he had insane eyes!

We partied at Michael Butler's house constantly. Michael lived high in the Hollywood hills where we could eat and swim anytime—and we did. I met the manager of North Beach Leather (Tony Good) and we fell in love. I had access to going to Hugh Hefner's mansion and partying with Sly and the Family Stone, just to mention a few. My boyfriend had clients who were more famous than anyone in our show!

I remember we were a family. No one was mean or jealous, except after I had been a tribe member for a year and they were letting me play Crissy. All of a sudden, they brought in a girl from the Chicago show and I was devastated. I did get the part later on and also understudied Teda Bracci as Jeannie.

Linda Faust was our Sheila. She fell in love with the bass player, Reinie Press. They have been married 30 years and have been with Neil Diamond all this time. The musical leader and drummer Cubby O'Brien (former Mouseketeer), was a drum student of my dad's. My dad was a big recording drummer in Hollywood when I was growing up.

Irv Kluger is his name, so Cubby and I had a reunion of sorts. Elaine Hill and I worked together in 1984 as backup singers for Englebert Humperdinck! We met up all those years later by coincidence!

Being in "Hair" was the best part of my life. I will never again be in a family of actors like that. I feel lucky to have been a part of its history

Peace and love ~ Jessica

Anita Krpan

Anita Krpan was a member of the National touring cast of *"Hair."*

Some things Anita remembers ~

These two stories are when I was in Mercury tribe in '71 and early '72:

The first one is when we opened in St. Louis (my hometown) in October of '71. Some of the bible belters were trying to keep the show out because of the nudity and because they thought we all would undoubtedly corrupt all of their sweet innocent children. Parents can sometimes be so naive about their own children. Little did they know the nude scene was probably the "cleanest" part of the show!

The show was booked anyway and there were threats of being arrested after the nude scene on opening night. The show was sold out thanks to all the publicity. The fight continued on through to opening night. "Ban the show from our city!" Others preached "Freedom of speech and expression!" The city was electric with anticipation and we were sold out for the entire run because everybody wanted to come and see the nude hippies.

There were police and picketing protesters in front of the American Theatre. Some cast members and I stopped and talked to the protesters, said hello, but didn't debate any show issues. We invited them in to see the show. They were a little taken back by us because they liked us. Well, maybe we wouldn't be condemned to an eternity in hell after all.

Rado, Ragni and Michael Butler flew in for opening night. Rado and Ragni came on stage and performed most of the show with us. All three of them did the nude scene with us! None of us got arrested and we went on to have a successful run. We were booked back for a couple more weeks in December!

The second story was from early 1972 in Atlanta, the New York of the South. We had been anticipating potential problems in Birmingham with all the racial unrest and civil rights problems, but we thought Atlanta would welcome us with open arms and open minds. The opening night show went smoothly into Act II. The audience was warming up and starting to finally let us know they were enjoying the show by being more vocal, laughing and applauding. We were all doing the slow motion walk during the song "Walking in Space," and just as someone was singing, "on a rocket to the fourth dimension," there was an explosion in one of the side balconies. We heard the collective gasp of the crowd. Most thought it was great pyrotechnics and was part of the show. But not the people in the balcony who were putting out the fire with their coats! Fire bombed in Atlanta, who would have thought?

We then traveled on to Birmingham, where all races, colors, nationalities, creeds, ages, sizes, shapes and sexual preferences welcomed us with open arms.

Anita

Ted Lange

Ted Lange was a member of the Broadway, Las Vegas and National touring casts of *"Hair."* He played the roles of Hud and Berger.

TED LANGE (Hud) Played "Henry VI" at the Colorado Shakespeare Festival in Boulder and *"Romeo"* with the New Shakespeare Company in San Francisco. He was in the San Francisco Company of *Big Time Buck White*, and directed *The Iron Hand of Nat Turner* at the Watts Writer's Workshop. Ted also taught at the Malcom X Center in Watts. ~ *From the HAIR Playbill on Broadway, August 1971.*

Some stories from Ted ~

Before getting involved with "Hair" I was a Shakespearean actor. We had started a Shakespeare company up in San Francisco called the New Shakespeare Company. I played Romeo in Romeo and Juliet in 1967 and in 1968 I went to the Shakespeare Festival in Colorado and played King Henry the Sixth in King Henry the Sixth Part II. Then I came back to San Francisco and got into a musical play called "Big Time Buck White."

While in that play one of the actors left to join the San Francisco Company of "Hair." His name was Charles Weldon. Through him, another guy named Phillip Michael Thomas and a girl named Jeannie Wood, I was introduced to "Hair." So I would go see the play as often as I could.

Then I went to LA with "Big Time Buck White," and some people from "Hair" in LA came to see the show. That was my entry into "Hair," with the LA cast. But I was already familiar with the play.

I thought "Hair" in San Francisco was a really good play. But then I saw it one time in LA with Ben Vereen as Berger, Frankie Karl as Hud, Gloria Jones as Sheila and Teddy Neeley as Claude. The people in San Francisco were good actors, but those people in LA had greatness. And when I saw all of them on stage, I understood the power of the play. Because they weren't good, they were great.

I joined the show in Vegas and I had 2 weeks to get my shit together. For the first couple of days I'm stage learning the songs. At the end of the first week, they put together who they felt was the cast for the tour. So the next week, they're firing people who aren't going to be in the show, others are leaving, and they put together the show.

Bob Cole, Frankie Karl and I were the Huds. I was the third backup and I knew that wasn't enough and I'd better get something else. So I went to management and said, "Let me do the young recruit." They said okay because they let everybody do whatever because they were always looking for backups.

I didn't even know the play, but I learned the young recruit. What I noticed after watching about three performances before I did it, was that they basically hit certain points and then they'd do their own little thing—whatever their own little thing was. If they could do a Russian accent, they'd do the young recruit with a Russian accent. If you were more of a dancer, you'd dance into the young recruit. Whatever their thing was, they'd do the lines, but put their own slant on it.

So I did this Black Panther, very street hip, young recruit. I had a little black walk, I came out and sat down, with attitude, you know. It went over like that; Bing, bang, boom! So when they put together the first tour, they put me in as the young recruit and James Brown. Then I had two things besides third Hud understudy.

So my big deal was the young recruit, not for playing Hud. I had a good Hud, but that was not my reputation. When I went into Vegas, it became very obvious to me you had to develop something special. They said, "Everyone can't go on the tour, so we're going to cut people. We're gonna take the best Berger and the best backup Berger. We're gonna take the best Hud and the best backup Hud and so on."

So after Vegas that's how we went out on the road. We had Patty Keene, Greg Karliss, Doug Rowell and I think Richard Baskin was there. He didn't go on tour with us but he was in the Vegas show. He worked with Barbara Streisand and they became an item. Richard was like 6' 3" and 250lbs, and he did Berger. In the scene where Berger jumps off the tower into everyone's arms, no one wanted to be there! But everyone one had to catch him cause he was so big man! And I mean he was fearless! I mean, he didn't say, "Will you catch me?" I was more like, "Catch me!!" Richard Baskin was a big deal in Vegas, because he was heir to Baskin Robbins.

Then we go to Indianapolis Indiana, the heart of the Midwest and we've now got a bond together. Some people are from Hawaii, from LA, some people from other tours; we're all here together to make the first national tour of "Hair." And we ran in Indianapolis for a month or more.

The thing I didn't like about "Hair" was that it was undisciplined. I came from the Theatre, with discipline, vocal warm-ups, body warm-ups and after about three months with "Hair" I stopped doing that myself. People were getting high onstage. There's scene in the show where they pass out joints and sometimes (not all the time) they were real joints.

We picked up one girl named Chopper, Helen Lowe. Helen Lowe was singing backup for Tina Turner in Vegas. So she left Tina to join our show. She also had a record under the name of Little Helen. So she came from the black world of rock and roll, and rhythm and blues. I came from theatre, Susan Allanson came from folk singing, we're all from all over the map, bonding in Indianapolis Indiana.

On the last day, a matinee, a girlfriend of one of the guys in the band, was standing by the stage. This girl was a stunningly beautiful blonde, in leathers, all clothes that she had made. She later became a costumer and won an Emmy. She was standing there with a palm full of pills, giving each person a pill as they came on stage.

So as I come on stage she says, "Do you want some speed?" I said, "No, no, I don't do drugs." She say's, "It's a matinee, it'll keep you up." I said, "No, you know I don't do drugs." So I go on and do my thing.

Now as the audience comes in we give them daisies, talk to them about love, peace, getting out of Vietnam, how are you doing and so on, for about 15 or 20 minutes before the show even starts. Then you hear the chimes and wherever you were you'd stop and go into slow motion. You'd turn towards the stage in slow motion, start climbing over the seats and the audience, as you made your way towards the stage—which is not in the script. Then you would hear the theme of Aquarius and Claude would burn his draft card, which was his driver's license. He'd burn the card, they'd pick up the urn and they'd walk off. Then whoever sang Aquarius would start singing, "When the moon is in the seventh house."

Now were doing this, we're in slow motion, walking towards the stage. And as were walking towards the stage we hear, "When the moon, agghhhh…. and the person starts crying. The guy who's singing the song started tripping. Turns out, those pills were acid, not speed. Now they all knew it was acid. Because I didn't do drugs they thought maybe I'd do speed. So what some of the leads and the cast decided was that they were going to have a communal, bonding experience on stage, where everybody dropped acid. There were five of us who didn't do it, because five of us were adamant about not doing any kind of drugs.

So, when this guy started tripping, someone else pushed him aside and continued singing the song. But then this other person started tripping. It was like popcorn all over the stage with people hitting their high, one after the other. We continued with the show, but everything was slower. The leads were fine because they had done it before—it was their idea, they didn't have a problem. They could maintain, they could focus, but the others were staring up at the lights, didn't remember their lines, or tripping on something else. One of those people was a girl named Helen Lowe, Chopper. She lost it. So rather than the stage manager assigning her bits and lines to others, the cast was doing it. Because the cast knew what was going on. Happening on stage, in the moment. If a line was missed, someone else picked it up.

The management found out what happened and they called Helen into the office. We were all going out to a between the shows dinner. She meets us at this restaurant in tears. We said, "Are you still high?" She said, "No, I'm not crying about that." We said, "Then what are you crying for?"

She said, "I got fired." We said, "Why'd they fire you?" She said, "They fired me for dropping acid on stage." "We'll everybody dropped acid on stage. They can't fire you without firing the whole cast." She said, "No, they fired me because I couldn't handle it."

So after dinner, Greg, Patty Keene and all those guys go back to the management saying, "You have to reinstate her because we all did it." They said, "Fuck you. She dropped acid, she couldn't handle it, and she's out of the show and on the next plane back to LA." We said, "Oh come on, give her a second chance." They said, "No, she's out of here."

So, all the cast got together in one of the dressing rooms. The situation was, they weren't going to rehire her, they were going to send her back to LA, and she only did what everybody else did. Everybody dropped acid and not everybody handled it well. We didn't think this was fair, so we opted to strike. And the smart thing we did was to put everybody in the chorus dressing room—because in a strike, someone's going to give in. So we all sat, all the leads, the cast, all in costume.

Now, it's the last night in Indianapolis, sold out, packed to the rafters. They say, "Okay, everybody on stage," and no one went on stage. The stage manager comes and says, "What the hell is going on?" We said, "We want you to rehire Helen." "No, we're not going to rehire Helen. You can't tell us what to do." "Okay, then we're not doing the show." He goes off and slams the door.

Then he goes and gets on the intercom, "Alright, we want everybody on stage. Everyone that's not on stage will be fired." No one left the room. Ten minutes go by. "Alright, we want the leads on the stage, now." No one leaves.

Now it's curtain, people are starting to freak. It's a packed house and no one's on stage. "Alright, if we don't get someone on stage now, the entire cast is fined a thousand dollars." Nobody budges.

Fifteen minutes go by and one girl jumps up and says, "I don't think this is right, I love Helen but, the show must go on." So she goes to the stage manager and says, "I'll do Sheila." But all the rest of us sat there. Now even though I didn't participate in the drugs, the cast was right in that it was 30 people out of 35 who dropped acid. And they were going to fire one person. To strike was the right thing to do.

Now we're a half hour past curtain. They're ranting and raving on the intercom. They're calling us assholes and everything else. Finally the stage manager comes and says, "Alright, we've come to a decision. We're rehiring Helen, but you will all be on two weeks notice. If anybody is caught doing drugs over the next two weeks, you're fired." That was fine with us. All we wanted was to get Helen rehired. We went out and did the show.

"Hair" revolutionized the American Theatre by the nude scene and by the people that it cast in the show. Rock and roll, it was rock and roll on Broadway. It was integration on Broadway. It was totally free. I mean it had songs like White Boys and Black Boys. And before you even got to those songs, we were all on stage hugging and loving each other. So the play was a revolutionary play. But now, because we're past the turn of the century, people take it all for granted. They don't understand the context in which the play was brought up. These things were just not done back then.

I did a production of Romeo and Juliet before I got into "Hair," and we couldn't get reviewers to come and see the play. Newspapers, legitimate newspapers wouldn't come see the play. You know, because it was an interracial Romeo and Juliet. You couldn't do that then, it was the times. We were trying to say, particularly as a black minority, that we want to be a part of the society. At the same time, the young white hip guys, who had dropped out, were trying to say they have a right to change the system. And if the systems not going to change, then they don't have to participate.

Another simple thing everyone takes for granted, blue jeans. Blue jeans were a revolutionary thing at the time and that's very much part of the makeup of the show. I remember when white guys took off their wing tip shoes and their Brooks Brothers suits, and they would just wear their jacket, with jeans and a tie. That was a big, big move against the establishment. People got pissed off. And then what the establishment cannot change, it then absorbs. So what happened was, if they can't get you to stop wearing jeans, they then go to the Calvin Klein's of the world and they make designer jeans. And that's what happens.

And we changed that. "Hair" changed the perceptions as part of the move forward. "Hair" helped change the times and that's what the people who are now forward don't get—because they're now the sons and daughters, or grandsons and granddaughters of people who helped to change it all.

The problem with the establishment is, they rewrite history. They rewrite it so they're in a better light. Okay, so we say we protested the war in Vietnam. And NBC news now tells you how they helped to change the perception of the war in Vietnam when they were at the very beginning, putting us down for marching and protesting against the establishment. I saw this guy on NBC news once say how they stopped the war in Vietnam. Those bastards painted picketing as communist, radical influence. Not as patriotic Americans trying to make the establishment do what is the right thing. So because of that, in the history books and documentaries now, they've slanted it in their favor. So when people pick up the script of "Hair," they don't get it—because history's been rewritten.

The play was a revolutionary play. So much so they were not called the cast, it was the tribe. The whole makeup of the show, from head to toe was a revolutionary thing. Homosexuality, bisexuality, interracial relationships, pregnant and single, Jeanie I mean. All the things the establishment did not want to hear, was in this play. And on top of that, it was a hit. It was in your face. It was a hit because the establishment was not vocalizing a large section of the country. A culture in the country was not being heard—because Nixon, LBJ and all those guys were doing something else.

Anyway, that's my thing, that it was a revolutionary piece. And now because we've passed it and they've played it down, people don't realize what a revolutionary piece it was. It almost seems dated. But if you put into the context of the times, blacks and whites on stage, homosexuals and straight guys on stage, I mean that was heavy. "Hair" slapped them in the face, that's what "Hair" did. And it kept slapping them in the face until the times changed. "Hair" helped change the times.

And racism, it's still there. It's evolved, it's more sophisticated, it's more deceptive and deviously done, you know. Because when we first said, "hell no we won't go," they didn't know how to deal with that. Now after saying it for four or five years, they figure now they know how to deal with that.

Well, that's what racism is. You guys are fucking racists. They say, "Don't lower yourself to calling me that." But the phone doesn't ring; you still won't give us the job. That's what I'm doing right now with the DGA. The DGA Television Industry hires less than 3% black directors, writers and producers. Yet on the other side is like, 25% of the things you see have black people in it—visually. But if you call them on it, they say, "We didn't do anything." Well yeah, we know they didn't do anything. That's the problem.

Another thing that made "Hair" so great for me was just sitting around on the stage with each other. There were no debates, no can we live together, and no can we work together. There was none of that. You visually saw people sitting on stage—white girls hugging black guys, white guys hugging black girls, Asians, Hawaiians, the whole nine yards. So if we could do this on stage, you can do this in life. That's what the play said. We're doing this on stage; you can do this in life.

Hud was a great part you know, it was a wonderful part. It wasn't just a black part because it was also a hippie part. Up until that time, if you look at plays of that period, the black thing was a specific thing that did certain things. This was a part where the guy was black and he was hanging out with white folks and it was a whole other deal.

Let me tell you how the play affected society. We went to Evansville Indiana and Evansville is the birthplace of the Ku Klux Klan. Our Hud, Bob Cole, who was from Hawaii, was married to a blonde girl. He started having nightmares that something was going to happen to him in Evansville. So, he gave two weeks notice before we got there. So, I'm third understudy, but now it's Frankie and me. Now I'm confident because Frankie's still here and I'm not going to go on as Hud, particularly on opening night in Evansville.

The night before we're supposed to open in Evansville Indiana, Frankie calls me down to his hotel room. He said, "Listen kid I'm flying. Tomorrow morning I'm heading for LA. I can't open the show, are you up on the lines?"

I said "Yeah. What do you mean you're leaving and you can't open the show? This is Evansville Indiana!"

He said, "I have a court date in LA for marijuana possession. I'm totally innocent and I have to appear in court. Don't worry, you'll be fine."

So I go to the stage manager and said, "What the fuck am I gonna do? I'm doing Hud in the heart of Ku Klux Klan and all of that." And they had already gotten threats. We found out later they burned a cross on the house managers or somebody's lawn.

The stage manager says to me, "Somebody could have a gun out in the audience, you know, with all the stuff we're doing on stage." I said, "I'd be the first person to get shot." The guy said, "All I can say to you is, keep moving. It's hard to hit a moving target."

Now, two black guys are gone out of the show. I have to do my stuff, the young recruit, James Brown and the other little bits, plus Hud. That opening night was the Ted Lange show because I was a ball of energy. I didn't stand in one place long enough for you to get a good shot. He said be a moving target, I was a moving target!

The next day in the paper was a glowing review about "Hair," how fantastic it was, and there's this major talent playing Hud—by the name of Frankie Karl. They didn't change it in the programs—they just left it. So I got the greatest review of my life under Frankie Karl's name! They printed a retraction about a week later on about page 796.

They burnt crosses in Evansville. The show had an effect that they were always trying to shut it down. That was the effect and the song that addressed racism was Colored Spade. I mean the song was a blatant indictment on the establishment. None of those words were ever said or sung on stage like that before.

There were some terrible things going on while on the road with people. Somebody tried to poison Danny Miller. He almost died from poisoning because of the show.

In Cincinnati Ohio they wouldn't pick us up. Bob Mandolph tried to get a taxi. Of course he was in leathers, beads and all of that. His Hair was big and he had a headband. The taxi driver said, "I'm not taking you." Bob says, "Because I'm black?" And the taxi driver says, "No, because you're in "Hair" and I'm not taking you." Bob said, "You have to take me because you're public transportation." The guy said, "I don't have to do shit."

We lived on Mount Adams, the hip section of Cincinnati. Bob went and got the cops and said this cab driver won't take me and I have to get home. So the cop says to the cab driver, "If you don't take him I have to fine you." The driver said, "Fine me." So he got a fine and Bob didn't get the ride.

The reason I first did the nude scene was because of an incident. We were in some city and these 2 girls in the show came to me and said, "Are you with us or against us?" I said, "What are you talking about?"

They said, "They're going to shut down the show and arrest everyone who does the nude scene. The fire department and the police department are going to be here and they're going to shut down the show."

I said, "They can't do that! The thing has gone before the court in New York and everything else. It's been okay. No, I'm with you."

So I got underneath that thing, took off all my clothes and I stood up there with no clothes on. I looked over and I saw firemen and policemen all over the theatre. And you know what they did? Nothing. They were just backstage to get a closer look! That's how I did the nude scene the first time, as a protest. Because I thought I was going to be arrested with the rest of the cast. It never happened.

We did a thing in Washington DC in a park where everybody got naked. We opened at the National Theatre and a lot of money came to see the show—all the politicians' wives and all of that shit. We did an outdoor concert in a park somewhere—there were other performers there, but I can't remember who. But when it came to us doing our thing, the people started taking off their clothes. They'd been drinking beer, whisky and things like that. So the audience got naked! They started dancing around, taking off tops, and we're going, "God they're getting naked!"

Rado I met, but Ragni, Ragni was the one because Ragni truly loved people. He was always earnestly interested in you, who you were and what you were about.

I'll never forget one day I was walking to the theatre and I saw Ragni sitting in the gutter with a homeless person, sharing a bottle of wine. He was engrossed in a conversation with a homeless person, sharing a bottle of wine. To me that was the essence of Ragni. He didn't care if you were the president of IBM, or you were a homeless person. He was interested in you and earnestly. So I was really anxious to be on stage with Ragni.

Ragni liked me but he knew I was cocky. I think he thought I needed to be knocked down a notch. Everybody knew my thing was the young recruit. So, I was going to show Ragni my young recruit. What I didn't know is he'd already seen it from the back of the theatre maybe 7 times before, but now I'm on stage with him. He's not doing Berger; he's just doing the show.

So I start doing the young recruit and sit down in the chair. Ragni comes over while I'm sitting in the chair. He has an Indian blanket wrapped around him and he comes and stands right next to me. He slowly opens the blanket and I turned and looked. He had painted his cock and balls with florescent paint. He then walked over to the foot of the stage, coat open. Now, who's listening to what I have to say? Not a fucking person in the theatre! As I'm talking he slowly walks, coat still open, down the aisle, all the way to the back of the theatre. Now I'm even trying to include the guy with the blanket in my thing, but no one hears me. Everyone's turning and watching him. He turns and slowly comes back up on the stage and stands next to me again. By this time I'm basically done with my young recruit.

He totally ruined the bit, but it brought me down a notch. But it's a great statement about Gerry. Who the fuck are you? You know, we're all in this together. Nobody's better than anybody else. You know? And just as you can take stage, you can be upstaged just like that. And he didn't say a word!

The deal was every once in a while Ragni and Rado would show up. But if one came on the other wasn't going to be there. Gerry would change lines and he'd add shit. He was the purest human being you would ever meet. Ragni was a free spirit. He was free spirit and you have to understand that he loves the world. He loves you, but he loves the world.

That's a story that has to be told, the Rado, Ragni, Galt MacDermot connection. Galt was like a middle class straight arrow. Another part of the story was Rado and Ragni and their relationship to each other. To me, Ragni was the play, in that the pure essence of the play is who that guy was. And I think Rado loved that about Ragni—a truly unique relationship.

Ben Lautman

Ben Lautman was in the Boston and National Touring companies of *"Hair."*
He later went on to be a member of the Broadway cast.

Ben's thoughts about Hair ~

When I first heard about "Hair," I was at a friend's house outside of Boston.
My friend asked, "Have you heard about the show "Hair?" I said I hadn't and
then he played me some of the music. I said, "Wow, this is a show?" He said
yeah, it's a Broadway show." I then said something like, "Fabulous, I'm going
to be in this show. It's in New York?" My friend then said, "Yes, but it's also
coming to Boston."

So later on in November or December of 1969, I saw an ad for "Hair" auditions. For some reason, I decided not to audition. I don't know why, maybe I
was chickening out. Later, while at another friend's wedding, someone mentioned I really should audition for "Hair." Reconsidering, I thought okay, I
will.

It was amazing; there was a line on Commonwealth Avenue in Boston that
went around the block, like twice. It was probably a three or four hour wait,
just to sign up! At the time I was singing with a rock group in Boston called
The Marsells. I guess I was pretty confident in my abilities as a performer and
a singer.

Anyway, when I finally got into the building, I noticed there were about
30, or 40 different people seeing those who wanted to audition. They had
many different compartments in this one office, with various stations. I sat
down and the guy that was taking my information said okay, tell me a little
about yourself. So I began to talk and while I was talking, a Joe Cocker song
came up on the radio. He said to me, "If you could sing like this, you'll be in
the show easy." I thought to myself, "no problem." Before I left, they said my
hair was a little too short and suggested I let it grow.

I was in my last year of college at the time and once again I decided not to
audition. I figured I'd finish up the school year and pass on being in the original Boston production of "Hair." I did however, take their advice and started
letting my hair grow. I also started going to the "Hair" office in Boston, getting acquainted with all the people and making friends. I would often ask if I
could come audition, if they had any openings, stuff like that. They told me

no, but eventually someone will leave and promised I'd get an audition if and when that were to happen.

They had these little yellow business cards that said "Hair" on it. One day I asked if I could have one and they said I could. I took one of the cards and wrote down the words "Claude understudy" on it. That evening, I went down to the Wilbur Theatre. I had been told if I waited around until intermission, I could walk in and see the rest of the show for free.

That night I walked into the theatre at intermission. The show was sold out so there were no seats available. I went upstairs to the balcony and sat in the aisle as close to the seats as possible. As I'm sitting there, one of the usherettes comes over to me and says, "I'm sorry, but you'll have to return to your seat." I said I didn't have a seat, that this was my seat here. She then asked, "What do you mean you don't have a seat?" I said, "Well, I'm the new Claude understudy," and then I showed her the card. She said okay and left.

About ten minutes later this guy comes over to me and says. "Excuse me, but who are you?" I said, "My name is Ben Lautman and I'm the Claude understudy." He said, "You're what? The Claude understudy? Can you show me that card you just showed that lady?" So I showed it to him. Meanwhile, this guy is reeking from smoke, not cigarettes, I mean, he's stoned. After looking at the card he cracks up laughing, almost uncontrollably. He say's, "Look, when the shows over I want you to come on stage. Promise me you'll come up on stage when the show is over." The guys name was Ken Farrell.

The funny thing about it was a couple of months later; I finally got a call from the "Hair" office. Somebody was leaving the show and they asked if I would like to come and audition. This time I said yes and it turned out the guy who came up to the balcony was actually the person who was leaving the show. I was auditioning to take Ken's place!

I ended up having about three or four separate auditions and still didn't know whether I was going to be in the show or not. Meanwhile, I was graduating that year from college, acting school. Some friends and I secured a theatre in Lynn Massachusetts to do our own summer stock company. We proceeded on with our plans and in the middle of rehearsal one day; I received a call from the stage manager for "Hair." They said they wanted me, pending on what sign I was. They asked what my birth date was and I told them. They then asked what my rising sign was, where my moon was, etc. All to which my answer was, "I don't know." Afterwards they said providing everything was okay with my astrology chart, they we're going to hire me. It was all very strange.

Apparently everything turned out to be okay with my charts as they called back and wanted me to join. I was already committed to doing the first show for "The Actors Colony," which is what we called our theatre group. I explained it to them and we agreed I would start as soon as the play finished its run. So the day following my last performance in the play, I started rehearsals for "Hair." Eventually, I did get to understudy Claude.

One of the most wonderful things about joining "Hair" was when they inaugurated me into the show. This may have been unique to Boston, but it was the most phenomenal, special experience I've ever had in the theatre. Maybe that I've ever had period and it's never been replicated, ever. As an ensemble group, everybody welcomed me in to the tribe in such a way that I can only describe as cosmic.

It began with a series of exercises, where first we would do something like yoga to get into a state of mind, almost hypnotic. Then, as a group they would lift me up, turn me around, throw me up in the air and spin me around. I'm by this time totally relaxed, floating, and completely trusting that nobody's going to drop me. I also remember lying on the floor of the stage and each cast member would come over, whisper something in my ear and touch me. Some would touch my hand, my hair and say different things to me. They'd say really beautiful things like love, peace and brotherhood. They not only made me feel welcome, but put me at a level where I felt like I was in space. I just assumed everybody went through this exercise. But this was the only time I had ever seen something like this. It never happened again. Everybody who came in after me did not go through this. Mine was probably the last time something like this was done.

The authorities shut down the Boston production for a few months just before I got involved. Like most people, I had read about it in the paper. There were objections to the language, how the flag was handled and of course the nudity. The strange thing about it was, right across the street from "Hair" (a very small street), there was a strip club. The club had strip teasers (not that I ever went in there), total nudity and they never shut them down.

I remember walking down the street once after the show with some other cast members. We went to this place called Jack and Mary's, a deli in Boston. As we were walking out of the deli, this guy drives by us and is looking at us like he's going to swear at us or something. So I yell over at him, "What are you looking at?" And he yells back, "Weren't you in the show tonight?" Caught off-guard I said, "Oh, Yeah." He then said something like, "Oh, you were great," to us. Here I was expecting to get hassled and it was really a fan of the show.

At one point, I sort of got tired of people just associating me with being a "Hair" celebrity. I just wanted to be my own person, as opposed to, "Oh this is Ben, a member of the cast of Hair." I would think, why don't they just say, "Oh this is Ben." "Hair" had become part of my identity at the time and I just got a little tired of it. One of the only times I appreciated it was when my father introduced me to his friends as, "This is my son, he's a member of the cast of Hair."

My parents did come to see the show. I had got them really good seats in the orchestra section. My mother told me that just as the nude scene was happening, my father looked at her and said, "I'm getting out of here!" They weren't expecting it at all. I guess I should have warned them. He gets up and starts to leave and my mom pulled him back saying, "Get back here, you're going to embarrass everybody."

When Boston finally closed for good, there was a little list on the bulletin board that said who was going where. Some were going to various tours and those who weren't listed were on their own. I had already made plans to move to New York, but for many people, when Boston closed, that was it. They never got involved with "Hair" or any other theatre at all.

There were a couple of guys in the show whose favorite thing to do was to drink. They would do the show, go out and spend the money they made (we got paid pretty well) on booze and would not have any left. The show closed and there they were, with no source of income. That was probably their last taste of theatre. There were many people I'm sure with similar stories.

When I moved to New York, I lived right near the "Hair" office at 55th and Broadway. I would periodically go up to the office to find out what was going on. Once, someone was taking a vacation for two weeks in the Broadway show and I was asked to fill in, which I gladly did. I had been auditioning for many things while in New York and one of the films I was up for was The Godfather. This one particular agency mislead me by saying they were definitely going to use me for the film. While I was waiting for word on when filming would begin, I was asked to join the Mercury tour. I joined Mercury, but the whole time I was on tour, I had to keep on checking back with the agency. Each time they would continue to say they would be needing me soon. Not wanting to miss an opportunity for a major film role, I quit the Mercury tribe and went back to New York. After I got settled in, the agency told me the director decided to use a real Italian actor. Had I known earlier, I probably wouldn't have left "Hair." I learned a great lesson about showbiz from that experience. I eventually re-joined the Broadway cast of "Hair" during its last few months.

The show had so much impact for the times. It was more than just a play, especially in Boston. It was like a statement, it was so important, such a noteworthy thing to be involved in. I've been a part of many great plays and theatrical experiences, but they were nothing in comparison to "Hair." In theatre, it's difficult sometimes to keep a show fresh. Performing eight or more times a week, how do you say the same lines in a similar way without getting stale? It's difficult to stay fresh and with "Hair" especially, you're supposed to be having fun. The thing about "Hair" was—the show never remained the same, every night was different.

Somehow, I was aware every night on stage, that as wonderful as "Hair" was, it would also come to an end. I wanted to be able to capture those moments and get the most I could out of them. After each performance, I would conscientiously try to take away something relevant in the message of "Hair" that affected my own life. I think I was able to do just that. To take away a different message, a different element of the show and incorporate it into my total life experience.

Although I came into the show believing the concepts of peace, love and brotherhood, "Hair" reinforced them. It also added to my own self-esteem, being part of a something as successful as "Hair." To be able to accomplish something I set out to accomplish. I think "Hair" became a major influence in how I feel about myself.

Ben

Sharmagne
Leland-St. John

Sharmagne Leland-St. John was a fan, friend and honorary member of the *"Hair"* tribe. Sharmagne also worked on the "Hair" movie.

Here's what Sharmagne remembers about Hair ~

I first met Michael when I went to visit Peter Yarrow, who was a houseguest at his Rising Glen home. "Hair" had just opened in LA and we were briefly introduced by Peter. I thought Michael was the "cats meow!" In fact he was gorgeous! He asked me if he could ring me sometime to invite me to a movie. I almost fainted dead away right there in the entry hall! I gave him my phone number but he never called.

A few years later I had a girl staying with me on Lookout Mountain called Phyllis Major. She was raving about this guy she had met in Paris who had invited her to a christening. It was for Susie Sunflower's baby, Michael Red Wind, and it was at Michael Butler's home up on Rising Glen. Michael Butler was to be the godfather and she asked me if I would like to go as her guest. It was a potluck and she was going to make cream cheese pie. I guess her mother told her "the way to a man's heart was through his stomach." Well my mother taught me a few different tricks!

I made an aphrodisiac as my contribution to the afternoon. It was disguised as a rose petal cooler made with real rose petals. What better entry into "The Snag Michael" contest than a beverage with flower petals floating on top of wine made from roses. As it turned out, Phyllis never showed up but I crashed the party anyway!

The tribe was so sweet to me. They hugged me, gave me incense, flowers and acid. I loved them all instantly and decided I had found my way home. Throughout the day, Michael kept looking at me and smiling like a Cheshire cat. Finally late in the afternoon he said he was going to go into his room to take a nap and would I like to join him. I said I would and he led me into a large room with a gigantic bed, with tie-dye sheets and mirrors all over the walls and ceiling. There were several other people in there taking a nap too! It was kind of like being in Kindergarten all over again, the innocence. One of the things I love most about "Hair" is that it reminds me that it is OK to take off your clothes and run naked through the sprinklers like we did when we were kids and no one will judge you or pay it any mind.

It wasn't long before Michael and I became an "item." I became his girl-friend and official hostess at Rising Glen and unofficially at many of his other homes around the world. After "Hair" shut down in L.A., I signed several members of the Tribe to my new management company. Most notably Corinne Broskette (who got an airline commercial out of it), Janis Gotti (who got a Bell Telephone billboard) and Teda Bracci (a role in the movie "Frances"). There were others but this is not a résumé it is a souvenir of an incredible time period in my life.

In the late 70's I was technical advisor on the movie "Hair" and also wrote the treatment for the Love-In sequences. Apparently I was one of the few people alive that particular day on the set, who had actually attended the now famous Easter Sunday Love-In in Central Park. I wrote all that I remembered of that incredible spring day in the Sheep Meadow of New York's Central Park and it was amazing for me to see it up there on the silver screen.

I remember so many fun times as if they were yesterday. Painting the floor of the Fool Room at Rising Glen with Barry, Yoshi, Simone, Marieka and others and learning what space eggs are! (Don't ask!) The "Hair" reunions, which I am more apt to be upset about missing than my own High School Reunions. Going with the Tribe to see the Rocky Horror show in London and having Hayward (Michael's butler) don a hump on his back under his jacket, when he served tea to Michael and a very important guest! At the time Michael handled it very well as he only did a double take. But later, Michael admonished Hayward to never do it again! Being with tribe members at Smith's Lawn in England and having Her Majesty Queen Elizabeth come over to tell us she really enjoyed having the "Hair" clan at polo because we added so much color to the stands! Being included in Christine's wedding beneath the weeping Willows at Oakbrook, IL. Toilet papering Michael's sister Jory's home before her big event of the year "The Polo Ball." Dressing my brother Jasper in full drag, with flowing frock and picture hat croquet mallet in a gloved hand at Montecito. Then introducing him to Paul Jabara as this "croquet playing beauty" named Jasmine. Paul spent the entire weekend searching for the elusive Jasmine! With Michael just shaking his head and clucking at us and our shenanigans!

With the new company of "Hair" at the Candlefish theatre a few years ago came the realization of how important a part of my life the Tribe has always been and always will be. It has been suggested that I will play the role of Silver

Indian in a new company of "Hair" and that will really make me feel as if I am truly "blood brothers" to all of you.

Peace and Love, Harmony and Laughter,

Sharmagne Leland-St. John-Sylbert
(Walks Far Woman of the Confederated Colville tribe of Nespelem, Washington)

Annabel Leventon

Annabel Leventon was a member of the London and Paris productions of "*Hair*."

ANNABEL LEVENTON (Sheila) was born in Hertfordshire. While at Oxford she made several appearances at the Playhouse and toured France in the OUDS production of *Othello*. She then joined *The Fourbeats* pop group and played in *The Scarecrow* at the Edinburgh Festival. On obtaining her BA she gained a grant to LAMDA and made her professional debut in *Dante Kaputt* at the Phoenix, Leicester. Various repertory roles followed as well as television appearances before leaving for America in December 1967. There she joined Tom O'Horgan's La Mama Troupe in New York and worked with them for several months before returning to England. ~ *From the London HAIR programme.*

A few anecdotes from Annabel ~

After the London opening of "Hair," Robert Stigwood (British Producer) planned a grand opening night party at a lavish estate in town. The problem was the cast was not to be invited to this party. Not only was the cast snubbed from this event, they were also not given any tickets to the opening night show for friends and relatives. They were not even given the opportunity to purchase any tickets that night. Needless to say, tribe members were very hurt by this indiscretion.

Director Tom O'Horgan was equally upset over this situation and informed the management the cast members must be invited to the party and also should have tickets available to the opening. Management didn't agree so Tom gave them an ultimatum, if the cast was not to be included, then he would not attend either. Management gave in and included the cast in all the plans.

After the London production was open for a few weeks, one of the young male cast members became ill, couldn't sing and stayed out for a few days. The management didn't believe he was really ill and decided to follow him about one day.

This particular day, they observed him coming out of a recording studio with a tape in hand. Seeing this, they approached him and thinking they caught him in the act of deceiving them, they fired him on the spot. No notice was given, no warning, no chance to prove otherwise.

The cast was appalled and complained to management, saying this person should not have been terminated and should be allowed to present a doctors notice to validate his claim. If he could not do so, then the management would be in the right to fire him. The management wouldn't budge so the cast approached the acting union. The union, not wanting to ruffle the feathers of "Hair" management, did not help this young actor. Even though the rules stated that if he could provide a written excuse from a doctor, he would be within his rights.

It was over this event, that Annabel can recall the cast really becoming a tribe. The tribe decided to strike and all were as one. Unless this person was reinstated into the show, they would not perform. Strength being in numbers, the young man was brought back into the show.

Annabel was later sent to Paris to re-direct the show and to play Sheila. The Paris Company was a very unique presentation of "Hair." There were numerous fights among cast members both on and off stage. There were also occasions where audience members would wander up on the stage during the show without being invited, and it was tolerated.

During one period of her stay, there were seven different Berger's appearing in the show within about nine days. During the "Easy to be Hard" scene, Sheila gets slapped by Berger. This is intended to be a staged event, not a real slap. In Paris however, each one of these gentlemen, really slapped Annabel hard on the face. The cast was generally unfriendly to her and was not into the spirit of the tribe as she was accustomed to in London. Consequentially, she was very unhappy, didn't feel welcome and cried often.

One night after being slapped by Berger very hard, Annabel broke down in tears. While singing "Easy to be Hard," she had a very difficult time in getting any notes out at all. Later after the show, a woman who was an audience member approached Annabel to say she was very moved by her performance of "Easy to be Hard." She went on to say that throughout the song, she could hear the drip, drip, drip of her tears falling on the microphone.

Annabel

Helene Masiko

Helene Masiko also known as Helene Morrison was a member of one of the later American tours of "HAIR."

Helene thinks back ~

I had the pleasure of being part of the Rock Talent Productions Tour in '74. One story I can recall is when we were playing in Huntsville, Alabama. The word got to all cast members but me that the nude scene was not permissible and the alternate scene was to be done.

I couldn't quite make out what Lucy (another cast member) was trying to tell me under the parachute after the "Be-In," so I quickly whispered back, "Sorry Lucy—I can't hear you. Tell me later." And out I went, nude and all alone, except for a fully clothed Claude (Ed Force) singing "Where Do I Go?" I knew it would be ridiculously distracting if I dodged back under cover, so I stayed and sang with purpose, verve and conviction, as if this was how it was supposed to be. Got a nice ovation during intermission too! It's one of my favorite stories.

I now have three children (young adults) who are happy little hippies in their own way. I've raised them to love and respect God, nature and mankind. I often tell them that I got a better education on my "HAIR" tour, than I did in all my years of formal (Catholic) education. I am truly grateful for the experience.

Just today I saw an audition notice for a production of my beloved "HAIR" at a local theatre. Even though I'm probably much too old to do so, I'm going to try to participate in some capacity—I must.

I've held up well over the years, or, at least, don't have the good sense to look, act or feel my age.

Peace and Love ~ Helene Masiko (nee Morrison)

Kevin Mason

Kevin Mason was a member of the original Seattle and Miami productions of "Hair." He played the role of Margaret Meade.

KEVIN MASON (Scorpio) is an expert skier who feels that all is one—love is a guide. He has recorded several songs and sung with "The Chancellors" and "The City Limits." His nickname for the past seven years has been "Hair." ~ *From the HAIR program at the Coconut Grove Playhouse, Miami August 1970.*

Kevin recalls ~

A story I recall was the time in Coconut Grove when I was taking pictures in a park across from the apartment house we lived in. It was during our line rehearsal. I was randomly shooting photos of our line rehearsal and I happened to point my camera at this guy who was trying too hard to look cool. I still have those photos by the way, as if a lace shirt on this guy was cool (it wasn't). Anyway I didn't take his photo but he came over to me and said,

"You took my picture, give me that camera."

Shocked I backed up and said, "No I didn't take your picture," at which time he said again, "Give me the camera."

Well Arthur Dillingham heard this and came over and said, "You want to take his what?"

And the guy in the lace shirt said, "You shut up nigger or I will blow your head off!"

Well to say the least we were all dumbfounded by what he said. Then Michael Rhone walked up and said, "He (Kevin) is not going to give you the camera."

Right then the guy turned to Arthur, put his hands on Arthur's chest and said, "You are under arrest!" He never showed a badge or said he was a cop, he just said, "You are under arrest!"

Well then I did start taking photos of the guy. Then, magically, all of a sudden about 15 cops showed up—all within minutes. How they all happened to get there so quickly was really pretty odd. There was some pushing and shoving, some swinging and all that kind of stuff going on. I got some good photos and then gave my camera to one of the girls and said, "Take this camera and hide it."

Finally they showed us their badges. I don't remember if guns were drawn but I do remember that a bunch of us got arrested. They put us in 3 different cop cars with 4 people in each car. All of us were handcuffed with our hands behind our backs.

We took off from that little parking area and started driving towards Miami. There were the 3 cars we were riding in, led by 2 other cars in front of us and another couple of cars behind us. So there was this huge line of cop cars. About a mile down the road—after we had gotten away from the fracas (we had collected quite a crowd from all this), they turned on to this dirt road. Then they started driving down this dirt road and they kept driving and driving, and the whole time were thinking—oh man, this doesn't look good. What the hell are these cops taking us down a dirt road for?

We finally got to the end of the dirt road where there was a clearing. The cops sort of circled the wagons and while we were all sitting in the cars, they got out of the cars and were having a pow wow over in the center of this big dirt clearing. Now we are way out in the middle of nowhere, I mean there's not a house—there's nothing to be seen.

I turned to the guy who was next to me (I can't remember who it was) and said, "You know, if nothing else, we know this was not by our doing. This is something they set up and our vibes are good." I was kind of anticipating the worse, who knows—these guys could dump us in the Everglades for all we knew. It all seemed so setup, so contrived, that so many of them would show up so quickly.

We're sitting there sweating because its super hot out and they wouldn't roll down the windows for us. It's getting really hot in these cars but we're there, all handcuffed behind our backs, just waiting while they're outside talking all this time. Right about that moment we look around and in comes Heather MacRae, her car screeching and skidding into the middle of the circle. The cops, they kind of jump out of the way and I remember a big cloud of dust bellowing over it all from the car skidding in the dirt. The car door opened and she came flying out of that thing like a wildcat. She shouts something like, "If you touch a hair on one of their heads I'll have every one of your damn jobs!"

Of course she was Heather MacRae, Gordon and Sheila MacRae's daughter. Well somebody knew something and knew who she was. They ended up arresting her because she went right up to them (the sergeant or whatever) and got right into his face. Once she knew that they had taken us down this dirt road, it kind of blew their cover. So obviously they had to decide that they were going to take some other tact.

Next they called in for a paddy wagon and down the dirt road it came. They placed Heather in a car, handcuffed, but they didn't rough her up. I'll never forget what happened next. As they got ready to put us in this paddy wagon, they took us out of the cars and walked us all up into a line to get us in. I remember a guy just putting his shoe against one of the guys, I think it could have been Arthur and he just kicked him into the paddy wagon! Now he's handcuffed with his hands behind his back, so he can't stop his fall. And it's all metal on the inside of that thing, just a solid metal box.

So I said, "You don't have to do that. You don't have to play the violence thing with us." The cop turned to me and glared but he didn't do anything, he didn't hit me or anything like that.

So they got us all into the paddy wagon and this is where the real show began. Because here's the cops, driving that paddy wagon down this dirt road and we could see through this little window, the driver was actually forcing the wheel to turn radically from left to right, and right to left. And we're just loosing balance, slamming into the sides, the floor and into each other. We're flying all over the back of this thing and they are laughing. They are literally laughing!

Then, he'd slam on the brakes, causing all this dust to blow in through a hole in the back. And it's choking us because we can't get any fresh air. Then he'd firewall it again and we'd all get thrown back. And these were cops doing all this—uniformed cops!

But it didn't stop there. Once we hit the regular street, he was still doing all this. Now, whether or not he was doing it in a place where there were no houses, we couldn't really see that. But we knew we were on the street.

Anyway, we finally showed up at Dade County jail and they took us out and walked us in one by one. Well the one guy in "Hair" who was totally a straight arrow was Marcus Mukai. He didn't ever smoke anything, never took drugs. Just as Marcus was walking into the jail, he felt something getting stuffed into his back pocket. So he reached around back there and pulled a film can out of his pocket. He looked back, saw this film can and just dropped it. Somebody, as he was walking in, reached around and stuffed it into his pocket at the last minute. He didn't know what was in it, but someone obviously planted something on him. Of all people to plant something on, Marcus was the straightest of them all.

Once we got into the actual jail cell, it's me, Otis Stephens, Marcus Mukai, Arthur Dillingham, I think Tyrone Miles, Michael Rhone—I can't remember everybody that was there. But we were in the cell feeling, "Hey we didn't do anything wrong so we don't have to be all down in the mouth." So we started singing. Well in the jail cell, the walls are cavernous and the music just floated through that place. It just sounded great; it was like an echo chamber. So here we are, all great singers and we're singing our hearts out with harmonies and everything.

Some brothers down the cellblock heard us and yelled out, "Hey, who are you guys?" We said, "We're in the Hair cast." Then they decided they wanted to kick in and do some singing too. Now we're really changing the vibe. So these guys started singing, then we would sing another one, and so we'd trade songs back and forth.

Then of course as it turns out, someone on Hair's Management staff got the call and quickly hired one of the best lawyers in Miami. He ended up getting everything cleared. Of course we had the pictures, which showed that Arthur's hands were down at his side, while the cop was grabbing him. The pictures showed exactly who started what.

Once we got out of the jail, man here's AP wire photo and everybody's all walking backwards as we're walking out. The pictures and story went out nationwide and of course my dad opens up the Seattle Times the next day to see, "Hair, busted in Miami."

They did get us out in time for the evening performance. What a wild day that was.

Kevin

Arnold McCuller

Arnold McCuller was a member of the National touring productions of "Hair."

ARNOLD McCULLER (Tribe) Arnold has been with the National Company for only three months. An amateur actor, originally sang with a well-known gospel group in Cleveland called *The Prestonians*. He left the group to join the cast of *"Hair"* and plans to stay with the company until the last performance has been given. ~ *From the HAIR Scene magazine for the Royal Alexandra Theatre in Toronto, July 1971.*

Arnold shares some thoughts ~

The period of the sixties was too heavy for me. I only know if it were not for this period I might not be as well adjusted as I am today. I feel the confrontational aspect of the play brought us under fire, but toughened us up. I do think a lot of us lost touch with the author's original intention from time to time. We often used the drugs and partying to an extreme and subsequently many of us are now in recovery of one form or another.

Before joining "Hair" I was singing in church and school choirs, and working for the Erie Lackawanna Railroad as an office clerk. I could relate to "Hair" because it dealt with racial issues that hit close to home, sexual issues that I felt passionate about, and I was totally against the war in Vietnam.

I auditioned in 1971 for the Mercury touring company on their first stop in Cleveland Ohio, after leaving their sit down in Chicago. I was one of 200 people to tryout and only four of us were hired. I Played Hud, Margaret Mead understudy and every possible solo and Duet or group vocal—Aquarius, What a Piece, Electric Blues, Dead End, Colored Spade, etc. My audition song was "Bridge Over Troubled Waters." I wore a Navy shirt and pants, and looked really thin! I was hired the next day. I was also in the Venus tour. Considering both, I was on the road with "Hair" for 2 solid years.

I can vividly remember the hotel fire in Cleveland and the sadness I felt after. I was new and these were my new friends, and it immediately drew me close to the tribe. I remember taking wonderful trips with my friends in the company on days off (Mondays usually) and always having some of my expanding drug experiences.

I first met Gerry Ragni when we played St. Louis and were told we would be arrested if we did the nude scene in their town. Gerry and Michael flew in to be hauled off to jail with us, but nothing happened. The cop scene after was really affective though.

When we played St Louis I loved meeting Michael O'Hara, a local singer who auditioned for the show and blew everyone in the company away with his songwriting, singing and all around beauty. He was the real thing, the son of a preacher-man, and of course his dad would not allow him to go off and join the circus. We were so disappointed, especially the black members of the company, because he was so damn soulful!

"Hair" was my introduction to show business. And unlike many of us I have had the honor and gift to be able to continue and always work. I had a regular job for about 6 months, working for Ralph Ginsberg's Moneys worth Magazine Subscriptions, but I've been singing somewhere since 1970 and I am still going strong.

I must add that meeting and singing with David Lasley was the richest experience I remember. We sang, "What a Piece of Work is Man" from the beginning and now he is my oldest friend. We still sing together with various artists including James Taylor who we've worked with since 1977.

After leaving "Hair," I left the Venus tour, which was really Bus and Truck at that point and moved to New York to pursue a career in Musical Theater, but only did a few Off-Off Broadway things that did not make much money. "Hair" spoiled me financially; we made good money for kids. I moved to hells kitchen in mid Manhattan, paying $55.00 a month for a studio walk-up and from there walked to auditions, dance class and music lessons. I learned my craft and became more confident and eventually became a studio singer, getting hired for all the Disco records that were soon to follow.

I've since completed five solo recordings and worked with every possible artist known to man around the world. I have been really blessed and I never take that for granted.

Always,

Arnold McCuller

Barry McGuire

Barry McGuire was a member of the Broadway cast of "HAIR," playing the roles of Berger and Claude.

BARRY McGUIRE ~ Born in 1935 in Oklahoma City. I like everything, don't like nothing. ~ *From the Broadway HAIR program.*

BARRY McGUIRE (Claude and Berger) has been a construction worker, a milkman, a fisherman and a pipe fitter before he invested in a guitar. Three months later, he had mastered it and twelve songs, which he sang five hours nightly in a Santa Monica club. He was with *"The New Christy Minstrels"* for four years, then recorded *"Eve of Destruction,"* the first war protest song to make it big. He dropped out for two years to spend the $200,000 he had made from the record, a million-and-a-half seller, and a movie, *"The President's Analyst."* He was busted recently for swimming nude in Topanga Canyon, California, where Topanga Canyon's finest climbed down a 200 foot cliff to make the arrest. ~ *From the HAIR Playbill on Broadway, October 1968.*

Barry's comments ~

There are so many stories I could tell you about my days with Hair. I could write a book of my own.

From my first contact, I was sitting with John Sebastian on the edge of Cass Elliott's swimming pool. Cassie stuck her head out the window and hollered,

"Hey McGuire, you've got a call from New York."

I said, "Who is it?"

She disappeared for a couple of minutes, stuck her head back out the window and said,

"It's a Broadway show called Hair."

I said, "What do they want?"

She said in a very Cass Elliott pissed-off kind of way,

"What am I, your goddamned secretary—you come and ask them what they want."

So I asked John, seeing as how he was from New York, what Hair was all about. He told me it was a Broadway musical about the hippie scene that was happening a couple of years ago in the streets of New York.

So off I went, not to do the show, but to take advantage of a free round-trip ticket to New York where I could see all of the old friends I hadn't seen in a couple of years. That's how it started for me.

The spiritual enlightenment I received while doing the show was a major step for me in my search for ultimate truth. One major thing I discovered was in order to find out what works, you have to know what doesn't work.

Barry

Danny Miller

Danny Miller was a member of the original Detroit Company of "Hair," and played the roles of Woof and Berger. He also played the same roles in the Broadway and National Touring productions of "Hair."

DANNY MILLER (Tribe) Loves monkeys, motorcycles, strohs, poppy, mom, dad, Lind, Mert, Bert, friends, and family. ~ *From the HAIR Playbill on Broadway, October 1971.*

Danny looks back ~

In the mid sixties I had a band and I also was one of those guys who stood out in front of the pool hall and sang acappella. I didn't like school, so I quit in my senior year in 1966. I walked out, was into the drugs like amphetamines, drinking and lots of singing—in a blues band of course. My original band in 64 and 65 was like Motown, Beatles, sock hop, and stuff like that. Later on, I did the blues, acappella and the oldies.

Then what happened is they had the draft lottery and my number was number one. September 14th came up the first number, so I was picked first and I was 1-A. My good friend's brother was at the University of Michigan and was actually a draft-dodging counselor. He told me, "Just go back to high school, because then they can't take you for the draft. I really didn't want to go, but only because a guy from the neighborhood came back from Vietnam and he told me, "don't go." Otherwise, I would have gone, I was just that crazy, I didn't care.

I was still 1-A while I was in "Hair." I was dodging the draft by writing crazy letters and coming up with schemes. I came up with this incredible scheme that if I had warts on my fingers, I couldn't shoot a gun. So I'd go to these theatre doctors in each city, give them a couple of tickets and say, "Can you write me a letter about these warts, that my hands are incapacitated?" and they did. So when I finally did take the physical in 1973 they said, "We're going to give you a year to get rid of those warts." From that year it all changed though.

In 1970 I auditioned for Motown Records and they wanted to groom me for a two record deal. They flew me to New York to see "Hair" because they wanted me to get into the show for more exposure. Then they flew me to Pittsburgh to be onstage with the Temptations. So right before "Hair" that's what I was doing. Once I got cast in "Hair," because of my insanity and my inability to be managed, I dropped the Motown deal and just did the "Hair" thing. Not realizing I could have probably done both. So they kind of dumped me like a hot rock. I think they were grooming me for a song called "Get Ready." Rare Earth did the song and two or three guys from Rare Earth were in our band in the Detroit show.

I remember my first audition in Detroit. It was like the American Idol thing. There had to be like two or three thousand people there. I pulled up in a full dressed Harley, complete with a saddlebag, windshield, and I was wearing a helmet that had holes drilled in it like a whiffle ball. I pulled my bike right up into the lobby, got off, shook my hair out and Gerry Ragni came over to me and said, "Boy I sure hope you can sing."

The only time I could put both feet on the ground with my bike was if Meat Loaf got on the back. He always liked to ride on the back. We ended up living in a house together, with Stoney (Shaun Murphy). Shaun Murphy is now a member of the band Little Feat.

There were several auditions over a few weeks and they cast me as Woof. That kind of scared me because I had never acted, but Jonathan Banks worked with me on a daily basis. He took me under his wing and led me right through the whole process. Once I do something over and over, I do it well.

While in Detroit, a bunch of us went up to Montreal to see their opening of "Hair." Myself, Meat Loaf, Jonathan, Stoney, I guess about eight of us went. They didn't open though because of all the political stuff. So we're all in the motel room drinking and Jonathan says, "Hey Danny, do think you can do Berger?"

I say, "Sure, I can do Berger."

This is Sunday night and he says, "Okay, you're doing it Wednesday Matinee."

So I was doing Berger and after doing the part for about six weeks, Michael Campbell's parents were in town and he asked to do Berger on the Sunday night second show. I said, "Sure, I'll do Woof, you do Berger." And we were having a brand new premiere on Tuesday, with new lights, me doing Berger, like a new show. I started drinking, my timing was way off and I broke my ankle on stage. So the Tuesday night premiere was like the same show they'd seen when it was first previewed. It wasn't good and that was because of alcohol.

As Berger in Detroit, I remember when I was singing "Donna," I'd swing from the rope and go up about fifteen feet, let go, and Meat Loaf would catch me while I was still singing.

During the draft card-burning scene, I was burning real draft cards. I burned all my own and then I took real draft cards and letters from the audience and would burn them. We had the props, but I would burn the real thing and people knew I would do that.

We had a couple of bomb threats in Detroit. They evacuated the theatre and I remember David Patrick Kelly taking a guitar, singing a song we all had sung with him before on an album, and we just followed him out of the theatre like he was the pied piper. The audience followed and everybody was singing along until they let us back in the theatre. David Patrick Kelly was the one in Detroit who really pulled the show together. He was an actor, he knew all the lines, he knew the blocking, he could sing and he could dance. Most of us weren't actors; we were mostly singers and dancers.

I think my fondest memory was in the very beginning of the Detroit show when we did the sensitivity stuff. Most of the black kids had never been around whites and visa versa. I had where I grew up, but a couple of the black girls said they'd never been that close to a white man ever. The cast was so tight then. We were one, we really were. I don't know how they did it—I don't know if they strived to do it, or if it was just happening. If we had problems, we worked them out.

I was pretty close to Gerry Ragni. We were so similar, he was a Virgo, I was a Virgo, we both always had a thing about changing shirts, we had a lot of similarities. He kind of took me under his wing a little bit and I think he was also surprised I wasn't gay, but it didn't stop our friendship. He was just brilliant. I don't remember Jimmy Rado that much except in the beginning, but Gerry was always at the auditions, the rehearsals, and he was always around.

I remember doing Berger on tour when I was in Pittsburgh. Joe Mantegna's dad died and he had to go home. Michael Rudder got stuck in Canada and couldn't get back to do it and Doug Rowell was ill, so they had me do Berger. Nobody knew I did Berger except the Detroit people. They were surprised, but the role was more my personality, it was probably me.

There were these fans, young girls in Pittsburgh. I couldn't even go out into the audience because they'd rip my jacket, my clothes and take my beads. Even when I left the stage in the back, I'd have to wet my hair and put it in a ponytail. They'd be looking for the cute guy with the big hair, while I was sneaking out with my ponytail and a hat. They even had my picture in a poster shop, so I had a little bit of a following there.

I also had these death threats in Pittsburgh. I was playing Woof and there was a guy who was angry I wasn't gay. He was angry that a straight guy was playing the part. He would write me death notes and send them up with the ushers. He would also call my room and tell me everyplace I'd been all day. We couldn't figure out who he was, this guy just kept calling. I would have my calls screened and my number changed, but he'd still get through to my room. It didn't bother me, I wasn't afraid. As a matter of fact I kept saying to him when he would call, "Can't we just meet man? I'll buy you dinner. He agreed to meet me one morning but never showed up. So Jon Banks always had a couple big guys with me when I went out.

Wilmington Delaware, that was a crazy town. We went there right after Pittsburgh. Three limousines were taking us to a party about thirty minutes away. We get in the limousine and all of a sudden this tall black guy gets in. I didn't think anything of it; I was with Michael Brown (she was my wife at the time) and Debbie Andrews. We're all in this limousine and I hear this voice I kind of recognize but I can't place it.

So we get to the party at this big beautiful mansion and the tall black guy is following me around. He's being friendly, no big deal, I thought he was a friend of Michael's and maybe she had invited him. I took a half a drink of a beer and got violently ill. They called the doctor and they rushed me back to the hotel. I had been poisoned. By the time the doctor got there everything was out, everywhere. Later, the others told me it was very strange when they left the party to come back, this guy, whoever he was, asked to be dropped off at the Greyhound bus station.

Wilmington Delaware was the whitest city in the world. During the peace march, when the some of the cast is in the isles with signs, somebody jumped up and actually tried to attack Michael Brown and a couple of the girls. We came off stage in a hurry though and nailed them first. They had to stop the show because of the ruckus.

Another incident was during the nude scene; every light in the house came on. Every single light! I'm talking about overhead lights, exit lights, the spot-lights, and in the first row you're hearing, "It really is a nude scene."

I started laughing because Bobby Mandolph runs off the stage holding his breasts, totally forgetting that "other" parts are exposed. I was laughing so hard I couldn't stop. Jon Banks came out and he had this leather hat. He puts it over me and he takes my microphone and we walked off the stage with the hat over my rear end. The cast is screaming and I'm laughing. We knew they did it on purpose.

I joined the Broadway Company when Alan Braunstein went to Jesus Christ Superstar. A funny thing I can remember from Broadway is that I broke one baby toe on Billy Alessi one night and I broke my other baby toe on Bobby Alessi in the same scene the next night.

On another night Greg Karliss was playing Berger, I was playing Woof, I think Robin McNamara was Claude and Larry Marshall was Hud. Greg, Myself and one of the Alessi twins (Billy I think) were in the flag scene. Greg and I got into one of those moments where you look at each other and just start laughing. We were laughing so hard we couldn't stop and Billy had to sing the song all by himself.

One night four of us (I won't tell you which four) we're up on the third floor in the Biltmore snorting heroin. I was an IV user then and was up there to get some more. We all nodded out, it's like 8:15 and they couldn't start the show. Finally we all came to, ran down and they started the show. I was singing bad and could hardly keep my head up. The stage manager called me in after the show and I thought I was getting fired. He said, "Danny, I really like the way you did that show tonight. You were mellow.

I thought, "Oh that's nice, you're giving me permission now to use heroin. Thank you very much." I was strung out on heroin back then and in my Broadway career I kept getting hurt on stage because of my drug use.

The last thing I did musically was in 1975. I was to front a band in Detroit called the Sammy Sanders Band. It was a pretty popular band but the best I could do for them was get their drummer strung out on morphine. So I got kind of black balled from the music business in Detroit. I went on a rapid road of drugs and in 1978 I got clean for the first time, which lasted for five and a half years. Then I thought I could drink alcohol like a "normal" person, but ended up back on my drug of choice—heroin.

Nine and a half years ago I came to California from Detroit with a heroin and methadone addiction. I kicked it cold turkey and found a spiritual life, which I never had before. I was from the God is dead generation, that was me, I was an agnostic, I was God as I understood him. After finding a spiritual life, my ego was finally smashed and I was able to clean up all my wreckage.

Today I supervise six drug and alcohol recovery houses, I'm chairperson for the Orange County Sober Living Coalition and we represent almost two thousand beds in Orange County California. I also work at a performing arts high school and we provide high school diploma classes for recovering addicts and alcoholics. To date, we've enrolled over eighty recovering addicts and alcoholics to get their high school diplomas.

I'm also writing a musical called "R.A.T.H., The Romantic and The Hero-ine," which is about recovery. I started writing it in 1981 as a fictitious book, did some more research on it, and turned it into a musical. The things I wrote that were fiction have now come to fruition. That's not my priority though.

My priority is still to help the addicts and alcoholics who are suffering and I have a certain passion now to help the adolescents because they're getting lost. There are only sixty county funded beds for adolescents in Orange County and we need six hundred beds. My mission is to produce a play about recovery to receive monies to help the adolescent community. We're working on a drug and alcohol rehab site for adolescents in sober living, where they can come through our own system and then go to the sober living houses. By the time they're eighteen, they can even be a certified counselor.

Looking back, I think from the very beginning "Hair" was a perfect play for me. It was my personality, what I was. Besides the fact that "Hair" was a great opportunity for my career, I remember it changing people's lives. They would come up on stage, hugging us, with a new awareness. A lot of people in those days thought we were the people spitting on the veterans coming back, but we weren't those people at all. We were the ones who were accepting them back with open arms.

Your Friend in Peace….Danny

Susan Morse

Susan Morse was an original member of the Los Angeles cast of "*Hair.*" She later appeared in the Broadway production as well. Susan played the roles of Sheila and Jeanie.

SUSAN MORSE (Sheila/Jeanie) Capricorn. The third member of the cast from Quintano High in New York. Appeared in *Jimmy Paradise*, the national company of *The Sound of Music*, and summer stock. Collects antiques and thrift shop clothes, and reads about the supernatural. "I wish that people would look at different colors of the skin like different colors of the rainbow." ~ *From the Los Angeles HAIR program.*

What Susan remembers about Hair ~

I remember recording the DisinHairited album, like it was yesterday, going into the studios at RCA. I even have a picture of us recording in there, a Polaroid that somebody took. There's Leata, Beverly, Barbara Lauren and myself.

I was seventeen when I joined "Hair," and had already been singing professionally and acting since I was seven years old. So when I got into "Hair," I was already a member of Actors Equity and AFTRA.

I used to get the trade papers and I used to go to auditions after high school. After school was out, I would go to every audition I could go to. One day I had seen an audition for a show I absolutely knew nothing about and they were holding auditions at the Public Theatre.

So I went down there and I even remember what I wore. I looked like Marlo Thomas from the show "That Girl." I did not look like a hippie at all—I was dressed more mod. When I went in, there was nobody there auditioning. It was like an open audition, you could go in any time, the whole day. And I remember seeing a table with two guys, Jim and Gerry. I had never met them before. I thought Gerry was the oddest person I'd ever seen in my entire life.

Walking in with my little black portfolio, I showed them my pictures and I also had an acetate of a recent demo I had recorded. I was telling Jim and Gerry I had just recorded this thing and they wanted to hear it. So I remember walking with Jim to look for a phonograph to play it on. We walked all over the Public Theatre together, just to find one so they could hear my demo. We never found one though.

They called me back later and I got to sing "Going Out of My Head." I wasn't nervous, I didn't know anything about anybody, I didn't know what I was embarking upon, it was just an opportunity to audition. I did really well and they were extremely complimentary and they were very cool. They made me feel very comfortable. They called me back again, but I didn't get it.

A couple of months later I read in the paper that the show was now going to be on Broadway. And I thought I gotta check it out. I remember those guys—they liked me. I must have had ten auditions. I think the very last audition was at the Henry Hudson Hotel. This was with Tom O'Horgan and was the final cut. It was really late at night and at the tail end of the audition, they split the finalists into two groups. I remember seeing Diane Keaton who had her dog with her, Leata Galloway, Ronnie Dyson and all the people who were chosen to be in the original cast.

To make a long story short, I was not in the group that made Broadway. I was in the other group. I was heartbroken. I took the subway home to Queens and cried the whole way home. On the subway, I was absolutely determined, one day I was going to be in "Hair."

"Hair" held their rehearsals at Variety Arts rehearsal studios. Every time I'd go there and I'd see on the bulletin board they were rehearsing for "Hair," I would try to listen in. I went to see it on Broadway when it opened and it was the most amazing thing—I was totally impressed. I was even more determined because up to that point, I didn't know much about it. I was so upset about not being in the show and getting in became an obsession.

So when I read in the paper they were going to be doing an L.A. company, I had to audition again. I knew I was going to make it this time—they had always liked me. After many auditions I got a phone call from the stage manager, Fred Reinglas, saying I had been selected for L. A. I was very excited.

Well my mother was not happy—I was only seventeen. My mother knew about the four letter words and the nudity and she was very upset. I said, "Mom, I've been in show business all these years. Since I was a kid I've worked really hard and I have an opportunity here. I have to do this." Anyway, my parents decided they were going to let me go out to L.A., so I went.

I remember they met us with a limousine at the airport. And I had said to someone, "God we get to ride in a limousine?" The only time I had been in a limousine was at a funeral.

The Los Angeles cast was a real mixed group of people. There were the people from New York—who besides me were Ben Vereen, my friend Jim Carroza, Denise Delapenha, Randy Fredericks, Carol Miller, Elaine Hill and Bert Sommer, who was my high school buddy. Bert and I were in the same class. Then there were the people from L.A. There was Jennifer Warnes, a wonderful singer. She was sort of the "apple of the eye" of Tommy Smothers and Ken Kragen, who were managing her career. She was Sheila and a lovely, lovely woman. And people like Gloria Jones and Delores Hall; I got to share a dressing room with both of them. Also a lady named Rhonda Oglesby. She was beautiful—Rhonda was Ms. Arkansas.

There was Jerry Combs, Willy Weatherly, Jobriath Salisbury (who was amazingly talented), Alan Braunstein and Kay Cole—who I had also known as a young girl in New York. She had done a lot of Broadway previous to "Hair." There was Keith Carradine, Greg Arlin and Teda Bracci. Oh my God, Teda is a wonderfully, colorful person. And then there was Bob Corff, Ted Neeley (who I've lost track of) and Lee Montgomery, a wonderful singer. Joey Richards was another person I knew from high school. His father was a famous songwriter, Joe Richards who wrote the lyrics to "Young At Heart."

Gina Harding was a good friend of Mary Wilson of The Supremes. Mary used to have parties and invite us to her house. How cool was that? Do you know how cool that was for me? I mean I got to meet a Supreme! I had all their records—they were my idols!

I was like in the pocket of the music business and all that great stuff was happening. When I'd get to meet these people, I was in awe of all of it! I thought it was so cool, I still think it is cool!

There were the people who did a lot of drugs and then there were the people who didn't do drugs. I did not do drugs. I did do the nude scene once. I was absolutely horrified wondering how I could find my clothes in the dark to walk back to my dressing room. That was more of a horror than standing up there in front of people nude. But I had to try it because I knew one day I'd be sitting here talking to you and I could say, "I did it." That was one of the things I promised my parents I wouldn't do, so please don't print this okay! No it's okay, I don't care.

I lived at the Hollywood Landmark Hotel. The Landmark was on Franklin Avenue and was a place where lots of rock musicians stayed. Janis Joplin, who was a hero of mine, lived there and died there. It was a remarkable experience at seventeen, to walk up the steps to go to my room and have Janis walking the opposite way. It was breathtaking to me.

At the beginning, I remember working with Tom O'Horgan and going through those sensitivity exercises. That was all so wonderful, working with Tom, Galt McDermott, Jimmy and Gerry. Jim Rado was one of the sweetest people I had met in "Hair." I always loved him and thought he was an incredible actor and singer. He always had such goodness about him. I was never really that close with him, but I had this little schoolgirl crush on him. I got to play Sheila quite a bit. I was so young and Jim was so much older. He would say things like, "I feel like I'm robbing the cradle," and I'd be so insulted. I don't know how old they were, they always seemed a lot older than me, but they're also kind of ageless. I saw a picture of Jim recently and he's just as beautiful and timeless as I remember him. He had an interest in me as a performer and I think, as a young person when somebody shows that kind of support it feels good. Like when you're growing up and you have a teacher who makes you feel kind of special. Well he did that to me, that's how he was. I love you Jim Rado. I didn't really know Gerry that much. Gerry hardly ever paid any attention to me.

We had a great band in L.A. Cubby O'Brien was the drummer and had been a member of the original Mickey Mouse Club. Reinie Press was the original bass player and his wife Linda Press was also in the show. I also remember John and Michelle Philips of the Mama's and Papa's. They used to have some really wild parties at their house in Bel Air that we were invited to. There were a lot of drugs and people walking around nude, lounging around nude, it was real scary to me.

One time Frank Sinatra was coming to the Aquarius Theatre. He wouldn't go into the dressing rooms until they disinfected it. He did not like hippie people or anything to do with hippies. We had to take everything out of our dressing rooms.

There was an incident with Bert Sommer; Bert was a troublemaker. One day he was teasing Rhonda and Rhonda got really pissed off at him, smacked him right in the mouth and he started to cry. She said in her little Arkansas accent, "Don't push me Bert." But he kept at it and was really annoying her, so she turned around and hit him. It was very funny and I know that Bert is looking down now and laughing, "Yeah I did that alright, I was a bad boy."

I had a dog named Frank Mills who was part poodle and terrier. She was my companion and I named her Frank Mills, but it was a she. I used to bring Frankie to the theatre and keep her in the dressing room when we had to go onstage. There were a lot of dog lovers in the cast, so other people started bringing their dogs. Jobriath and Jennifer would bring their dogs to the theatre, so during the quiet moments in the show, you could hear the dogs barking. Which had nothing to do with the show at all and I'm sure some of the audience must have been saying, "Why do I hear dogs barking?" Then one time I brought my dog to a rehearsal and my dog pooped on the stage, and Ted Rado got really mad at me. Eventually, Ted Rado said we couldn't bring our dogs to the theatre anymore and anybody who did would be fired.

My parents were really beside themselves that they allowed me to come out to L.A. at seventeen. I used to get these letters in my mailbox at the theatre. The letters would say that if I didn't come home, they were going to disown me. So, the letters would put me in a bad mood before the show. I would sit in my dressing room and I would start to cry because I missed my parents. I didn't know what to do because I was having a great time; I had a lot of pressure. But people really took care of me. I mean I was the baby of the show. People would tell me its okay and Ted Rado was like a dad to me. He got me in the tribe on Broadway, which was a bizarre, bizarre scene—much more than in L.A.

I only lasted three months on Broadway because I found it to be so bizarre. They didn't give me the opportunities I was hoping to get there. They told me at one point I could be Crissy, then another time they said I could be Sheila, and then they wouldn't let me do anything. On top of it, there were a lot of drugs, a lot of inappropriate sexual behavior, while the show was going on. I was taking a cab home every night to Queens, which wasn't very cost effective. I wasn't happy with the show anymore and thought, "What am I doing this for?" It was a combination of many things, but I thought I just didn't want to be a part of it anymore.

But I did meet some really nice people there. I'm still in touch with my friend Beverly Bremers. We spend Christmas together every year. Melba Moore was a doll and a fantastic singer. We shared a dressing room and she turned me on to soft shell crab in Chinatown between shows on matinee days. I gave my notice and moved on. I went on to do Jesus Christ Superstar, Godspell and the Rocky Horror Show.

"Hair" was just one of the greatest experiences for me, being in L.A. anyway. Once I went to New York things got different, old and out of control. The opportunity of being with and meeting so many wonderful people—how lucky we all were. I don't think there has ever been or will be anything quite like it again, at least in my lifetime. I'm glad I was part of it all.

Susan Morse

Allan Nicholls

Allan Nicholls was a member of the Broadway cast, as well as some later touring productions of "HAIR." He played both Claude and Berger.

Allan's thoughts ~

I was in a rock band in Montreal Canada and our New York manager suggested that I audition for the Broadway show, "Hair," in order for us to get the
band into the USA market, which had been denied us because of our inability
to obtain work visas.

It was 1969 and I auditioned for Galt and two stage managers (Tom Kelly
and Bob Currie, I think). There was this accompanist Patty who was incredible and I sang two of my original compositions.

Unaware that there would be other auditions required, I thought that it
went so well that I was in. I spent the next month and a half waiting to hear
and doing other auditions. It became an extremely pressured situation as the
press in Montreal, where our rock band was extremely popular, announced
(prematurely) that I had gotten in the show.

So there I was waiting and sleeping on my manager's sofa in NYC with all
of Montreal thinking I was in "Hair." Finally, I got the word and I enjoyed
more than two years performing on Broadway as Claude and Berger. I have
been told that I was the only one who performed both Claude and Berger on a
regular basis on Broadway, which is either a testament to my split personality
or someone's lack of decision-making. All I know is that I enjoyed both rolls
equally. I got to perform them both with Gerry and Jim on opposite sides of
me and that was a treat.

There were a couple of incidents that should be remembered. It was during
an anniversary performance and some had set the Berger rope on the wrong
knot, after it had all ready been preset. They were putting balloons in the theatre for the celebration. So, during the song (Going Down) where I swung
down from the scaffolding, I just dropped into the audience. I recall looking
up on the stage and seeing the entire cast staring out at me for a split second. I
continued singing and checked for bruises later. I was fine. Thank you padded
theatre seats.

Another rope incident was when Red Shepard was playing Berger and he
misjudged a swing on the rope and smashed into the lip of the stage. I was
playing Claude and sitting in front of the fire meditating and Red was crawl-

ing off the stage, I thought where's his understudy? Wait I'm his understudy! I ran off the stage, changed into Berger garb, I think Teddy or Robin took over as Claude and I resumed the show as Berger. That was wild!

My manager had brought me down to audition (as I was telling you), the band never followed and so I started a solo career. I recorded the single Goin' Down which I produced with The McCoys and another "Coming Apart" (that featured everyone who was available from the cast on background vocals) and even another "The Joke" a Cat Stevens song. All had little or no success here in the USA, but my home country, Canada, gave them a little respect, but not too many sales.

Broadway and the various rock shows that I was doing, combined with my move into film, slowly ended my recording and rock and roll career, which I sorely miss these days. I revived it for a while when living in LA and involved a bunch of "Hair" alumni, who were out there at the time.

It started out as a midnight show at the Westwood Playhouse, which I rented from Ted Rado, at the nominal sum of $365.00 for one performance on a Friday night at midnight. It was suicide as LA goes to bed at 10:30, but we managed through the efforts of friends to sell out.

The group included, singers; Heather MacRae, Cliff De Young, BG Gibson, Debbie Dye, Steven Scharf, myself, Jo Anne Harris, Dorian Harewood, Marty Gwinn, and a great band put together by Tony Berg. It was a great evening that parlayed itself into two later spectacles at The Roxy and the group was featured in a film I wrote with Altman called "A Perfect Couple."

I am telling you all this to illustrate how my associations with "Hair" spanned all these years and held up. How all these friends from "Hair" came together and put on this great show, out their love for music and each other…. the common bond was that which was missing in all of our lives at the time…the music. This was in 1979, ten years after I first when in the show. What a great memory.

Allan

Sally Shafer

Sally Shafer was Michael Butler's secretary in the international office of "Hair" in New York.

Sally remembers these things about Hair ~

I look at "Hair" as a vehicle which offers to the world an interpretation of how to think and live outside the box—-the fun of it prompts you to sing and dance—the pain of it, depicting man's ongoing inhumanity drives you to sadness—put it altogether and you have the choice...extreme sadness, outrageous gladness and/or absolute madness!

<u>It's about the freeing the free spirit.</u>
<u>It's an organic thing.</u>

1968...NYC...Hank had a NYC Fireman's badge and every Friday and Saturday night we'd walk right up to the doorman/bouncer of the nightclub of choice and Hank would deliver his spiel about making a fire inspection and we were in the door! We'd dance 'til closing. One night the bouncer at EARTH, INC.—a spiel maker himself—thought Hank's spiel was so good, he invited us to an after-hours party. There I met Brenda who is, to this day, the person I call my Best Friend. As she was grooving on the cracks in the ceiling—she asked what kind of work I did. Me? I'm a Legal Secretary working for one of those huge corporations on the top floor of an Eastside skyscraper. (On a windy day, you could actually feel the sway of the building!) Anyways, Brenda said the House Legal Counsel at the "Hair" office was looking for a secretary—why didn't I give him a call?

Next week I did—his name was Bill Bramlette, Jr. We had an interview set but he got caught-up somewhere and phoned the "Hair" office to apologize for not being there and asked did I "take shorthand?" I said, "Yes" and he said "Can you do this letter for me, please?" How's that for an interview!

The office was a two-story walk-up on West 54th Street—also known as Joe Cavallero's acting studio. A small space with enough room for 4 desks to be lined up on each side of the room, facing a little stage, which had a desk and lots of phones and chairs. The stage is where we'd have the tribal council office meetings.

The wall at the back of the stage was draped in a black curtain, flush to a Chinese restaurant on the other side. You could always smell the cooking! If you were in the office late at night, though, you could see the four-legged nocturnal scavengers climb down the curtain and cruise the office. Millie, our cleaning lady from Puerto Rico, taught us to be sure to bang our metal trash cans real loud if you happened to be there late at night! It became too hard to work though and bang a trash can at the same time!

Everyone painted their desk their favorite color—what rebels we were! When the San Francisco show opened, they sent us two little turtles in one of those cute little plastic turtle bowls with a little green plastic palm tree. They lived on Brenda's white desk. One day there were tracks on Brenda's white desk—one day there was only one turtle and one day there were no turtles. Until now I never thought about a connection to Leonardo and the Ninja Turtles and Master Splinter!

We eventually moved to larger quarters on West 55th Street. It was Brenda Howell, Jeannie Altson-Linhart, Barbara DiSalvia-Siomos, LaVerne Reed, Bonnie, Stanley Soble, Carey King (whom we lost to AIDS), Dr. John Bishop, Brooke Lappin and yours truly, me (Sally Shafer). This was actually the Natoma Productions part of "Hair." We looked after and kept track of Michael Butler and were the center of operations for all the other "Hair" companies running simultaneously in the United States (about 10) and overseas (about 5). It was a constant beehive of activity!

We had what must have been one of the first fax machines where you put the phone handset in the machine and dialed away. We also had a telex machine. You could dial up anyone else who had one (it's the way we communicated with most of the overseas companies because of the time differences) and type away or cut a ticker tape and run it though. When we'd receive telexes it would come off this big yellow roll of paper.

When Michael was in Morocco or somewhere when he could take the time to consult the "I Ching" we'd come in the office in the morning and find a deep pile of printed yellow roll telex paper with Michael's daily guidelines from the "I Ching" which he'd have us pass on to the other tribes.

The Countess Maria Crummere—Tribal Astrologer

Michael always consulted Astrologer Countess Maria Crummere for his opening day dates and his travel dates. Whenever Maria would call the office for Michael, we immediately put her through to him. We never ever questioned her Countess-ship—she just was "The Countess."

I remember I went to The Countess for a private reading. It was after work one evening and I took her a bottle of brandy. It was kind of hot and stuffy in her apartment and as we sipped on the brandy and she told me all about myself—I got kind of sleepy. I didn't want to miss a word—my shorthand was real good at the time—and as I nodded, I jotted her every word. A year or two later I read my notes and absolutely everything she had forecast had happened down to the exact days I would meet certain people and certain things would happen. It really took my breath away.

The Gorilla Suit

Occasionally in the office we'd hear the Gorilla suit wasn't where it was supposed to be for the show...or it was spotted on the subway...or at a party...you just never knew!

When the "Hair" movie was filmed and they did that portion in Washington, DC, that's where I was living at the time. There was an ad in the newspaper calling for anyone and everyone to come be an Extra and sit on the Lincoln Memorial steps and pretend it was the 60's! Not a problem for me or anyone I knew!

At the end of the movie where all the crowds of people are rushing across a field singing, "Let the Sunshine In"...that's DC. That day there were concerts all day long for all of us "Extras". The scaffolding for the cameras seemed about four-stories high...and there, at the very top of the scaffolding (I promise I did not dream this), I spotted the gorilla suit! (Someday I'll find the photo I took of it!)

The Flasher

Probably everyone from New York will remember "The Flasher". The guy would come in the Biltmore lobby wearing a trench coat and show what he had inside...nothing—or no clothes, that is! He became sort of an icon—when "Putney Swope" was filmed, he even got a part.

One day in the office on West 55th Street—bubbling blonde little Jeannie, all of 95 lbs, was the receptionist. It was your average day—5 phone lines ringing—people coming and going like Grand Central station, the telex machine clicking away and the yellow paper roll piling up all over the place. (Jeannie had a chair but I don't think she was ever able to sit down.) Anyways, one day she flew back to my desk—like the bouncing smiley yellow ball she was—about to burst: The Flasher himself was at reception! He wanted to be in "Hair" so he'd brought his resume! The resume was a photo of him and his "Putney Swope" movie credit! No, he didn't flash and yes, we were very gracious to him.

Scumbag

There was good ole "Scumbag". He was a man who sat perched on a box on Broadway at about 52nd Street. To every single individual who walked by he would utter and growl and call them "Scumbag" or "F" something. He was just ALWAYS there…then one day he was gone. We heard in the office that some of the tribe members (we always thought it was Paul Jabara) took him out to dinner and brought him to the show and that he was a changed man.

Working for Michael

I worked for Michael as his secretary on different occasions over the years—beginning in the NYC "Hair" office 1969—1971. Then Jon Banks and I got sent to Australia by Producer Harry M. Miller. Jon directed "Grease" in Melbourne and I was the Orchestra Manager for "Jesus Christ Superstar" traveling show and the grand opening in Sydney. Jim Sharman (later "Rocky Horror") was the director. Then I worked again for Michael in New York mid-70's, again in Santa Barbara and at his home in England. His dinner guests there would be anyone from George Harrison to Lord Waterford. I worked for Michael again in NYC when he produced a beautiful piece of musical theatre called "Reggae".

Michael Butler was always a very hard-working individual, extremely involved with his projects and consistent about what he expected from his staff members. If he was out of town and he'd call in to see how everything was, I quickly learned that even if everything was under control and you told him, that's not what he wanted to hear. He wanted to know absolutely every phone call, every blurb—every single thing that was going on. He always had "lists" of things he needed you to get done. Talk about multi-tasking—Michael could run on several different tracks at a time. Michael could be very stubborn. I loved working for him and will always feel grateful even knowing someone like him——a true visionary, so colorful—a beautiful person with a heart of gold.

Since then I've continued to have a blast and have had the most wonderful experiences. Back in DC I worked for the House Judiciary Committee during the Impeachment Inquiry; in the Reagan White House Personnel Office; for the #2 man at the VA, Everett Alvarez, who had been a Vietnam POW for 8 ½ years; and for the President of the Baltimore Orioles; and in Florida at the Marlins Spring Training Complex and currently for a bridge engineer, who has had some input on nearly every huge-scale bridge in the US over the last 40 years.

My most special and privileged opportunity has been single parenting my daughter, Lauren. I moved to a little beach town in Florida when she was 6, picking out a place because I overhead some people say they didn't lock their doors here! With fresh air and blue skies and year-round outside sports (although too low salaries), it's really been a good place. Lauren graduated from high school 2002 (she was Prom Queen) went off to college having earned academic and soccer scholarships.

These days I try to run and stay fit and am one very grateful human being!

Love and God Bless ~ Sally

David Taft

David Taft was a member of the Australian cast of "HAIR." He was in the Melbourne and Sydney productions of the show.

DAVID TAFT (Tribe) Leo, born in the year of the tiger. Melbourne freak. If I had wings no one would ask me should I fly. ~ *From the HAIR program in Melbourne Australia, May 1971.*

David's reflections ~

I suspect my story is not too unusual. I was a university student, interested in student theatre and playing in a rock band. I knew the songs from "Hair" (I had the soundtrack album) and was aware that the show was on in Sydney.

When they announced auditions for a Melbourne show, I offered to go along with a university friend who was too uncertain of herself to go, but dearly wanted to try out. I took my guitar and accompanied her. While I was there, I was asked if I wanted to audition and on the spur of the moment, I said yes. I was cast without a callback so I must have done okay.

My friend, who has gone onto a very successful career as a singer, actress and radio personality, didn't get in and never fails to remind me of that fact. Most recently she did so on a morning radio show—this after nearly 30 years!

I went to Sydney for the last few months of the show's run there, together with the 6 or so new members of the cast to join those who were travelling with "Hair" to Melbourne. I stayed with the show here in Melbourne for the whole 10-month run and was a member of the Tribe all that time. I did rehearse for the role of Claude but never played it.

Because there was doubt about the show opening in staid Melbourne for morality reasons, the producer was taking no chances at upsetting an already sensitive police force, then under investigation of charges of corruption. We were therefore given very strict warnings about drugs in the theatre and in fact a couple of members of the cast never made it to opening night in Melbourne because they had been smoking grass in the theatre during rehearsals. On opening night there were still letters to the paper calling for the show to be banned because it encouraged poor moral behaviour, but nothing ever came of it. My recollection was that we didn't get high in the theatre, though we did often perform in various states of highness. On warm night, the roof of the building outside the dressing room window was a prime place for a pre-show smoke.

I know that some of my contemporaries went through huge changes as a direct result of being in "Hair"—long theatre careers, marriages, breakdowns, suicides, coming out of the closet etc. In some ways I could say it changed my life too, but in a more convoluted way than that.

One of the members of the Melbourne cast was originally from Germany and after the show finished in Melbourne she went back to visit her mother in Hamburg. At that time I was sharing a house with her boyfriend and she wrote to us that she had been in contact with the producer of the German touring production, who was planning to assemble an international cast to put the show on during the 1972 Munich Olympics and was inviting us to apply. I had graduated from university by then and thought it a good chance to travel and my friend was finishing up in the TV show he was in—so we both went.

It is a long story, but in the end the show never materialized. By then I was in London and as I knew several people there anyway, stayed. I worked in the theatre for a while and then moved into television production (which I still do) and lived in London until 1988. I did try out for "Hair" in London, but unfortunately about that time the roof collapsed at the Shaftsbury Theatre and I think the show was cancelled.

The rest is all just pleasant personal memories. We spent a lot of time together socially—movies, parties, picnics etc. I was very involved politically with the anti-war movement at the university and successfully mounted a conscientious objecting claim to my call-up for the draft. I don't think the rest of the cast were much interested or involved. Most were interested in a career in the theatre rather than living the life. I was studying for a science degree and although I did go on working as an actor for a while, did not see myself on that particular path.

All the best

David

Voices of the Tribe

~ To be continued ~

Visit the
HAIR ONLINE ARCHIVES
For more Hair stories, pictures, and memorabilia at
http://www.michaelbutler.com/hair/holding/Hair.html

or visit http://www.goodhairdays.net

Love Will Steer The Stars
THE "HAIR" TRIBE

In "Hair," we had no stars. Seriously, from its earliest beginnings "Hair" was considered an ensemble, a tribe, but not a cast. We were told that although there were leading roles as defined by union rules, no one was considered to be in a "starring role." Although many of us believed and held fast to this doctrine, in reality this was not really the truth. The fact remains, the more bits you did, or if you played a leading role, you were paid much more and you also had the opportunity to shine more.

Even nowadays, more than 30 years later, former cast members will appear to cringe at the mere mention of stars in the show. Even so, it can't be denied that the show was a major stepping-stone for many stars. "Hair" was an incredible magnet for talent in the 60's and 70's, and many of these young people went on to great heights within the entertainment world.

When I first created this section of the book, I listed separately all those people who I thought deserved "star" recognition, along with their "Hair" bios. I was never happy with the outcome though, mostly due to my fear of leaving someone out. My strongest instinct was to include everybody. It was all a daunting task in that the definition of a "star" is so subjective.

In the end, I decided the best way to handle the "star" issue was to let you as a reader decide for yourself. I will list just a few of the well known names and then you can browse through the following list of names in the "Hair Tribe" to discover on your own the many talented people who have been involved with "Hair."

Joan Armartrading, Keith Carradine, Nell Carter, Tim Curry, Dobie Gray, Paul Jabara, Diane Keaton, Ted Lange, Joe Mantegna, Barry McGuire, Meat Loaf, Melba Moore, Joe Morton, Teddy Neeley, Richard O'Brien, Kenny Ortega, Elaine Paige, Vicki Sue Robinson, Stan Shaw, Donna Summer, Meshach (Bruce) Taylor, Phillip Michael Thomas and Ben Vereen were all in "Hair." Look through the list and see how many more you can find. Believe me, you will be surprised as to how many more there are.

Happy star gazing!

THE *"HAIR"* TRIBE

Continuing an old tradition, by honoring all those special folks who helped "HAIR"
grow from between 1967 through 1975

Stephen Abbott, Arta Abele, Sammy Abu, Tina Abu, Ricardo Acosta,
Christine Adams, Jonelle Adams, Audley Adkins, Robert Adsit, Gary Aflalo,
Roberto Aguilar, Guillermo Aguirre, Ugur Akdora, Teoman Akinci,
Michael Alassa, Steve Alder, Mart Aldre, Theoni V. Aldredge, Billy Alessi,
Bobby Alessi, Michael Alexander, Pernell Alexander, Alice, Sue Allanson,
Jonelle Allen, Mike Allen, Peter Allen, Seth Allen, Richard Almack,
Brooks Almy, Nevin Alp, Shelley Altman, Jeannie Altson-Linhart,
Murilo Alvarenga Jr., Enrique Alvarez, Brent Alverson, John Aman,
Inez Amaya, Jonathan Ames, Andrea Anderson, Blake Anderson,
Evadne Anderson, Gary D. Anderson, Jeannie Anderson, John Anderson,
Maureen Andrew, Debbie Andrews, Derek Andrews, Jonny Andrews,
Margalit Ankori, Bill Anstatt, Robert Anthony, Ynez Anthony,
Mette Antonsen, Raul Arellano, Julie Arenal, Michael David Arian,
Greg Arlin, Joan Armartrading, Gabriel Arnell, Leon Aronson,
Martin Aronstein, Billy Arrington, Jerry Arrow, Sebastião Arruda,
Jeannie Arthur, Frances Asher, Johnson Ashley, Leni Ashmore,
Elena Ashton, Elizabeth Assarson, Steve Atha, Toad Attell, Bill Atwood,
Vaughn Aubrey, Charles Austin, Carlos Avalos, Arsenio Avizado,
Guliz Aydemir, Gillian Aylen, Brandy Ayre, Nolan J. Babineaux, Gene Babo,
John Bacher, Birthe Backhausen, Joe Baerga, Keith Baggerly, William Bagley,
Laurie Baker, Lynn Baker, Araci Balabanian, Jennifer Baldwin, Lani Ball,
Keith Ballantyne, Ann Ballester, Lee Balterman, David P. Band,
Laura R. Bank, Jonathan Banks, Rose Marie Barbee, John Barber,
Paul Barber, Robert Barberis, Alan Barcus, Thurman Barker, Clive Barnes,
Doug Barnes, Marjorie Barnes, Michael Barnes, Robalee Barnes,
Mary Barnett, Don Barnhart, Neil Bartley, Lloyd Baskin, Richard Baskin,
John F. Bassett, Susan Batson, Lyvia Bauer, Roberta Baum, Beverly Baxter,
Daghan Baydur, Richard Bayne, Resit Baysan, Felipe Baz, Luis Baz-Heredia,
Elisabeth Beafritz, Danny Beard, Minnie Cushing Beard, John Beatty,
Jerry Beaumont, Maxine Beaumont, Kay Beckett, Perry Bedden,
Iduna Beenken, Ian Beeton, Rose Jean Bell, Marilyn Bender, Robert Bender,

Cari Bengtsson, Floella Benjamin, Brian Bennett, Jeannie Bennett,
Karen Benson, Ronald Benson, Erleen Bentley, Sally Bentley, James Benton,
Elisabeth Berger, Jonnie Berger, Jonathan Bergman, Hanus Berka,
Cyril Berlin, Lelan Berner, Betty Berr, Paul Berriman, Charles Berry,
Michael Berz, Jurgen Beumer, Otto Bezloja, Vikki Biggins, Ruth Bilbert,
Bob Bingham, Ronnie Bird, Zeynep Birsel, Jor Holmberg Birthe,
Lars Bisgaard, Paul Bishop, Dr. John M. Bishop, Cynthia Bixby,
Terrance Black, Harry Blackstone Jr., John Blake, Peter Blake,
Carolyn Blakey, Harry Blassman, Louie Block, David Blossom,
Nancy Blossom, Roscoe Blount, Sara Blumenthal, Eugene Blythe, Bobiel,
Mecki Bodemark, Armando Bogus, Robert Boehm, Jay Boivin, Kenny Bolds,
Larry Boman, Roberto Bonanni, Chango Bongo, David Bonnier,
Erroll Booker, Yavuz Boray, Ulf Borge, Ferne Bork, Tom Bowden,
Skip Bowe, John Bowman, Ricardo Boyd, Teda Bracci, Sarah Brackett,
Walter Bradin, Sonia Braga, William A. Bramlette Jr., Derek Branch,
William Brand, Walter Brandin, Buddy Braun, Josef Braun, Alan Braunstein,
Obie Bray, Joe Brazil, Beverly Bremers, Sandy Briar, Tisha Bricko,
Alexander Bridge, Casey Bright, Chuck Bright, John Bright, Sal J. Briglia,
Enrique Brik, George Brimo, Karyl Britt, Aldora Britton, Nancy Broadway,
Kim Brodey, Kenn Brodziak, Doris J. Brook, Alma Brooks, Jo Ann Brooks,
Corinne Broskette, Linda Brotherton, Charles C. Brown III, Genie Brown,
Light Brown, Michael B. Brown, Michael Brown, Miquel Brown,
Penny Brown, Rudy Brown, Dennis Browne, Suzanne Browne,
Jo-Ann Brown-el, Joseph (Tito) Broz, Angela Bruce, Ron Brugiere,
Soren Brunes, Ulf Brunnberg, Kate Bruschini, Hazel Bryant, Fred Buda,
Aydan Budak, Kate Buddeke, Rober Bulgan, Tom Bullock, Dick Bunn,
Steve Burkey, Donnie Burks, Paul Burns, Veronique Burri, Warren Burton,
Thommie Bush, Mirta Busnelli, Christina Bustamente, Jorge Bustamente,
Joseph Campbell Butler, Michael Butler, Paul Butler, Ziggy Byfield,
Luie Caballero, Ena Cabayo, Tony Cafrelli, Joyce Cairns, Robert Calder,
Robert Callely, Alfredo Elias Calles Jr., Lee Callet, Larry Calvert,
Norma Calvin, Carl Cambell, Yager Cantwell, Maria Celia Camargo,
Cher Cameron, Jimmie Cameron, Kevern R. Cameron,
Vella Maria Cameron, Nuvit Camlibel, Alice Campbell, Charles Campbell,
Craig Campbell, Michael (Champion) Campbell, Ron Campbell,
Sharon Campbell, Robert Camuto, Arthur Cantor, Anne Capek,
John Capon, Mark Arion Cardosa, Patrick Carlock, Ric Carlock,
Michael Carlos, Les (Claude) Carlsen, Carroll Carlson, Corrina Carlson,

Rusty Carlson, Otis Carr, Keith Carradine, Jimmy Carroza, Kid Carson,
Russell Carson, Floyd Carter, Gloria Carter, Jimmy Carter, Nedra Carter,
Nell Carter, Jack Carver, Pat Casey, Jimmy Cassidy, Bertrand Castelli,
Peppy Castro, Robert Castro, Michael Caton, Walter Cavalieri,
Joe Cavallero, Elizabeth Caveness, Celttoras, Engin Cezzar, Idit Chaim,
Sue Chaloner, Catherine Chamberlain, Michael Chandler,
Jean-Guy Chapados, Bob Chapman, Helen Chappell, David Charkham,
Eva Charney, Ben Chavez, Lyle Cheatham, Nick Chelton, Sammy Chester,
Warren Chiasson, Christine Chilcott, Demetrius Chistopholus, Ulli Chivall,
Avril Chown, Nicole Christian, Norman Christian, Unni Christiansen,
Joel Christie, Julienne Ciukowski, Ted Clancy, Jean Clark, Joe Clark,
Rosalind K. Clark, Dorian Clarke, Robert Clarke, Tiki Clarke,
Grady Clarkson, Ada Clay, Isaac Clay, Beverley Clayton, Sven Cleemann,
Robert Clench, Julien Clerc, Maurice Cockrell, Pat Coffin, David J. Cogan,
Harriet Cohen, Reiner Cohrs, Bob Cole, Joe Cole, Kay Cole, Malcolm Cole,
Ethel Coley, Ann Collin, Charlene Collins, Rufus Collins, David Collison,
Bill Combs, Jerry Combs, Chris Comer, Linda Compton,
Zenobia Conkerite, Lynn Conner, Ed Constagna, John Contardo,
Glenn Conway, David Conyers, Colin Cook, Charlette Cooke,
Malcolm Cooke, Ian Cooksley, Dennis Cooley, Burt Cooper, Gary Cooper,
Clayton Coots, Don Copeland, John Coppola, Olivier Coquelin,
Maria-Elena Cordero, Robert Corff, John Corkill, Joe Correro, Jim Corrozo,
Guy Costa, Jorge Costa, Sue Costin, Debbie Cotton-Walker, Bob Coughlin,
Armand Coullet, Pat Coulter, Jerry Cournoyer, Gil Courtemanche,
Isabelle Courts, Helene Cousineau, The Cowsills, Ken Cox,
James Forrest Craig, Nick Craig, Ellen Crawford, Michael Craydon,
Ed Creed, Meriel Creser, Rudy Cresto, Tim Crighton, Jan Crites,
Crosley Crosby, Charlotte Crossley, Ed Crowley, Nicky Croydon,
Maria Crummere, Roger Cruz, Frank Csaszar, Wayne Robert Cull,
Jennie Cullen, Steve Cummings, Carolyn Cunningham, Dell Cunningham,
Robert Currie, Nancy Curry, Steve Curry, Tim Curry, Charlotte Curtis,
John Wayne Cushing, Dagmar, Susanna Dales, Chuck Dalton, John Dalton,
Cristal Dane, Joan Daniels, Kaipo Daniels, Walker Daniels,
Gerald Danovitch, Michael Danso, Olu Dara, Dary, Jacquie David,
Jennifer David, Jamie Davidson, Billy Davis Jr., Delano Davis,
Henderson Davis Jr., Lorri (Mary) Davis, Valentina Davis, John Day,
Waldyr De Barros, Carol De Carter, Coelho De Castro,
Stephen De Ghelder, Geraldine De Haas, Rene De Knight,

Marcela De LaFerrer, Carlo De Mejo, Candace Louise De Puy,
Luisa De Santis, Andre De Sheilds, Susana Migliore De Vega,
Willy De Wit Jr., Cliff De Young, Dennis Dean, Steve Dean, Linda Deater,
George Deber, Susan Debert, Philipe Decaux, Jay Dee, Michael Delano,
Denise Delapenha, Michael Deluca, Doug Demeerlerr, Phillip Denman,
Denni, Sally Dennison, Serge Descheneaux, Frank Desmond,
Philippe Desprats, Destiny, Clinto Dexter, Bill Dial, Niola Di Staso,
Franco Di Stefano, A. W. Di Tolla, Freddy Diaz, Georg Diaz, Peter Dibble,
Dan Dick, Simon Dickie, John Dickson, Gunther Dietrich,
Arthur Dillingham, Corky Dillon, Marie-Louise Dion,
Barbara DiSalvia-Siomos, Tish Diskin, Betty Dixon, Gale Dixon,
Nedra Dixon, Regina Do Santos, Clive Doak, Bill Dobbins, Janice Dobbs,
Peter Dobe, Christine Dobinson, Eddie Dodsworth, Erkan Dogan,
Michael Donald, Star Donaldson, Elaine Doniger, Mindi Donner,
Joe Donovan, Bruce Douglas, Pamela Douglas, Helen Downing,
Earle Draper, Leslie Drayton, Jan-Anne Drenth, Peter Drescher,
Jacky Drews, John Du Pont, Merle Dubufsky, Dan Dugan, Dylan Dunbar,
Jeffrey Dunn, Gary Duoos, Sid Durbano, Norm Durkey, Debi Dye,
Rooth Dye, Ronald Dyson, Candice (Candi) Earley, Reece (Kookie) Eaton,
Robin Eaton, Sally Eaton, Cecilia Eaves, Jim Edison, Edward,
Vince Edward, Juan Edwards, Barbara Eff, Mark Egger, Felipe Ehremberg,
Patrick Eimon, Pelle Ekman, Jennifer Elder, Bill Elliot, Robert Ellis,
Leo Elmore, Patrick Elmore, Charlie Elvegard, Jim Emanuel,
Natascha Emmanuels, Margaret Enchelmaier, Ben Enghoff, Charles English,
David Enraght, Bulent Erbasar, Nur Erkut, John Erlenson, Moacir Ermel Jr.,
Justice Esri, Bob Etienne, Turhan Eteke, Steve Ettleson, Tom Eure,
Bryan Evans, Dick Evans, Hal Evry, Matthew Faint, Denny Fairchild,
J. V. Falcetti, Annie Fargue, Will Farish, Leo Farland, Wayne Faro,
Annie Farque, Robert Farrant, Fred Farrel, Ken Farrell, Bob Fahsbender,
James Patrick Farrell, Robert Farley, Wayne Faro, Mia Farrow,
Carolina Fasulo, Wesley Fata, Claire Faulconbridge, Roland Faulkner,
Linda Faust-Press, Michel Fauteau, Marsha Faye, Michael Feast,
Michael Federal, Marcello Federici, Bella Fehrlin, Bill Feingold,
Jim Feliciano, Luis Felipe, Sandy Fellman, Jeff Fenholt, Stephen Fenning,
Lucy Fenwick, Audrienne Ferguson, Bobbie Ferguson, Irene Ferguson,
Jose Fernandez, Raül Fernandez, Luiz Fernando, Greg Ferrara,
Bruno Ferrari, Sussan Ferrer, Jean-Jerome Ffoulke, Lindsay Field, Jim Fields,
Tomay Fields, The Fifth Dimension, Margaret Figucio, Emin Findikoglu,

John Finlay, Bill Fisch, Ed Fisher, George Fisher, Jules Fisher,
Paul Fitzgerald, Robert Fitzpatrick, Carol Fletcher, Patrick Flynn,
Alfonso Fonseca, Alan Fontaine, William Fontaine, Horacio Fontova,
Ed Force, Antonio Formihella, Andy Forray, Brett Forrest, Stephen Forrest,
Bill Forrythe, Don Forst, Colin Forster, Chester Fortune, Kim Fortune,
Robert X. Forza, Noelani Fowler, José Luiz Franca, Jose Franciso,
Pierre N. Franckel, Hawkey Franzen, Randy (Brooks) Fredericks,
Gerald Freedman, D. French, Karl-Heinz Freynik, Merle Frimark,
Bob Frissora, Ken Fritz, Aaron Frosh, Robert Gabriel, George Gaffney,
Andrea Gaines, Linda Gaines, Tadg Galleran, Leata Galloway, Steve Gamet,
Robert Ganshaw, George Garcia, Jose Garcia, Karen Gardner,
Patrick Garland, Gale Garnett, Kate Garrett, Dee Garvin, Lilian Gatrell,
Gary Gauger, Laura Gauthier, Jack Gaver, Ray Gay, Barbara Gayle,
Susan Gaynes, Bruce Gelb, Gratien Gelinas, Michel Gelinas, Judith Gendel,
Joe Geores, Kimo Gerald, Bernard Gersten, Samuel Gesser, Sheila Gibbs,
Frederick J. Gibson, Robert Gibson, Ed Gifford, Michael Gifford,
Dr. Benjamin A. Gilbert, Eileen Gilbert, Helga Gillette, Steve Gillette,
Tressa Gilliland Jr., Goeff Gilmour, William Ginsberg, Agneta Ginsberg,
Keith Glass, Milton Glaser, Denis Glezos, William Glover, Bettina Goings,
Serge Godinho, Paul Godkin, Louise Gold, Bobby Goldberg, Fred Golden,
Robert Golden, Margaret Goldie, Gloria Goldman, Mosche Goldstein,
Acácio Gonçalves, Alfonso Gonzales, Jorge Gonzalez,
Marie (Witch) Gonzales, Jim Goode, Kim Goody, Brenda Gordon,
Michael Gordon, Tony Gordon, Janis Gotti, Robin Gould, Dr. Gourson,
Bruce Govan, Gary Graham, Jeffrey Graham, Richard Graham, Rick Granat,
Nathaniel (Nat) Grant, Sean Grant, Carol Gray, Dobie Gray, Vivien Gray,
Richard Grayson, Denny Greco, Barbara Green, Jack Green,
Albert Greenberg, Michael Greenblatt, Barbara Greene, Ken Gregory,
Cleo Griffin Jr., Gerri Griffin, Kenneth Griffin, George Grogan,
Paul Grosney, Shelly Gross, Richard Groulx, Peter Gruschka, Lee Guber,
Lynda Gudde, Christine Guenther, Ademar Guerra, John Gulliver,
Christine Günther, Francios Guy, Stefan Haag, Linda Haas, Betty Hadler,
Kenny Hakansson, Delores Hall, Larry Hall, Pamela Hall, Bettie Hallett,
Aila Halminen, Max Halpern, Gary Hamilton, Kenny Hamilton,
Deborah Hampton, Charles Hamrick, Edmund Handy, Abigale Hanes,
Gayle Haness, Dwight Hankins, Ann Marie Max Hansen, Bud Hansen,
Floyd Hansen, Gyda Hansen, Ian Hanson, Wendy Hanson,
Timothy Harbert, Gina Harding, Pamela Hardman, Pippa Hardman,

Fritz Harewood, Rebekah Harkness, Jessica Harper, Bende Harris,
Dickie Harris, George Harris, Herb Harris, Jo Ann Harris, Leonard Harris,
Margaret Harris, Preben Harris, Shawn Harris, Valentino Harris,
Walter Michael Harris, Niels Harrit, Alex Harvey, Maureen Harwood,
Bernard Hassel, Linda Hassler, Mona Hays, Henry Hay, Gayle Hayden,
Murray Head, Thomas Healy, Delia Haeussler, August Hecksher,
David Hedges, Ula Hedwig, Marta Heflin, Aila Heikkilä, Susi Heine,
David Heinemann, Catherine Helbling, Maria Helena, Herb Hellman,
Jimmy Helms, Peter Helms, Ann Helstone, Barbara Hempleman,
Judith Henderson, Roger Henderson, Bob Herring, Bob Herrmann,
Daniel Hersch, William Herter, Anita Hertz, Martin Herzer, John Herzog,
Bent Hesselmann, Henry Hewes, Carol High, Alan Hill, Carolyn Hill,
Elaine Hill, Jeffrey Hillock, Stan Hilton, Marcia Hines, Fluffer Hirsch,
Michael Hirst, Robert Hirst, David Hixon, Thomas Hock, Patricia Hodge,
Jannie Hoeg, Maurice Hogenboom, Randy Hoey, Barry Hoffman,
Maarten Hoffman, Milton Hohaia, Ricci Hohlt, Alexander Hold,
Anthony Hollows, Bentine Holm, Jim Holmes, Gary Holton, Alana Hopkin,
Pixie Hopkin, Gilly Hornby, Clint Houston, Live Hov, Debbie Howard,
Doug Howard, Brenda Howell, Phillip Howells, Keith Hubbard,
Pamela Huberman, Sy Hubscher, Al Fred Hughes, Mike Hughes,
Tim Hughes, Sidney Hull, Lynn Humphrey, David (Pappy) Hunt,
Marsha Hunt, Tracy Hunt, Danny Hurd, Harold Hutchinson,
Verlynne Hutson, Paul Huttel, Bruce Hyde, Helena Ignês, Keld Ipsen,
Charles Irwin, Bob Isle, Albert Isler, Barbara Isley, Frank Iversen, Paul Ives,
Paul Jabara, Abe Jacob, Rachel Jacobson, Chris Jagger, Billy James,
Derek James, Robert James, Sylvia James, Stephanie Janecke, Udo Janson,
Corrine Jarvis, Roger Jenkins Jr, Linzi Jennings, Dick Jenson, Stanley Jerome,
Yves Jobin, Pamela Joel, Patrick John, Anchy Johnson, B. J. Johnson,
Ben Johnson, Bob Johnson, Chris Johnson, Emanuel Johnson, Joan Johnson,
Jonathon Johnson, Kathleen Johnson, Lennie Johnson,
Melissa Lynelle Johnson, Robin Lynelle Johnson, Tabby Johnson,
Clayton Johnston, Howard Johnston, Kjell Jonasson, Donald Jones,
Fred Jones, Gillian Jones, Gloria Jones, Paulette Ellen Jones, Ronnie Jones,
Roy Jones, Signa Joy, Bobby Joyce, Hellen Joyce, Juanco, Richard (Kass) Kaal,
Bunny Kahanamoku, Ursuline Kairson, Carolyn (Coco) Kallis,
Osman Kalmuk, Jolie Kanat, Lyle K'ang, Danny Kantner, Frankie Karl,
Gregory Karliss, Oswaldo Kaslauskas, W. Katwinkel, Ann Kavanagh,
Teru Kawaoka, Shiro Kawazoe, Byron Kaye, Barry Kearsley,

Kimberley F. Kearsley, Diane Keaton, Franz Keck, Micky Keene,
Patty Keene, Hiram Keller, Lynn Kellogg, Colette Kelly, David Patrick Kelly,
Tom Kelly, Gregory Ken, Linda Kendrick, Joe Kennedy, Michael Kennedy,
Shirley Kennedy, Peter Kern, Junior Kerr, Jo Kester, Gary Kettel,
Audrey Keyes, Gary Keyes, Johnnie Keyes, Randy Keys, Chris Keystone,
Robert Kiernan, Carl Killebrew, Randy Kim, Carey King, Lee King,
Michael King, Milton King, Hinemihi Pipiana Kingi, Tyrone Kinlaw,
Paula Kirby, Hanny Kirchhoff, Tahir Kiziltepe, Steven Klatch,
Annette Klingenberg, William Kloman, Jessica Kluger, Peter Knapp,
Robin Knapton, Peter Knight Jr, Cheri Kohler, Kutay Kokturk,
Ayban Kolhofer, Peter Kondal, Pohai Kong, Fred Kopp, Paul Korda,
Elke Koska, Paul Koslo, Ken Kragen, Leo Krakow, Gudrun Kramer,
Jonathan Kramer, Peter Kriegner, Gene Krischer, Sonja Kristina,
Anita Krpan, Dora Krummnikel, Peter Krushka, Jan Kudelka, Peter Kunkle,
Huseyin Kutman, Ann Karin Kvamme, Patrick Kyle, Abraham Laboriel,
Charles Lackman, Llewellyn Lafford, Andre Lafolie, Adela Lafora,
Denis Lagace, Tony Lake, Pat Lambert, Sue Lambert, Norman Lambertsen,
Charlotte Lambeth, Bob Langdon, Ted Lange, Marlena Langston,
Diane Langton, Joseph LaPlaca, Brooke Lappin, Tobi Lark, Paula Larke,
Harold Larkin, Hal Larsen, Claude Larson, Vilma Laryea, Anthony Larweth,
Helen LaShaunne, David Lasley, Vince Lateamo, Gino Latorre,
Daniel Laufer, Ben Lautman, Kent Laundre, Lacques Lavallee, Stan Lavalle,
John Phillip Law, Linda Lee Lawley, Barbara Lawren, Danny Lawyer,
Nancy Lazariuk, Damien Leake, Alannah Lee, Cindy Ann Lee, Donna Lee,
Doug Lee, Ed Lee, George W. Lee IV, Howard Lee, Jane Lee, Jennifer Lee,
Ming Cho Lee, Otja Lee, Sandra Renee Lee, Alan Leigh, Donald Leight,
Peter Leitch, Orlando Lelienhof, Gunnar Lemvigh, Joey Lent, Robin Lent,
Louise Leon, Annabel Leventon, Jane Levin, Morris Levine, Howard Levy,
Shuki Levy, Victor Levy, Jimmy Lewis, Ron Lewis, Jean Leyris,
Marie-Josee Leys, K. C. Li, Carl Libin, Paul Libon, Raymond Lignowski,
Alice Lilly, Altair Lima, Medeiros Lima-Pingo, Goran Lindgren,
William (Billy) Lindner, Peter Link, Marjorie LiPari, Karen Lippolt,
Clifford Lipson, Carmen Litke, Stephen Henry Little, Susan Little,
Anabel Littledale, Jerry Livengood, Helen Livermore, Reg Livermore,
Rosemary Llanes, Betty Lloyd, Frances Lloyd, Walley Loate, Dick Lock,
Richard Lockwood, June Lockhart, Shirley Lodrick, Judy Loe,
Alletta Lohmeyer, Ina Londahl, Bobby London, Judy Long, Helli Louise,
Billy Love, Charlie Love, Chopper (Helen) Lowe, Jim Lowe, Cia Lowgren,

Jack Lowther, Carlos Lozano, Glen A. Lucas, James Lucas,
Lawrence Allan Luczko, Jerry Luke, Hedi Lund, Lasse Lunderskov,
Robert Lusalor, R. Robert Lussier, Dolf Luteyn, Caroline Lyndon,
Len Lyons, Maby, Iaon Macalpin-Gunn, Gil MacCahill, Galt MacDermot,
Gregory MacDonald, Joyce Macek, Nina Machlin-Dayton, Linda A Mack,
Reggie Mack, Christine Günther MacKenzie, Morris Macklin,
Sperry MacNaughton, George MacPherson, Armelia MacQueen,
Gar MacRae, Heather MacRae, Mary Maddocks, Susan Madley,
Margaret Magennis, Anna-Karin Magnusson, John Maguire,
Sergio Makaroff, Peter Malick, Lee Mallory, Bruce Maltby,
David Mandarino, Henry Mandel, Robert Mandolph, Ehud Manor,
Enzio Mansfeld, George Mansour Jr, Joe Mantegna, Nancy Manville,
William Manville, Jack Manuel, Donald March, Robert Marcum,
Bruce Marder, George Marek, Neusa Maria, Rosa Maria, Paul Marichal,
Marijane Maricle, Pablo Maricmal, Antonio Marin, Don Marks,
Emmaretta Marks, Marla Marlow, Carolyn Marn, Sue Marn,
Allen Marrinson, Berys Marsh, Clement Marshall, Larry Marshall,
Alan Martin, Luci Martin, Michael Martin, Roberto Martinez,
Gene Martynec, Bob Mason, Joe Mason, Kevin Mason, Danny Mathewson,
Bodil Mathiasen, Edith Matisek, James Matousek, Graham Matters,
Wayne Matthews, Renate Mauerer, Laurie Maund, Michael Maurer,
Sundiata Mausi, Paula Maxwell, Mayita, Paul Mazzio, Richard McAllister,
Jean McArthur, Shawne McBride, Gil McCahill, Ronnie McCain,
Mary Beth McCarthy, Stelina McCarthy, James McCloden,
Arnold McCuller, Rohan McCullough, Mary Ann McDonald,
Rory McDonald, Scott McDonald, Curt McGettreck, Rosemary McGraw,
Barry McGuire, Frank McKay, Sandra McKenzie, Galen McKinley,
Jack McKinley, Chuck McKinney, Robert McKinney, John McKinnis,
Donna McLaughlin, Larry McLaughlin, Dottie McLlhenny,
Horace Greeley McNab, Robin McNamara, Mildred McNichols,
Billy McPhail, Robin McPherson, Michael Meadows, Meat Loaf,
Ulf V. Mechow, Victoria Medlin, Mecki Mark Men,
José Albino Pestana Medeiros, John Menching, Howard Mendelsohn,
David Mendenhall, Mary Mendum, Steve Menkin, Lee Menzies,
Robert Meredith, Bente Merete, Lawrence Metzler, Linda Meyers,
Peter Meyers, Stan Michaels, Stefan Michel, Vanina Michel,
Caroline Middleton, Edward Middleton, Linda Marie Milburn,
Tyrone Miles, Richard (Kim) Milford, Allen Miller, Carlyle Miller,

Carol Miller, Danny Miller, Eric Miller, Fred Miller, Harry Miller,
Ian Miller, John Miller, Maurice Miller, Pat Miller, Peter Miller,
Gilles Millinaire, Francine Mills, Carlos Milton, Jimi Milton,
Sergio Minervini, Bartholomew Miro, Audrey Mitchell, Fiona Mitchell,
Jack Mizrahi, Pyret Moberg, Wendy Moger, David (Kalani) Molina,
Erik Moll, Mike Mones, Marius Monkau, Michael Montell, Jean Monteray,
Lee Montgomery, Grover Mooney, Stella Mooney, Amanda Moore,
Barbara Moore, Frank Moore, Melba Moore, Melvin Moore, Mona Moore,
Francisco Mora, Pancho Mora, Alfonso Morales, Lloyd Morales,
Carmen Moreno, Soni Moreno, Cassandra Morgan, Harvey Morgenbesser,
Chris Morice, Bruce Morley, Warren Morrill, Delores (Sakinah) Morris,
John Morris, Leo Morris, Nathaniel Morris, Helene Morrison,
Laerte Morrone, Susan Morse, Borge Robert Mortensen,
Svend Age Mortensen, Mathilda Mortimare, Joe Morton, Natalie Mosco,
Ted Moses, Michael Moshier, Sam Moskovic, Patti Mostyn, Ira Mothner,
Richard Mowdy, Columbia Moya, Marcus Mukai, Buddy Mullaney,
Mike Mulloy, Anna-Bella Munther, Edward Murphy Jr,
Shawn (Stoney) Murphy, Edgar Murray, Hugh Murray, Ken Myers,
Linda Myers, Suzie Mylecharane, Rivka Nachoma, Greg (Flash) Nagasawa,
Barbara Nahass, Marshall Naify, Russell Nafus, Peter Narroway, John Nasht,
Max Nass, Mary Nealon, Holly Near, John Neary, Teddy Neeley,
Debbie Nehring, Christopher Neil, Chris Neilson, Glen Neilson,
Margaret Nestor, Pamela Nestor, Edoardo Nevola, Morris Newcombe,
Del Newman, Linda Newman, Peter Newton, Anna Nicholas, Paul Nicholas,
Allan Nicholls, Nia Nichols, Freddie Nicolaidis, Mauro Nicoletti,
Glen Nielsen, Lykke Nielsen, Maxine Nightingale, Sherry Nijima,
Ann-Sofie Nilsson, Bo Nilsson, Suzannah Nilsson, Kathy Nixon,
May Helene Njoten, Peter Noble, Terry Noonan, Tony Noons, Anne Nord,
Eva Nordli, Cecelia Norfleet, Cisco Normand, Suzannah (Evans) Norstrand,
Lesley North, Roy North, Hugo Norton, Ivar Norve, Michal Noy,
Louis Nugue, Vicky Nunis, Kirk Nurock, Carl O'Brien, Cubby O'Brien,
John Edward O'Brien, Richard O'Brien, Terry O'Brien, Julio Ocampo,
Juan Carlos Ochipinti, Anne Beate Odland, Maurine O'Donnell,
Ernie Oelrich, Deborah Offner, Michael O'Flaherty,
Rhonda (Coulet) Oglesby, Scott Ogelsby, Jill O'Hara, Eileen O'Hare,
Tom O'Horgan, Bill Ohrstrom, Robert Ojeda, Okyay Okan, Jack O'Keefe,
Kim O'Leary, Célia Olga, Peter Oliver, Eduardo Oliviera, Lotte Olsen,
Byron Olson, Jorgen Olsen, Oystein Selenius Olsen, Nancy Olson,

Charles O'Lynch, Eamon O'Neil, Florence O'Neil, Discos Orfeon,
Angie Ortega, Debbie Ortega, Kenny Ortega, William Orton,
Richard Osorio, Robert Ossenfort, Ronnie Osterberg, Darron O'Sullivan,
Alice Ottawa, Helle Ottesen, Linda Otto, Adam Russell Owen,
Michael Owen, Fusun Ozben, Selcuk Ozercan, Mithat Ozyilmaz,
Angela Pagano, Howard Page, Mike Page, Elaine Paige,
Marja-Leena Paimensalo, Bruce Paine, Pekka Pajula, Gerard Palaprat,
Renata Pallottini, Ray Papai, Joseph Papp, Norrie Paramor, Debi Parker,
Dennis Parker, Stephanie Parker, Ted Parker, William Parker, Bud Parkes,
Ted Parkins, Jenny Parkinson, Tom Parkinson, Robert Parr, Bernice Parrish,
Edward Parrish, Stephen Pascal, Tadeau Passarelli, Jean Pastorelli,
Patty Patience, Bill Paton, Karin Patterson, Phillip Patterson,
Sandra Patterson, Reijo Paukku, Fred Payne, Jimmie Payne, Carol Peabody,
Jody Pearlman, Seymour Peck, Mogens Pedersen, Ricky Peebles, Brent Peek,
Robert Peitscher, José Luiz Pena, Celelia Pencak, Carol Penner, Ariclê Perez,
Ed Perez, Donnie Perkins, Si Perkoff, Harry Perry, Carol Peters, Jim Peters,
Karen Petersen, Charles Peterson, Colleen Peterson, Claudio Petraglia,
Ricardo Petraglia, Peter Petricone, Yasmin Pettigrew, Kirsten Peuliche,
Rick Pfleeger, Harvey Phillips, Lydia Phillips, Peggy Phillips, Peter Phillips,
Edwige Pierre, Neil Phillips, Peter Phillips, Zwicka Pick, Vernon Pickering,
Bob Pierson, Bernie Piltch, Jose (Yipi) Lopex Pinto, Lynn Pitney,
Mauricia Platon, David Plattner, Lyla Pliego, Shelley Plimpton,
Shelley Plotkin, Richard Pochinko, Di Polk, Helen Pollack, Erica Pomerance,
Herb Pomeroy, Jimmy Ponder, Richard Ponte, Andy Pool, Larry Pool,
Gus Popiel, Arturo E. Porazzi, Pat Porter, Sol Posnack, Dorothy Poste,
Gary Potter, Ian L. Potter, Nancy Potts, Frederic Poursain, Janet Powell,
Shezwae Powell, Dennis Powers, Jon Laurence Powers, Howard Pratt,
John Prescott, Reinhold Press, Sidsel Prestbakmo, Charles M Preston III,
Kathy Preston, Cedric Price, Marianne Price, Dorothy Priest, Rocco Principe,
Robert Propper, Colin Prowell, Ron Pryble, Hector Puhuy, Dennis Purcell,
Laura Purdy, Linda Purdy, Robert Pusilo, Louise-Marie Quelette,
Gitte Raae, Norman Racussin, James Rado, Ted Rado, Joyce Rae,
Bennett Raffer, Gerome Ragni, Irene Ragni, Claire Raine, Eddie Rambeau,
Penny Ramsay, Stanley Ramsey, Nancy Randolph, Sonya Rangan,
Victor Rapaport, Juha Räsänen, Zora Rasmussen, Merolyn Ravetz,
Preben Ravn, Nola Ray, Irving Raymond, Vanesa Ready, Sharon Redd,
Bernd Redecker, Alaina (Tiny) Reed, LaVerne Reed, Ken Reeder,
Clare Rees, Linda Rees, Maria Regina, Darryl Reid, Fred Reinglas,

Ruth Reisin, Horacio Reni, Gloria Rennalls, Fernando Reski, John Revson,
Lance Reynolds, Mara Su Rez, Michael Rhone, Terrill Rice, Roger Richard,
Jeff Richards, Joey Richards, Betty Richardson, Henry Richardson,
Karl Richey, Marlies Richrath, Frank Ricotti, David Riddick, Gayle Riffle,
Doug Riley, Ray Riley, Fred Rios, Linda Rios, Jack Ritchie, Walter Rivera,
Mary Ann Robbins, Carlos Roberto, Barry Roberts, Chapman Roberts,
Billy James Robertson, Darrel Robertson, Eric Robertson, Gwene Robertson,
John Robertson, Cara Robin, Alma Robinson, Bobby Robinson,
Charles Robinson, Ed Robinson, Erik Robinson, Kath Robinson,
Leighton Robinson, Paulette Robinson, Troy Robinson, Vicki Sue Robinson,
Barbara Robison, Dennis Roche, Ruspoli Rodriguez, Dennis Roe,
Betty Roelofs, Fred (Skip) Rogers, Florence Rollin, Rolo, Jerry K. Rose,
Jehudit Rosenberg, Per Rosenquist, Joseph Rosenzweig, Bill Rosevear,
Merria Ross, Lino Rossi, Tracy Rosten, Robert Rothman, John C. Rowe,
Doug Rowell, Tera Rowell, Sheila Royster, Robert I. Rubinsky,
Michael Rudder, Joel Rudnick, Michelle Rupena, Bruce Rusin, Kevin Russell,
Peter Russell, Birgit Rüssmann, Carol Ruth, Rod Ruth, Tom Rutley,
Clint Ryan, Paul Ryan, Pirkko Saanakorpi, Jobriath Salisbury, Carol Salmon,
Zoe Salmon, Annie Sampson, Victor Samrock, Vidar Sandem,
David Sanderson, Ron Sandilans, John Sangster, Jane Sannemo,
Melody Santangelo, Neil Sardelli, Bill Sargeant, Ray Sassetti,
Marianne Sauvage, Paul Saunders, Sherine Savan, Carl Sawyer, Les Saxon,
Franco Scarli, Maurice Schaded, Stephen Scharf, Bill Schimpf, Joan Schirle,
Werner Schmid, Al (Farmer) Schmidt, Tyrone Schmidling, Enno Schnetz,
Matthew Schoenwald, Reiner Schöne, Max Schonke, Arlene Schreer,
Thom Schuyler, Billy Schwartz, Robby Schweider, Tilo Schweinitz,
Carl Scott, Earl Scott, Mike Scott, Tyrone Scott, Scumbag (LaRee),
Fred Seagraves, Ronny Seballo, Sebastian, Dan Sedgwick,
Susan V. Sedgwick, Leonard Seeds, Raye Anne Seely, Rafael Segovia,
George Seighe, Bilge Sen, Minoru Serezawa, Bill Serjeant, Jose Pepe Serna,
Colin Setches, Rhoda Seven, Jose Sevilla, Kenny Seymour, Mary Seymour,
Maurice Shaddad, Dan Shadle, Ron Shaeffer, Sally Shafer, Humberto Shaik,
Denny Shanahan, Nat Shapiro, Jim Sharman, Stan Shaw, She She,
Kathy Shearer, Thomas Sheehan, Edward Sheftel, Red Shepard,
Eugenia Sheppard, Lowell Sherman, Gershen Shevett, Ken Shields-Alleyne,
Rosa Shiels, Gloria Shiers, Rick Shorter, Gaby Shushan, Anne Sidney,
Herbert Sidon, David Siegel, Jukka Siikavire, Aleta Silva, Bene Silva,
Lana Silva, Marilene Silva, Vicky Silva, Don Simmons, Junius Simmons,

Sid Simms, Nina Simone, Rita Simonini, Dennis Simpson, Gena Simpson,
Sid Sims, Anthony Sinclair, Belinda Sinclair, Barry Singer, Ibrahim Sirin,
Rolf Skogstrand, Eddie Skoller, David Slagter, Esther Sleska, Aleta Slivwa,
Gail Slobodkin, Hylan Slobodkin, Michael Smartt, Babette Smith,
Carol L. Smith, Claire Smith, Dennis Smith, Gregory Smith, Joshua Smith,
Kate Smith, Leslie Smith, Lynn Smith, Merlene Smith, Michael Smith,
Michael J. Smith, Nettie Smith, Orlando Smith, Otis Smith, Wende Smith,
Tom Smothers, Thomas Smythe, Ronald Snellenber, Robert Snieciniski,
Peter Richard Snook, Virginia Snow, Stanley Soble, Arthur Solomon,
Bert Sommer, Avery Sommers, Shelley Sommers, Michael Sorafine,
Dale Soules, Martin Speer, Alice Spencer, Bryan Spencer, Clint Spencer,
Linbert Spencer, Richard Spiegel, Norman Spiller, Victor Spinetti,
Michael Springfield, Linda Squires, Creena St. Clare, Ron St. Germain,
Kirk St. James, Susan St. James, Wayne St. John, Barrie Stacey,
John Stainton, Michael Staniforth, Aggie Tell Stanley, Al Stanwyck,
Brenda Stark, Starlee, Rusty Steiger, Oatis Stephens, Keith Sterling,
Michael Sterling, Suzi Stern, Geff Stevenson, Stephen Stevenson,
Ellen Stewart, Gloria Stewart, Greta Stewart, Phyl Stewart, David Stidwell,
Robert Stigwood, Christel Stocklinger, Christopher Stone, Freddy Stone,
Toby Stone, Tom Stovall, Peter Straker, Barbara Streisand, Myrna Strom,
Clive Stuart, Shelagh Stuttle, Danny Sullivan, Donna Summer (Gaines),
Oney Sunio, Supa, Bob Surga, Gulriz Sururi, Peter Sutherland,
Kingsley Swan, Margot Sweeny, Maureen Sweeney, Bill Swiggard,
James Swijert, William (Oliver) Swofford, Catherine Sydee, Rick Sylvester,
Ronald Syson, David Lee Taber, Eron Tabor, David Taft, Vincent Tajiri,
Neil Tate, Kenan Tatli, Howard Taubman, Jeannette Tavernier,
David Patrick Taylor, Kathy Taylor, Keith Taylor, Meshach (Bruce) Taylor,
Graham Teear, Jay Telfer, Minoru Terada, Tulay Terem, The Fool,
Oscar Thiede, Guy Thomas, Paca Thomas, Philip Michael Thomas,
Christie Thompson, Don Thompson, Jay Thompson, Shirley Thompson,
Brian Thomson, Sandra Thornton, Colleen Thorton, Maureen Thorton,
Ove Thue, Clevon Ticeson, Tie Dye Eddie, Jose Francisco Tijerina,
Tuhi Timoti, Semra Tinaz, George Tipton, Donald Tirabassi, Bernd Tischer,
Eva Tissell, Oliver Tobias, David Toguri, Nicholas Tomaselli,
Veronica Tomlinson, Ronnie Tongg, Bob Tootelian, Aniton Tootell,
Franca Tosato, Philip Toubus, Mira Trailovic, Janinia Tredwell,
Tom Trenkle, Todd Tressler, Maria Trinder, Mikolaj Trutnik, Jimmy Tsai,
Tien-Yung Tsai, Helge Tuft, Ahmet Tugsuz, Serap Tuna, Gulay Turker,

George Turner, Robin Turrill, Horst Twieg, Robert Tylor, Ray Uhler, Joanne Unkovskoy, Luis Vacantes, Frances Valentine, Cecile Valery, Irene Valua, Gilda Vandenbrande, Bill Van Dijk, Garry Van Egmond, Arlene Vanko, Monique Van Voorhan, Edwin Van Wyk, Suki Vasquez, Roberto Vega, Tata Vega, Teddy Vega, Martha Velez, Willy Velthaak, Argia Venturino, Ben Vereen, James Verner, Albert Vescovo, Emilio Vigo, Robert Villefranche, Terry Villis, Barbara Virgil, Hannele Virta, Bibi Vogel, Dag Vognstolen, Gerhard von Halem, Uli von Mochow, Arlene Vrhel, John Waddell, Mike Wade, Derek Wadsworth, Edward Wagemans, Robin Wagner, Fred Walker, Freda Walker, Joyce Walker, Mike Walker, Burke Wallace, David Wallace, Vioretta Walle, Bengtarne Wallin, Helena (Lady) Walquer, Ewart Walters, Louis Walton, Laurel Ward, Trevor Ward, Orgad Wardimon, Reudor Wardimon, Rachella Waring, Fred Waring Jr., Elaine Warner, Sherman Warner, Jennifer Warnes, Glen Warren, Bill Washer, Lamont Washington, John Wassens, John Waters, Cathy Watt, Jason Watts, Rebecca Watts, Herve Wattine, Arthur Waxman, Norman Wayne, Willie Weatherly, Eric Weber, Erik Wedersoe, Freya Weghofer, Mark Weiner, Jutta Weinhold, Scott Weintraub, June Weir, Harry Weiser, Verina Weiss, Anna Weisz, Charles Weldon, Jonathan Welsh, Jorgen Werner, Linda Wesley, Barney Westall, Tom Westerman, Naomi Wexler, Jacki Whelan, Andrew White, Bruce White, Dave White, Ebony White, Joanne White, Liz White, Paddi White, Robin White, Joan Whitehead, Barbara Whiting, Joan Whitman, Bill Whyte, Mort Widdifield, Harry Wieser, James Wigfall, Le Roy Wiggins, Kym Wilhelm, Arnold Wilkerson, Sheila Wilkinson, Charles Williams, Earl Williams, Eddie Williams, Freida Williams, James Williams, Philip Morgan Williams, Ronnie Williams, Sharon Lee Williams, Singer Williams, Sunday Williams, Teddy Williams, Valerie Williams, Yvette Williams, Marion Willis, Victor Willis, Karry Wills, Don Willson, Bill Wilson, Earl Wilson, Mike Wilson, Terrance Paul Wilson, Willie Windsor, Julie Winn, Hattie Winston, Jean Winston, Jimmy Winston, Lucy Winters, Tammy Winters, Frederick Winton, Bruno Wintzell, Jenny Wise, Manuel Wispe, Andy Wiswell, Brian Withers, Ken Wolen, Gabriel Wollen, Kimi Wong, Lillian Wong, Jeannie (Jurgen) Wood, Marge Wood, Philip Wood, Tony Wood, Susan Woodnick, George Woods, Peter Woolf, Johnny Worthy, Wini Wowor, Christopher Wren, E. Wright, Kathryann Wright, Michael Wright, Nathaniel Wright, Terry Wunder, Christina Yakobian, Kevork Yakobian, John David Yarbrough, Peter Yarrow,

Julide Yazansoy, David Yip, Terry Yirsa, Winston Yong, Daniel Young,
Ken Yovicson, Michael Ysebaert, Carl Yucht, Morris Yuter, Michel Zacca,
Zane Paul Zacharoff, Margalit Zanani, John Zaradin, Zardok Zarfati,
Vivienne Zarvis, Jack Zaza, Cathy Ziegele, Birgit Zinn, Tony Zito,
James Zorrozo, Steve Zweigbaum

THE TRIBAL COUNCIL

I offer my deepest thanks and gratitude to the following people who assisted me along the way while putting this book together. Their friendship, thoughts, encouragement, advise, stories, memorabilia, pictures, proof reading, etc., was and will forever be appreciated.

All My Family, Michael David Arian, Beverly Bremers, Corinne Broskette, Michael Butler, Robert Camuto, Bob Corff, Charlotte Crossley, Merle Frimark, Tracy Harris, Walter Michael Harris, Ula Hedwig, Lyle K'ang, Jolie Kanat, Jon Keliehor, Jessica Kluger, Anita Krpan, Ted Lange, Ben Lautman, Pierre Lehu, Sharmagne-Leland-St. John, Annabel Leventon, Nina Machlin-Dayton, Larry Marshall, Helene Masiko, Kevin Mason, Arnold McCuller, Barry McGuire, Robin McNamara, Danny Miller, Susan Morse, Allan Nicholls, Linda Rees, Sally Shafer, David Taft, David Patrick Taylor and Dawn Worrall

The Rest Is Silence

In loving memory of those tribe members we have lost along the way. Although invisible to our eyes, you will always be in our hearts.

Christine Adams, Michael Alexander, Seth Allen, Arsenio Avizado,
Danny Beard, Hanus Berka, Michael Berz, Otto Bezloja,
Harry Blackstone Jr., Tisha Bricko, Paul Butler, Tony Cafrelli,
Yager Cantwell, Carroll Carlson, Corrina Carlson, Otis Carr, Nell Carter,
Armand Coulet, Barbara Cowsill, Maria Crummere, Kaipo Daniels,
Walker Daniels, Denise Delapenha, Ronald Dyson, Leo Elmore,
Steve Ettleson, Tom Eure, Jose Fernandez, Jim Fields, Andrea Gaines,
Gratien Gélinas, Michael Gifford, Rick Granat, Margaret Harris,
Alex Harvey, Elaine Hill, Maurice Hogenboom, Gary Holton, Paul Jabara,
Melissa Johnson, Robin Johnson, Teru Kawaoka, Patty Keene, Hiram Keller,
Shirley Kennedy, Gary Keyes, Carey King, Pohai Kong, Jonathan Kramer,
Brooke Lappin, Jimmy Lewis, Rosemary Llanes, Carlos Lozano,
R. Robert Lussier, Donald March, Michael Maurer, Galen McKinley,
Victoria Medlin, Richard (Kim) Milford, Bartholomew Miro Jr.,
Suzannah Norstrand, Joseph Papp, Robert Peitscher, Colleen Peterson,
Gerome Ragni, Irene Ragni, Stanley Ramsey, Sharon Redd, Fred Reinglas,
Michael Rhone, Joey Richards, Gayle Riffle, Vicki Sue Robinson,
Barbara (Sandi) Robison, Jobriath Salisbury, John Sangster, Carl Sawyer,
Maurice Schaded, Stephen Scharf, Earl Scott, Denny Shanahan,
Nat Shapiro, Nina Simone, Bert Sommer, Bryan Spencer,
Michael Staniforth, David Stidwell, William (Oliver) Swofford,
Graham Teear, Nicholas Tomaselli, Jimmy Tsai, Lamont Washington,
James Wigfall, Jimmy Winston, Bruno Wintzell, Andy Wiswell,
Lillian Wong, Jeannie (Jurgun) Wood

References

Hair, book, lyrics and music ~ © 1966, 1967, 1968, 2004 by James Rado, Gerome Ragni and Galt MacDermot. All rights reserved.

Hair, logo and art work courtesy of Michael Butler, © Used with permission.

Hair, New York Shakespeare Festival LP, RCA PRS 319

Disinhairited LP, Broadway cast, RCA LSO 1163

Hair, Original London cast LP, Polydor 583043

Fresh Hair LP, London cast, Polydor 245501

Divine Hair Mass In F LP, Broadway cast, RCA LSP 4632

Hair, Original Mexico cast LP, Orfeon

Haare, Das Ganze Hair, German LP, Polydor 2630025

Haare, Deutsche Originalaufnahme Hair, German LP, Polydor 249266

Hair, Original Israel cast LP, CBS S 70074

Hair, Original Brazilian cast LP, Fermata FB 265

Hair, Original Australian cast LP, Spin SEL 933544

Hair, Original French cast LP, Philips PHS 600329

Hair, Original Japanese cast LP, RCA SRA 5168

Hair, Original Swedish cast LP

Hair, Original Broadway Souvenir Program, Natoma Productions, Inc. © 1968, 2004.

Hair, Worldwide Souvenir Program, Natoma Productions, Inc. © 1968, 2004.

Hair, Original Los Angeles Souvenir Program, Natoma, KSFI Productions, Inc. © 1968, 2004.

Hair, Original Australian Souvenir Program, Harry M. Miller and Michael Butler © 1969, 2004.

Hair, UK National Tour Souvenir Program, Dewynters Ltd. © 1969, 2004.

Hair, UK Holiday Tour Souvenir Program, Dewynters Ltd. © 1969, 2004.

Hair, Original London Souvenir Program, Dewynters Ltd. © 1969, 2004.

Hair, Rock Talent Souvenir Program, Rock Talent Associates 1974, 2004.

Showcard Magazine, The Knack, The New Theatre, August 1965.

Playbill Magazine, Lion In Winter, May 1966.

Playbill Magazine, Hair, Cheetah Theatre, December 1967.

Playbill Magazine, Hair, Biltmore Theatre, various issues, 1968 through 1972.

Playbill Programme, Hair at the Shaftesbury Theatre, London 1968.

Theatre Print Programme, Hair at the Queen's Theatre, London 1971.

Theatre Print Programme, Hair at the Queen's Theatre, London 1974.

Playbill Magazine, Hair, Shubert Theatre Chicago, various issues, 1969 through 1970.

Playbill Magazine, Hair, Blackstone Theatre Chicago, December 1970.

Playbill Magazine, Hair, Wilbur Theatre Boston, various issues 1970.

Performing Arts Magazine, Hair, American Conservatory Theatre San Francisco, Geary Theatre, various issues 1969 through 1970.

Hair program, Orpheum Theatre San Francisco, 1970.

Playgoer Magazine, Hair, Aquarius Theatre Los Angeles, various issues, 1969 through 1970.

Stage Magazine, Hair, Vest Pocket Theatre, Detroit, June1970.

Scene Magazine, Hair, program for the Montreal production, September1970.

Scene Magazine, Hair, Royal Alexandra Theatre Toronto, various issues1970.

Two On The Aisle Magazine, Hair, Moore Theatre Seattle1970.

Miami Marquee, Hair, Coconut Grove Playhouse Miami1970.

Hair Programme, Winter Gardens Pavilion Theatre, Blackpool UK1970.

Hair Programme, Empire Theatre, Liverpool UK1970.

Hair Programme, Hippodrome Theatre, Bristol UK1970.

Hair Program, Circle Theatre, Indianapolis1970.

Curtain Call Magazine, Hair, Shubert Theatre, Cincinnati 1970.

Hair Program, Brown Theatre, Louisville1971.

Playgoer Magazine, Hair, Nixon Theatre, Pittsburgh1971.

Playbill Magazine, Hair, Palace Theatre, Milwaukee1971.

Playgoer Magazine, Hair, Shubert Theatre, New Haven1971.

Hair Program, Capri Theatre, Kansas City1971.

Hair Program, Palace West Theatre, Phoenix1971.

Hair Program, Civic Center Theatre, St. Paul1971.

Dramapage, Egyptian Theatre, DeKalb1971.

Playbill Magazine, Hair, Hanna Theatre, Cleveland1971.

Playbill Magazine, Hair, Shubert Theatre, Philadelphia1971.

Hair Program, Ohio Theatre, Columbus1971.

Playbill Magazine, Hair, National Theatre, Washington DC, April1971.

Stage Magazine, Hair, Morris A. Mechanic Theatre, Baltimore,June1971.

Playbill Magazine, Hair, National Theatre, Washington DC, July 1971.

Scene Magazine, Hair, Royal Alexandra Theatre Toronto, July1971.

Hair Program, American Conservatory Theatre, Geary Theatre, San
Francisco1971.

Stage Magazine, Hair, Morris A. Mechanic Theatre, Baltimore August1971.

Hair Program, Mary E. Sawyer Auditorium, Wisconsin State Univ., La
Cross,1971.

Hair Program, Page Auditorium, Duke Univ., Durham,1971.

Hair Program, Eastman Theatre, Rochester,1971.

Hair Program, Eastman Theatre, Rochester,1971.

Stage Magazine, Hair, Morris A. Mechanic Theatre, Baltimore April1972.

Playbill Magazine, Hair, Shubert Theatre, Philadelphia1972.

Hair Program, Tulsa Municipal Theatre, Tulsa,1972.

Playgoer Magazine, Hair, Aquarius Theatre, Los Angeles, July1972.

Playgoer Magazine, Hair, Aquarius Theatre, Los Angeles, September1972.

Chicago Tribune, May 22, 1969. Butler: The Message Of Hair, by Clarence
Petersen.

Chicago Tribune © copyright 1969, 2004. From Michael Butler's Journal

Courier-Journal, Louisville KY January 1971. What else could bring together playgoers, Christians for Decency, four policemen and one heckler?…It's 'Hair!' by, Bryan Woolley © 1971, 2004.

Courier-Journal, Louisville KY January 1971. Play review, 'Hair' is beautiful, dazzling to eye, ear By, William Mootz © 1971, 2004

Courier-Journal, Louisville KY January 5, 1971. Cast Lives "Hair" on stage and off By, Sally Bly © 1971, 2004.

Hair Original Los Angeles Souvenir Program, 1968. Tom O'Horgan's Sensitivity Exercises. Making Hair Fly, by Jay Thompson. © 1968, 2004.

New York Times, October 30, 1967. The Theatre: "Hair," a Love-Rock Musical, Inaugurates Shakespeare Festival's Anspacher Playhouse. Contemporary Youth Depicted in Play, by Clive Barnes. © 1967, 2004.

New York Times, November 14, 1967. "Hair" and the 20's. Pert Musical on Lafayette St. Recalls Another Era's Off Broadway Revues, by Howard Taubman—Critic At Large. © 1967, 2004.

New York Times, April 30, 1968. Theatre: "Hair"—It's Fresh and Frank Likeable Rock Musical Moves to Broadway, by Clive Barnes. © 1968, 2004.

New York Times, August 11, 1968. Performer In Hair Critically Injured. ©1968, 2004.

New York Times, August 26, 1968. Lamont Washington Dies at 24; Actor Had Played Hud in Hair © 1968, 2004.

New York Times, February 5, 1969. "Hair" Holds Up Under 2d Look, by Clive Barnes. © 1969, 2004.

New York Times, April 12, 1969. Actor-Authors of "Hair" Barred From Theatre, by Richard F. Shepard. © 1969, 2004.

New York Times, April 18, 1969. Two Stars of "Hair" Are Back in Show As Feud Is Ended, by Sam Zolotow. © 1969, 2004.

New York Times, April 16, 1969 Princess Anne Dances On Stage During "Hair" © 1969, 2004.

New York Times, January 29, 1970. Moratorium, Garden Thronged for Songfest In Aid of Vietnam Moratorium, Contemporary Youth Depicted in Play, by Mike Jahn ©1970, 2004.

New York Times, June 6, 1970. Astronauts Find Hair Offensive, Lovell and Swigert Walk Out After First Act of Musical © 1970, 2004.

New York Times, March 13, 1971. Opening of Hair in Capital Tops Hectic Week © 1971, 2004

New York Times, May 17, 1972. "Hair" May Close Sunday © 1972, 2004.

New York Times, July 13, 1991. Gerome Ragni, 48, a Stage Actor; Co-Author of Broadway's Hair, by Richard F. Shepard © 1991, 2004.

Newsweek, November 13, 1967. Making of a Theatre. © 1967, 2004.

Playbill Magazine, Hair, Biltmore Theatre, September 1968. How a small-time rock musical from Lafayette Street found Fame and Fortune on Broadway, by Colette Dowling. © 1968, 2004.

Playbill Magazine, May 1971. "Hair" Trusting The Kids And The Stars, by Colette Dowling © 1971, 2004.

Seattle Post-Intelligencer, "206 Magazine", April 10, 1970. "Hair" Tribe Rocks Rafters, Controversial Musical Opens Monday, Let the Sunshine In Northwest "Hair" Tribe Ready to Rock © 1970, 2004.

Seattle Post-Intelligencer, "206 Magazine," Friday April 17, 1970. "Hair" opens tomorrow at the Moore. Best Bets On Stage © 1970, 2004.

Seattle Post-Intelligencer, Thursday April 15, 1971, Renton Mother, Baby Lose Lives in Cleveland Fire © 1971, 2004.

Seattle Post-Intelligencer, "206 Magazine," August 13, 1971. Seattle Sprouts "Hair." "Hair" Groomed for Its Return to Seattle Stage 1971, 2004.

Seattle Times, April 20, 1970. "Hair" Is Happy Show, By Wayne Johnson, Arts and Entertainment Editor © 1970, 2004.

Seattle Times, Wednesday, May 27, 1970. "Hair" Flourishes at Moore, By Wayne Johnson, Arts and Entertainment Editor © 1970, 2004.

Toronto Daily Star Sunday Magazine, March 7, 1970. Hair: the loudest, gaudiest, sexiest, grooviest musical ever to hit Canada, by John Zichmanis. © 1970, 2004.

1442049

Made in the USA